# Classic Railroad Advertising

## RIDING THE RAILS AGAIN

**Tad Burness**

Published by

**krause publications**

700 East State Street • Iola, WI 54990-0001
715/445-2214 • FAX: 715/445-4087   www.krause.com

Please call or write for our free catalog of publications. Our toll-free number to place an order or obtain a free catalog is 800-258-0929 or please use our regular business telephone 715-445-2214 for editorial com-ment and further information.

Library of Congress Catalog Number:2001086716
ISBN: 0-87349-274-9

# TABLE OF CONTENTS

# A NOTE ABOUT THE ADS

The railroad and related-industry advertisements appearing in this book span the years 1917 to 2000, with most concentrated in the 1930s, 1940s and 1950s. Most of the ads appeared simultaneously in three, four or more different publications. Sometimes a given ad appeared in several publications over a span of several weeks or months. When possible, the earliest date that an ad appeared is given.

Quite a few magazines carried railroad advertising, including *National Geographic, Fortune, Life, Holiday, Time, Sunset, Travel, Newsweek, U.S. News, Saturday Evening Post, Look, Collier's* and others, including a few periodicals in which you would not normally expect to find travel advertising, such as business or art journals.

When more than one copy of a given ad was found, the copy in the best condition, or with the best printing on highest-quality paper, was used. From 1942 to 1946, the quality of paper used in several popular magazines suffered a noticeable decline because of war-created shortages in raw materials. Thus, a few of these ads appeared on dull or yellowed paper that has further deteriorated over time.

An attempt was made to select only those ads in fine to perfect condition. However, there were a handful of cases where a certain ad was much too important to be excluded in spite of some minor blemishes. Additionally, in a few cases, only a portion of an ad was available or usable, elements from multiple ads were combined, or elements were reorganized slightly to fit the format of the book.

The ads are organized alphabetically under the heading of the company sponsoring the ad, rather than the railroad featured. Railroads featured in non-railroad company ads are noted in parentheses in the page heading. Within each section devoted to a single railroad or company, the ads appear roughly chronologically, allowing you to see the progression of marketing messages over time, and within the context of world events (such as World War II and its aftermath). Note that one heading, *California Zephyr*, is neither a company nor a railroad, but rather a train jointly operated—and jointly advertised—by three railroads (Burlington, Rio Grande and Western Pacific).

# ACKNOWLEDGMENTS

Though all the older advertisements and illustrations for this book came from the author's large private collection, special thanks is due to Amtrak for its cooperation in supplying helpful advertising material from 1985 to 2000.

Special thanks also is due to the following persons and organizations for their help in gathering certain needed information or photos needed for this project:

◆ Bob Campbell

◆ Don Gulbrandsen

◆ James Kavenaugh

◆ Dale Baker, Discovery Travel

◆ Pacific Grove Travel

◆ Association of American Railroads

◆ And, of course, thanks again to Amtrak for keeping railroad passenger service available in North America.

# INTRODUCTION

## By Brian Solomon

For more than eight decades beginning in the 1830s railroads dominated American land transportation. In that time more than two hundred thousand miles of railway line were built connecting nearly every town and city in the nation. It was a dynamic time of visionary engineering, pioneering technology, corporate empire building and financial scheming. The advent of the railroad allowed people to move faster and easier than ever before, cutting travel times from days to hours. The railroads were more than just transportation, they were the very foundation of Big Business, setting precedents that are still followed today. In the early days, many railroads were just short lines connecting nearby towns and cities: the Camden & Amboy; Mohawk & Hudson, and Boston & Worcester to name just a few. Within a few decades, ambitious men started connecting these short railways, and built new ones, to create large, powerful networks that were the transportation arteries of America. Among the most important were the big Eastern "Trunk Lines," the Pennsylvania Railroad, New York Central, Erie, and the Baltimore & Ohio. By the turn of the 19th century, several Western lines had become rich and powerful. The Southern Pacific, Union Pacific, Burlington, and Santa Fe were among the companies that shaped growth in the West.

The great benefits offered by railroad transportation changed the way Americans lived. The railroads were integral in the country's transformation from an agrarian nation to an industrial world power, a change that became evident when America stepped in and rapidly brought a conclusion to World War I. By providing the United States transportation, the railroads wielded great influence in politics and the economy, and with this power came corruption and abuse. Railroad tycoons generated animosity and hatred among the public, who felt—and rightly so—that the railroads were taking advantage of them. The tycoons' abuses were both blatant and subtle. New York Central's Vanderbilt was misquoted saying, "The Public be Damned." While we know now this was a distortion of what he meant, those words so often repeated came to represent the attitudes of all tycoons and railroads in general. World War I was a turning point, not just in the role of the United States as a power, but in the role of the railroads. On the eve of the war, the tide finally turned against the railroad companies, and the stage was set for their long, slow decline. Federal anti-trust suits broke up some of the most powerful systems, and legislation was enacted to curtail the power of the railroads. During the war, the railroads—saturated with heavy traffic—bogged down under the tremendous burden foist upon them, forcing direct government intervention. For the duration of the war, American railroads operated under the control of the Federal Government's United States Railway Administration. In 1920, when the railroads were finally freed from the shackles of USRA control, they faced a changed world. The Golden Age of the railroad had ended, and from then on they faced serious competition. The advent of the affordable private automobile, motor truck, bus, and airplane, gradually eroded railroad's market share. Suddenly, faced with this competition, the railroads were compelled to enter a field they had never taken seriously before: Advertising.

So, as the railroad's Golden Age ended, the Golden Age of railroad advertising began. To better compete with highways and airplanes the railroads developed more powerful locomotives capable of hauling heavier loads at greater speeds. They tightened up passenger schedules and introduced new runs. Then when the Great Depression struck, the railroads watched in horror as their business melted away. Desperate, a few of the most influential railroads went about revolutionizing the American passenger train with the introduction of the Streamliners. These trains were so attractive, compelling, sleek and fast, that despite the weakened financial condition of the nation, people flocked to ride to them. The streamliner helped introduced a new type of engine to American railroads, the diesel-electric. While initially seen as something of a gimmick, the diesel soon proved its worth, and rivaled the power of the traditional steam locomotive. Then, as events in Europe and Asia flared, bringing a second global conflict, the railroads again found themselves besieged with tremendous traffic. This time they retained their independence, and had the will and the capability to accommodate the deluge of wartime business, helping the nation towards victory.

Each of these crucial episodes, and those that

followed, brought waves of colorful, creative railroad advertising, carefully designed to win the public's heart and trust. The railroads had the money and the clout to hire the best designers, and came up with some of the most memorable advertising of the time. The advertising reflected the dynamic changes America and its railroads were undergoing. These ads painted the picture the railroads wanted the public to see, a picture that showed trains in a positive light. The ads made the railroads seem colorful, innovative, progressive and modern. They were designed to dispel the negativity that the previous generation associated with the railroads, and create a new image of hope.

Traditional passenger trains were comprised of solid, heavyweight cars, and painted a variety of dark, morose colors—most typically drab 'Pullman green,' a color that seemed more black than green. Conventional steam locomotives, which for all their romantic appeal today, were seen as dirty machines that spewed soot and cinders. Furthermore most steam locomotives were slow, required regular servicing along the way, and had to stop every so often to restock coal for fuel and water for the boiler. A typical locomotive of the 1920s would routinely consume several thousand gallons of water an hour to make the steam that powered the engine. Water and fuel stops took time and slowed schedules. A few lines minimized the need for water stops by building elaborate enroute watering systems, consisting of long track pans between the rails and mechanical water scoops that enabled the locomotive to refill its tender with water at speed.

In the 1930s, the airplane, which had been little more than a sideshow novelty a decade earlier, had become the latest mode of intercity transport. In addition to being faster than trains, planes were new and exciting. They were a vision of the future, and people were fascinated by them. Today we take jet planes for

granted, but in the 1930s, the simple propeller plane was admired. Public enthusiasm for air travel was reflected by their willingness to embrace it. Despite the devastating effects of the Depression, passenger air travel expanded sixteen-fold during the ten years between 1930 and 1940. Likewise the private automobile, already popular by 1920s, continued to enjoy widespread public support. Before World War I, American Railroads had carried some 98 percent of all intercity passengers. By the 1930s, their market share had sagged and revenues had plummeted. Simply running the same old steam powered trains with their old fashioned cars wasn't good enough anymore. The railroads needed something new and exciting. Something fast and sleek. What they came up with was the streamliner.

To the public, the streamliner seemed to appear out of nowhere, overnight, without any warning. However, the streamliner was really a long time in coming. It was the result of melding of three innovative concepts: lightweight construction developed for the airline and automobile industries, compact internal combustion engines developed for U.S. Navy ships and subs, and sophisticated new streamlined styling.

The basis of the first streamliners, were self propelled gasoline-electric railcars, already familiar to American railroads. These funny looking cars, nicknamed "doodlebugs," had been puttering around on branch lines for years. They were cheap to operate, inexpensive to maintain, but not particularly appealing.

Two big Western railroads led the charge. Union Pacific and Chicago, Burlington & Quincy embarked on programs to develop internal combustion streamliners at the same time. These two age-old competitors had been dueling for domination of

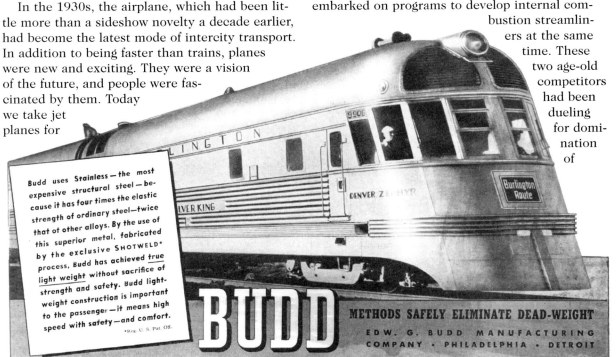

Budd uses Stainless — the most expensive structural steel — because it has four times the elastic strength of ordinary steel—twice that of other alloys. By the use of this superior metal, fabricated by the exclusive SHOTWELD* process, Budd has achieved true light weight without sacrifice of strength and safety. Budd lightweight construction is important to the passenger—it means high speed with safety—and comfort.

*Reg. U. S. Pat. Off.

BUDD METHODS SAFELY ELIMINATE DEAD-WEIGHT
EDW. G. BUDD MANUFACTURING COMPANY · PHILADELPHIA · DETROIT

Western traffic for decades. Whatever one railroad did, the other was soon to try to rival. And the two companies raced each other to see which one could first awe the public with its new streamliner. Union Pacific had Pullman build an aluminum train, while Burlington contracted with the Budd Company of Philadelphia for a shiny, stainless steel streamliner—both were new materials for train construction. For propulsion, the railroads turned to General Motor's Winton engine for a new compact, high-horsepower diesel design that was being developed.

Pullman's train was ready first. Since it was completed before the Winton diesel was ready, Union Pacific opted for an older, spark plug engine instead. It wasn't as powerful or as efficient as a diesel, but that didn't matter much so long as it worked. The train was fantastic—it looked like something right out of the pages of *Popular Science*. It was painted Armour yellow with golden brown trim, and had aerodynamic styling. The front of the train featured a vast grill that looked like a screaming mouth, and a turret like cab for the engineer to sit in that appeared like a row of demonic eyes. The body of the train had a low profile and its three cars, including the leading powercar, were articulated to form a single flexible unit. Union Pacific's new train debuted in February 1934 and was called, quite appropriately, the *Streamliner*. Dispatched on a nationwide tour, it raced from town to town, where people flocked trackside to watch it race past. The train was an immediate sensation. No one had every seen anything like it. The *Streamliner* was a striking contrast to the smoke belching steam train that had become an omnipresent element of the American landscape: it was new, modern, and, fast. It was an airplane on rails!

Burlington waited for Winton's diesel engine and debuted its shiny 'Silver Bullet' in April 1934, just two months after Union Pacific's *Streamliner*. This train was called *Zephyr*, named after the Greek God of Wind. It featured a stunning shovelnose profile, a shining silver body, and a rounded observation car at its tail. Like UP's streamliner, the *Zephyr's* streamlined form was the result of extensive wind tunnel tests, designed for speed. If the public was fascinated with UP's train, they were utterly thrilled with the awesome appearance of the *Zephyr*. Just imagine the excitement it caused racing across the Great Plains at more than 100 mph! The *Zephyr* was greeted by tens of thousands of people and cheered everywhere it went. After their publicity tours, both trains entered regular service. Union Pacific's *Streamliner* became the *City of Salina* and raced daily over the old Kansas Pacific, while Burlington's train became known as the *Pioneer*

*Zephyr* and worked a variety of high-profile runs, in addition to more obscure tasks.

Toy train manufacturer, Lionel, keeping up to date with current railroad fashions, released an O-gauge replica of the *City of Salina*. Envy the lucky child who came down Christmas morning and found a spiffy new Lionel streamliner racing around the tree! Envy the same child who finds the same train in the attic 65 years later. They are real collectors' items, and, in good condition, worth a small fortune today.

Streamliner fever infected American railroads. By the mid 1930s, railroads all across the country were ordering new streamlined trains. New England lines imitated the western streamlined pioneers. No surprise really, as both the *Streamliner* and *Zephyr* toured New England rails before racing toward Western skies. New Haven debuted its futuristic *Comet*, a blue-and-silver speedster built by Goodyear, while Boston & Maine unveiled its *Zephyr* lookalike, *Flying Yankee*. Soon the idea of using streamlined diesel-electric locomotives that were not incorporated in a fixed articulated train caught on. Baltimore & Ohio and Santa Fe were two of the earliest proponents of this new venue. Santa Fe's famous Super Chief was a deluxe extra fare streamlined train with a touch of class. It was the preferred choice for movie stars heading to Hollywood, as it ran from Chicago to Los Angeles across the Southwest. Migrant workers rolling west along Route 66, escaping the Dustbowl in their jalopies, might have seen the glint of the setting sun reflecting off *Super Chief's* stainless steel sleepers. Such a sight would have been a sign of hope in decade known for its dreariness.

Diesels were a novelty not embraced by more traditional lines. Southern Pacific debuted its colorful streamlined *Daylight*, Milwaukee Road its high speed *Hiawatha*, and *New York Central* its all new *20th Century Limited*, using new streamlined steam locomotives. These magnificent machines were the epitome of refined technology and combined a hundred years of research and development with the latest industrial designs.

The Pennsylvania Railroad had its own ideas for new trains. In the late 1920s it had begun electrifying its heavily used New York to Washington mainline. In 1934, it designed a new type of electric locomotive designated GG1, for both heavy freight and high speed passenger service. PRR gave industrial designer Raymond Loewy the task of cleaning up the GG1's streamlining. Among other refinements, Loewy, replaced conventional riveted design with a welded body, and added his trademark "Cat's whiskers" striping.

By the mid-1930s, dozens of the streamlined, doubled-ended GG1's were whisking passengers

"Better Trains Follow General Motors Locomotives".

between New York's Pennsylvania Station and Washington Union Terminal. By 1939, PRR's wire had reached Pennsylvania's State Capitol at Harrisburg. PRR also acquired a fleet of streamlined passenger cars and re-equipped its famous *Broadway Limited* to compete with New York Central's all new streamlined *20th Century*. Like UP and Burlington, Pennsy and Central were age old rivals. They vied for the best and fastest New York to Chicago run. Both the *Broadway* and *Century* were high status, all Pullman sleeper trains, and in their day they were the most pleasant way to travel. Most people couldn't afford the extra fare for these fancy flagship trains, and settled for the railroads' comfortable, but less-prestigious runs. Yet, the magazine advertising tended to stress the well known trains. The railroad's reasoning was simple: a railroad's flagship was the finest advertising that money could buy. The prevailing philosophy was that you put your best foot forward with your flagship train. This demonstrated to passengers the high quality of your service, but more importantly, demonstrated to shippers and stockholders that the company was in sound financial shape. The irony was that sometimes the shiny flagship was just a façade. In the darkest days of the Depression, the *Broadway*, for all its glory, often ran nearly empty between New York and Chicago.

Some lines couldn't justify the cost of all-new streamlined locomotives, and instead dressed up old engines in streamlined shrouds. Reading's *Crusader* featured Budd stainless steel cars, and a solid old Pacific wearing a new coat of armor. It might not have been all new, but the passengers didn't mind. Reading was a resourceful railroad and always and made the best of recycled equip-

ment.

Just as the railroads were re-equipping their passenger fleets with fancy new trains, and passengers were flocking back to the rails, the politics of war in Europe set the stage for another showdown. In the late 1930s, the railroads were all too aware that someday soon they might need to brace themselves for an onslaught of war time traffic. And this time they would be prepared, and not have to face the indignity of government control. Save for the odd new streamliner, during the worst days of Depression, most lines made do with their existing fleets of steamers, some already 25 or 30 years old. But now, on the eve of war, they were again buying new fleets of locomotives. Most lines looked to steam to haul their trains. Sure, diesels were nice for flashy advertising promos, and looked good on the streamliners, but when it came down to business, it was steam that did the real work. By the 1930s, Baldwin, Alco, and Lima had refined the steam locomotive into a powerful, reliable pulling machine, vastly more powerful than those of an earlier generation, and more efficient too!

General Motor's Electro Motive Corporation (soon to be its Electro Motive Division) had other ideas, and in 1939, introduced its model 'FT" freight diesel in competition to steam power. The FT spent a year marching around the country, hauling heavy freight up and down some of the toughest lines the railroads had. Some lines, such as the Santa Fe, were mightily impressed and quickly placed orders for the FT. Other roads turned around and ordered even more powerful steam locomotives. Union Pacific set out to build the 'world's largest' steam locomotive, its massive 4-8-8-4 'Big Boys'. UP seemed to say:

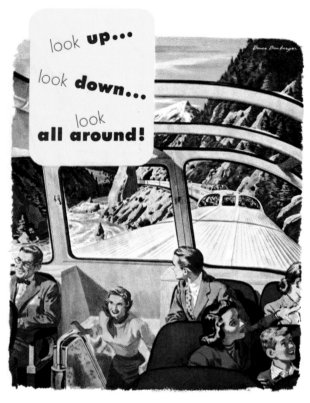

look **up**...
look **down**...
look
**all around!**

"Stand back FT, here's some real power!"

The first Big Boys arrived in 1940, a year after the FT diesels' public debut, and for a very short time, the Big Boys really were the world's largest. The Big Boys' builder, Alco, was also into the diesel business, and had designed its own road diesels to compete with Electro-Motive's. It hired industrial designer Otto Kuhler—one of Raymond Loewy's contemporaries—to handle the streamlining. Out on the West Coast, Southern Pacific was content with steam power, and was looking for more Lima 4-8-4's to haul its growing fleet of *Daylight* passenger trains. Lima locomotives were the real Cadillacs of steam, beautiful, precision machines that were a delight to behold, representing sheer power and industrial majesty. Southern Pacific wanted the best for its Daylight, which by the late 1930s was the most profitable passenger train in the United States—and entirely steam-hauled at that!

Although Europe and Asia were embroiled in full-fledged war, America had stayed clear of the fighting for a couple of years. The railroads continued to ready themselves for the eventuality of United States involvement, yet at the same time introduced more flashy new passenger trains. On a bright, clear December morning in 1941, New York Central debuted its all new streamlined *Empire State Express*, sending photographers and movie crews along the Hudson to photograph the train. It was hauled by one of New York Central's

acclaimed Hudson-type steam locomotives, and specially styled specifically for this run. Little did New York Central know, that the big publicity splash it had intended for December 8, 1941, would be totally overshadowed by a far more serious event! As the *Empire State Express* press run was making its way toward Buffalo, on the other side of the world Japanese bombers were aimed at Pearl Harbor.

America was again at war, and soon the railroads were flooded with more traffic then they had ever handled before. Industrial production was stepped up, troops were moving from coast to coast, and suddenly everyone was traveling! The railroads performed heroically in the face of adversity and unlike their failure in World War I, American railroads stayed abreast of the tide of traffic. Many lines wanted the new diesels they had tried in the months before the War, but were denied them because of strict government restrictions on valuable commodities needed for diesel production. Instead railroads were encouraged to order new steam locomotives, and they did, by the hundreds!

A few months earlier, railroads had been advertising in an effort to attract new passengers, but now the war had generated more traffic than they could rightly handle, and the tone of their advertising changed to reflect this. Railroad advertising was aimed to show how they were supporting the war effort by demonstrating how new locomotives and facilities were operating efficiently. Instead of showing flashy new streamliners, they showed freight yards and terminals, explained how signals protected and directed rail traffic, while urging people to curtail unnecessary travel, and of course, "Buy war bonds!"

Thanks in part to the ability of American railroads to operate efficiently during the war, America and its Allies were victorious. By 1945, the tide of traffic had begun to recede, and once the fighting had concluded, the railroads began to look toward resuming normal peacetime operations once again. Following the War, the railroads embarked on massive investment in new locomotives, new trains and new colorful advertising campaigns. Something had changed, though, in regard to motive power philosophy, after the War, very few lines were interested in new steam locomotives. They had seen what diesels could do, and understood the vast cost savings they could achieve by using them, so the railroads set out to discontinue the use of steam, and buy all new fleets of shiny streamlined diesels to haul both their freight and passenger trains.

So many new streamliners debuted after the war it would be impossible to even list them all! By 1950 there were more than 150 streamlined runs in America. Railroads that had ignored the advent of the streamliner before the war took notice on its conclusion. Northern Pacific re-equipped its famous *North Coast Limited* with an all-streamlined consist handsomely styled by Raymond Loewy, while NP's competitor, Great Northern, re-equipped its *Empire Builder*. Southern Pacific introduced its *Cascade*, and *Shasta Daylight*. The Burlington, Rio Grande, and Western Pacific railroads joined forces in 1949 and assembled one of the most famous of all Western passenger trains, the fabled *California Zephyr*. This sleek, diesel powered beauty featured a fabulous new type of car called the Vista Dome, which had a bubble-like, glass-topped observation lounge that allowed passengers to enjoy to passing scenery. The wonder of the dome was that passengers could see ahead, above the roof of the train—and for the first time see in all 360 degrees!

The *Vista Dome* was the vision of the Budd Company, the same firm that had built Burlington's original *Zephyr*. In the 1950s, Budd became synonymous with another type of passenger car, the self propelled rail diesel car, known by its initials as an RDC, or for its manufacturer as a 'Budd Car.' The Budd Car allowed railroads to economize their passenger services by eliminating the need for separate locomotives. This simplified operations and greatly reduced costs. The Budd Car was particularly popular on lightly used branch lines or on big city suburban services.

Despite tremendous investment in new long distance trains, railroads found that by the mid 1950s they still were losing market share to the airlines and automobiles. While the streamliners and the war had temporarily reversed these trends, the future did not look good. Since lightweight streamliners had done the trick during the Depression, the railroads tried this concept again, and in the mid to late 1950s, a whole new wave of lightweight trains were on the rails, included some based on Budd's RDC. Unfortunately, despite vigorous advertising, all of these trains failed to win the hearts of the passenger, and the saga of the American passenger train was nearly over. The advent of the Interstate Highway system and the jet plane compounded the railroads' problems. During the 1960s, the whole passenger network withered away. It appeared that soon there would be no passenger trains at all in America as the railroads were losing millions on the remaining runs, and desperately seeking ways to exit the passenger business altogether. By the late 1960s, the railroads were more prone to advertise their freight services, where they were generating nearly all of their revenue.

In 1971, the federal government stepped in and created Amtrak in order to relieve the railroads of the burden of running passenger trains. Since that time, Amtrak has provided the vast majority of intercity passenger service in the United States. In the tradition of the private railroads, Amtrak often advertises its trains. In December 2000, Amtrak set an important precedent with the first of the *Acela Express* high speed trains, whisking passengers faster than ever before between Boston, New York and Washington. In stretches the train operates at a top speed of 150 mph, making it the fastest regularly scheduled passenger train in North America. More importantly it introduces a significantly higher quality of service than offered on earlier trains. It is a bold step in the long tradition of the American passenger train, and, as expected, accompanied by imaginative railroad advertising.

## Built of ALCOA *Aluminum*
### this New Pullman "Travels Light" and Safely

Builders of riding comfort and safety for three-quarters of a century, Pullman takes another step forward with the new "George M. Pullman"—made almost entirely of the light, strong alloys of Alcoa Aluminum. Cutting 50% from the weight of the standard Pullman, Alcoa Aluminum makes for swifter, smoother riding with even greater safety, greater durability of structural parts. Alcoa Aluminum comes in every form needed for car construction—extruded shapes and sections, rolled plates, structural shapes in any desired

length up to 90 feet. For these reasons, too, *all* transportation units—buses, trucks, tank cars, mine cars, elevators—every form of mass in motion is rapidly being redesigned from the wheels up in Alcoa Aluminum.

The "George M. Pullman"—one of two all-aluminum Pullmans exhibited at A Century of Progress Exposition. Weight 96,980 lbs., including air-conditioning equipment. With ordinary materials it would weigh 180,000 lbs. Due to its light weight, it needs only 4-wheel trucks. (These are fabricated of Aluminum.) Yet it surpasses American Railway Association standards for strength and safety. Smart, modern decorative scheme in aluminum. Even the insulation is crumpled aluminum foil.

### All industry finds the going easier with Alcoa Aluminum

Bringing efficiency and economy to industry, saleability to industry's products, Alcoa Aluminum is finding its way into most progressive plants. Light in weight, yet strong as structural steel, non-contaminating, non-magnetic, a good conductor of heat and electricity, this is the ideal metal for production equipment. To the finished product, Alcoa Aluminum brings ease of handling, durability, attractiveness. In the plant itself Alcoa Albron as a paint pigment protects against rust, weathering, smoke and acid fumes—makes brighter working conditions.

There's a place in *your* plant and your product for Alcoa Aluminum. Let us show you how to use, form and handle this metal. Address: ALUMINUM COMPANY *of* AMERICA; 1802 Gulf Building, PITTSBURGH, PENNSYLVANIA.

**MODERN VENTILATION USES THE MODERN METAL**

Alcoa Aluminum makes this air-filter lighter, easier to install. This metal resists corrosion, isn't affected by moisture in the air, absorbs sound from vibration, not to mention its attractiveness, appearance and long life.

**SOMETHING NEW IN LIGHTING FIXTURES**

Here Alcoa Aluminum helps with its light weight, its light-reflecting surface. A color-filter gives this fixture the appearance of expensive translucent glass but the light is really indirect. Made of deep-etched aluminum, it is equally attractive day and night.

**FOR EYE-HAZARDOUS JOBS**

These goggle frames, made of Alcoa Aluminum, are light in weight, easy to wear through the day's work—yet strong. Alumilite finish gives them attractiveness, longer life and corrosion resistance—an important detail in many plants.

## ALCOA
# ALUMINUM

Because of the Great Depression's dreadful impact, Pullman sleeping car production nose-dived from 343 units in 1930 to only two in 1931. Only six Pullman cars left the shops in 1932, and the situation was even worse in 1933. However, the "George M. Pullman" and one other all-aluminum car were exhibited at the 1933-34 Chicago "Century of Progress" Exhibition. Shown in this November 1933 ad, the George M. Pullman solarium car is a rare transitional model that bridged the old style with the streamlined.

# Because Women Liked Kettles

I T IS TRUE that a man, and a bachelor at that, made the first commercial Aluminum. But it was the women of America who first gave it commercial importance. It seems incredible that, only fifty years ago, few homes in America contained a single ounce of Aluminum in any form. Today Aluminum ranks fifth in the great family of common metals. In the homes of 1936 there is hardly a room in which Aluminum is not serving, visibly or invisibly.

It all began with a teakettle.

Timidly, because men are creatures of habit and tradition, the young Aluminum industry ventured to make a teakettle of the new metal, because it would conduct heat so much faster than the older metals. The kettles were offered to women with some trepidation.

But women are bold spirits! They liked the kettles! The mere fact that the metal itself was new and comparatively unheard of, meant less than nothing to them, so long as they got results. They liked the kettles and they demanded other Aluminum cooking utensils that were light and bright and friendly to food.

This preference for lightness and brightness was quickly recognized by the men in the aggressive young electrical industry. Thanks to their enterprise, the teakettle and the shining Aluminum pots and pans soon had labor-saving electrical appliances as working companions.

The electric vacuum cleaner, the drudgery-banishing electric washing machine, the smart electric waffle mold, and a score of other electrical appliances for easier and more gracious homekeeping, all made use of one or more of the advantages of this versatile metal. With the coming of electric refrigeration ice cube trays were made of Aluminum to speed freezing.

It took more to make an industry than the discovery by Charles Martin Hall, in 1886, of an economical process for extracting Aluminum from the common mineral, bauxite. It took long, plodding years of research, and scientific and manufacturing development, to attain the strong capable alloys of today. Also it took generous co-operation from the engineering profession and the metal-working industry.

But when we who work in Aluminum are tempted to pride ourselves on the progress the industry has made in a brief half century, we are made properly humble by the realization that the modern streamline trains, the motor trucks and buses, the building facades now being constructed of Aluminum, are a tribute to the audacity of the homemakers of America; to them and to the enterprising household utility industries which have grown up to serve them.

Lionel's striking O Gauge version of UP's M-10000 shares the spotlight with an aluminum pan in this most unusual railroad-oriented ad from Alcoa, which first appeared in June 1936 in celebration of the company's 50th Anniversary.

# NEWS QUIZ!

*(Answers in box below)*

## TEST YOURSELF WITH THESE NEWS PICTURES...

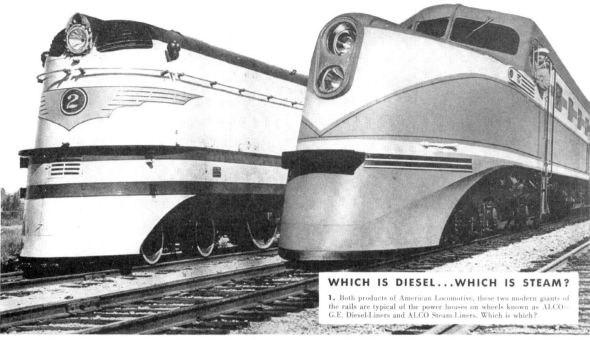

### WHICH IS DIESEL...WHICH IS STEAM?

**1.** Both products of American Locomotive, these two modern giants of the rails are typical of the power houses on wheels known as ALCO—G.E. Diesel-Liners and ALCO Steam-Liners. Which is which?

**2.** One of the gun-mounts built by the American Locomotive Company as part of the Defense Program. In which branch of the U. S. Army will it be used?

**3.** Another weapon now coming off American Locomotive production lines is the medium M-3 tank. How many men comprise the crew of this type tank?

**4.** This is what is called a Scotch boiler. It was built for Britain by American Locomotive far ahead of original schedule. In what is this type boiler used?

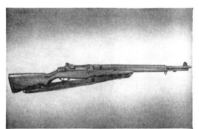

**5.** The American Army's new standard rifle, built with springs made by American Locomotive, can fire up to 100 shots a minute. By what name is it popularly known?

### HERE ARE THE ANSWERS
#### (NO FAIR PEEKING!)

**1.** On the left is one of the American Locomotive Company's modern Steam-Liners; the other is one of its ALCO—G.E. Diesel-Liners. Each is among the finest of its type and both types are serving the different needs of modern railroads today.

**2.** The gun-mount pictured on this page is being built for use in the Field Artillery.

**3.** The usual crew of the medium M-3 tank built by American Locomotive consists of seven men.

**4.** Scotch boilers are used in ships. This one was built for use in the British Merchant Marine.

**5.** This extraordinary rifle is generally known as a Garand, which is the name of its inventor.

# AMERICAN LOCOMOTIVE

### DIESEL    STEAM
### ELECTRIC

In December 1941, when this Alco ad appeared, America had just been attacked at Pearl Harbor and was fully involved in World War II. It was appropriate that Alco's various military products were shown, along with a steam and a diesel locomotive. The steam locomotive at left pulled the Milwaukee Road's streamlined *Hiawatha*; at right is a DL-109 diesel.

# AMERICA IN MOTION.... by Lowell Thomas
## News summary from national arsenal of mobile power

I'VE SEEN a locomotive over 130 feet long, speeding war material over mountain grades, and I'll never forget it! Now I'm here where 20 of them were born...the home of "The Big Boys," 7,000 horse-power, the heaviest and most powerful locomotives ever made...and I know now that some of the tanks and gun carriages on that train were made right here, side by side with "Big Boy."

I'VE WATCHED troops unloading from train after train, powered by fast Diesel or Steam-Liners. And now I understand how the railroads are able to handle this big job, biggest in history, so well. Here they build the most modern, streamlined locomotives in the world, both steam and diesel-powered. Build them fast. Build them to meet special wartime requirements. Build them to win.

I'VE FELT all along that power to produce is our greatest asset. But I never saw a speed-up so swift or so well directed as this. Men swarming all over a Diesel-Locomotive, building medium tanks... forging big-gun parts... skilled man-power under experienced directions. We Americans, we expect miracles. And by George, we get them!

I ASKED about power, and I got my answer in terms of diesels for the Navy ...Diesel or Steam-Liners for the railroads, whichever is needed to do a particular job best...tanks and gun carriages for the Army ...power to turn the tide of war against any enemy. A great country, this. And something I saw here tells me we're going to keep it that way.

# AMERICAN LOCOMOTIVE
## MANUFACTURERS OF MOBILE POWER
STEAM, DIESEL AND ELECTRIC LOCOMOTIVES

MARINE DIESELS, TANKS, GUN CARRIAGES AND OTHER ORDNANCE

Commentary by Lowell Thomas describes America's wartime railroad power from American Locomotive in April 1942. At that time, steam was still an important factor in new locomotive production.

THE **NEW HAVEN** R.R.

SERVING **NEW YORK** AND THE GREAT INDUSTRIAL STATES of **MASSACHUSETTS, RHODE ISLAND** AND **CONNECTICUT**

NEW HAVEN

## Quick - what's it pulling, boxcars or berths?

EVEN a railroad man couldn't tell—until he sees more than the locomotive.

For this particular locomotive—built by American Locomotive and General Electric for the New Haven—is the product of an important development.

You see, for years the railroads have had to bear the terrific expense of buying and maintaining different types of locomotives for freight and passenger service. But today—as a result of American Locomotive's hundred years of experience in railroading—this problem has been licked.

Locomotives are now being built that are *interchangeable*—that can haul fast freight trains one day

and crack passenger trains the next. And they may be Diesel-electric or steam or any modification of either type. It doesn't matter whether they use oil or coal —the important thing is economy of performance.

This development means big savings for the railroads, because it helps reduce the number of locomotives a railroad must buy and maintain. And that's important to you. For it is out of a railroad's *savings* that improvements in service can be offered.

This is just one of many developments that will contribute to finer postwar railroading. And it is significant that it comes from the Company that gave America its first Diesel locomotive, built the world's

largest steam locomotive, and has supplied an important share of the locomotives being used for war purposes by the United Nations.

**American Locomotive**

Alco

THE MARK OF MODERN LOCOMOTION

In April 1945 American Locomotive Company (better known as Alco) advertised a versatile new model of streamlined diesel locomotive. In the early days of diesel, manufacturers generally offered models specialized for either freight or diesel service; for example, passenger units usually were equipped with gear ratios suited to high-speed, low-tonnage pulling power and steam generators for train heating. Alco's DL-109, as ordered by New Haven, was touted as being suitable for both types of service, though in truth the 10 units featured 19:64 gearing, capable of 80 mph—actually Alco's standard for freight service. A New Haven route map is inserted at upper left. This is an example of a time-worn ad printed on interior wartime paper, but it's worth including in this collection!

# How many locomotives make a railroad?

HOW many locomotives a railroad needs depends on many factors—the size of the railroad, the kind and amount of load it carries, the nature of the territory it serves, and so forth.

Today, however, regardless of these factors, a railroad can do the same job with fewer locomotives—thanks to an important development.

You see, for years, the railroads bought and maintained different types of equipment for freight and passenger service. Locomotives powerful enough to haul freight trains have usually been too costly to operate on passenger runs—and locomotives speedy enough for passenger service haven't had the pulling power to haul freights.

But now—out of the shops of American Loco-

motive—are coming locomotives that are *interchangeable*. Locomotives powerful enough to haul freights, yet speedy enough to handle passenger trains, with low maintenance costs and high availability. Locomotives that reduce the need for "helper" locomotives in getting trains over steep grades.

The principles underlying this development can be applied to any type of locomotive—diesel-electric or steam or any modification of either type. It doesn't matter whether a locomotive is powered by coal or oil—*economy of performance* is American Locomotive's chief concern.

This is just one of many developments that will contribute to finer postwar railroading. And it is significant that it comes from the Company that

designed America's first diesel-electric locomotive, built the world's largest steam locomotive and has supplied an important share of the locomotives now being used for war purposes by the United Nations.

In August 1945 the war was nearly won when Alco presented this eye-catching display of motive power. Ready for the postwar rush to dieselize, the company had been developing models for a variety of uses—switching, passenger, freight, or even all of the above, hence the road-switcher. Starting with the Alco RS-1, road-switchers were the locomotives that spelled the end of steam. They were highly versatile, well-adapted to branchline service, and fuel costs were a fraction of what it cost to run a similar steam locomotive.

"GOOD MORNING. YOUR EGGS ARE FRYING, YOUR BACON IS CRISP, AND YOU'VE JUST

Amtrak's Coast Starlight near San Luis Obispo, California.

Since 1971, most intercity rail passenger service in the U.S. has been operated by government-sponsored Amtrak. For years, the carriers was strapped with worn-out equipment, and to economize made drastic reductions in the number of cities served. But despite constant challenges (especially to its relatively modest congressionally approved subsidies), Amtrak has kept American passenger trains rolling

TRAVELED 400 MILES."

While you were sweet dreaming on your pillow, Amtrak was whisking you 400 miles closer to your destination, and you didn't even bat an eye.

Now Amtrak's full service kitchen is preparing breakfast to your order, and it will be served with a smile and a passing view. Where else but on one of the most advanced passenger train systems in the world...Amtrak.

In the last 10 years, Amtrak has replaced 75% of its trains with all new equipment, and has refurbished the other 25%. We boast one of the best on-time performance records of any carrier in the transportation industry. Our computerized reservations system is second to none, and now there are over 10,000 travel agents at your service.

So come and feel the magic, as 19 million riders a year do. Call your travel agent or call Amtrak at 1-800-USA-RAIL. You'll find traveling so easy, you can do it with your eyes closed.

and has even managed to purchase new equipment and upgrade service. This February 1985 ad tells some of the story. The ad features the *Coast Starlight* on the SP near San Luis Obispo, Calif. Note the high-level Superliner equipment that has become standard on most long-distance Amtrak trains.

# Amtrak

Heritage Single Slumbercoach/Day

Heritage Single Slumbercoach/Night

Buffet Car

**Slumbercoach** rooms are designed for budget-minded passengers who want Sleeping Car privacy and comfort. (The modest price of Slumbercoach ticket does not include meals.) A **Single Slumbercoach** provides one seat for day travel, and a bed that folds down from the wall for sleeping. If you're traveling with a friend, the **Double Slumbercoach** provides two single seats for daytime, and upper and lower berths at night. All Slumbercoaches have lavatory facilities. Storage space is compact, so you'll want to check any large luggage, and just keep a small traveling bag with you. (We'll explain more about checking baggage in our Tips and Services section.)

**Buffet-style Dining Cars**—On Amtrak's Florida service and Auto Train, unique Buffet-style Dining Cars are operated. Passengers make their selection from an attractive choice of fresh-cooked entrees and tasty desserts. An Amtrak attendant then assists passengers in carrying meals to their table.

**Food Service Cars**—On a limited number of trains, the primary food service is offered by a combination dining and lounge car. Passengers choose from a variety of tasty pre-prepared tray meals at reasonable prices. Tablecloths, silk flowers, at-seat service and the American countryside, the hallmarks of Amtrak Food Service Cars, all make dining a unique experience.

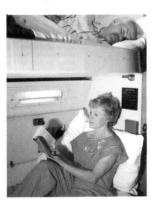

Heritage Double Slumbercoach/Day

Heritage Double Slumbercoach/Night

Call your Travel Agent or 1-800-USA-RAIL.

**Bedrooms** on full-service trains are designed for two adults, or one adult and two small children. Meals are included in the Bedroom fare. One type of Bedroom has two chair-style seats; the other has a long sofa. Both models contain one upper and one lower berth. Our Bedrooms are quite comfortable—although not everyone feels confident climbing a ladder into an upper berth. In such cases, we recommend reserving two Roomettes, for two lower berths. Each Bedroom has enclosed lavatory facilities. There's enough space to store two average-sized suitcases and one smaller traveling bag. A sliding partition combines two Bedrooms into a Suite, for large traveling parties.

Heritage Roomette/Night

Heritage Roomette/Day

**Roomettes** are enclosed First Class accommodations designed for seating and sleeping for one adult. By day, there's a chair with lots of legroom and, by night, a bed that folds out of the wall. Lavatory facilities are available in each Roomette. (To use the facility at night, the bed must be raised.) You'll have storage space for two average-sized suitcases. Complimentary meals are included in the Roomette fare.

Amtrak displays details about its 1988 accommodations, with Eastern trains at left, Western trains at right. The look is more modern compared with ads from an era, but the passengers still have the same smiles on their faces! At this time, most Western trains were using Superliner equipment, while the

**Western Route Accommodations**

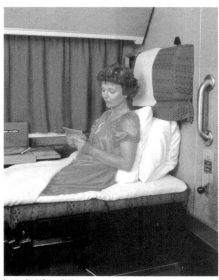

Superliner Special Bedroom/Night

Superliner Special Bedroom/Day

On the lower level, the Superliner **Special Bedroom** is a popular mid-priced option with convenient private toilet facilities. The Special Bedroom runs the width of the Sleeping Car, with two facing, reclining seats for daytime travel. Upper and lower sleeping berths fold down at night.

The Special Bedroom will accommodate the physically impaired, with ample space for wheelchairs and an accessible toilet. If you ask in advance, your attendant will be happy to deliver food and beverages to your room.

The ultimate in Sleeping Car travel is the Superliner **Deluxe Bedroom.** These rooms offer comfortable accommodations with a sofa plus an armchair by day, then an upper and an extra-wide lower berth by night. All Deluxe rooms are located on the upper level with a large picture window on one side and a curtained, windowed wall toward the corridor on the other. Sink, vanity and private toilet facilities are included. And, an exclusive feature of Deluxe Bedrooms is your own private shower!

A sliding partition allows two Bedrooms to be combined into a Bedroom Suite. The Deluxe Bedroom is **the** way to cross America in style.

Superliner Deluxe Bedroom/Night

Superliner Deluxe Bedroom/Day

Superliner Sightseer Lounge

# Call your Travel Agent
# or 1-800-USA-RAIL.

Eastern trains were using conventional passenger cars—in some cases aging Heritage equipment built before the Amtrak era. Subsequent equipment purchases have allowed retirement of the Heritage fleet, and allowed Superliners to be added to many Eastern routes.

**Eastern Route**

### Between Washington, DC and Florida

We can understand why you might want to have your car on vacation with you. For convenience, economy or if you plan on being somewhere for a long period of time (such as spending the winter in Florida).

**Auto Train** will take you, your car and all the baggage you pack in your car, between Lorton, Virginia (just outside of Washington, DC) and Sanford, Florida (near Orlando).

You'll travel in style and comfort while your car (with baggage safely stored inside) will be professionally handled and secured in enclosed car carriers.

Cars being loaded

# Want to use your car on vacation?

Table/Movie Car

The festivities begin in the **Auto Train's** Lounge Car two hours before the train departs. Here, you can enjoy coffee, tea and fruit drinks. Or, you can purchase a variety of sandwiches, snacks, sweets, soft drinks and alcoholic beverages.

Buffet Dining Car

Then, later in the evening, dinner is served in the Buffet Car. Your choice of several entrees, side dishes, salad and dessert along with coffee, tea and wine, is included in the price of your ticket.

**16**

Dome Coach

After dinner, you can enjoy a feature-length motion picture in the Table Car; stroll to the Dome Lounge Car where you can mingle with other travelers, play cards and join in the singing around the piano; or return to your Coach seat to read, write or relax. You can also view the moonlit scenery and the starlit sky from the glass-topped Dome Car.

# Just bring it with you

And when you feel like turning in for the night, just put your seat back, your feet up and your reading light out. We'll provide the pillow and the blanket. If you'd prefer more privacy, you can reserve a First Class one-passenger Roomette or two-passenger Bedroom. Both convert easily from seating by day to a sleeping compartment, with washroom facilities and individual temperature controls, by night. (See page 54 for sleeping accommodation descriptions.)

Next morning, whether you travel First Class or Coach, you'll start the day with a complimentary continental breakfast. And before you know it, you'll be at your destination, in your car and on the road. Relaxed, refreshed and ready to go.

**Things to do while you're waiting to go...**

If we can take you back to the beginning of your trip for a moment...it's true that you have to be at you boarding station at least two hours before departure. If you find yourself arriving with extra time to spare, we recommend visiting historic Occoquan, near Lorton, Virginia, or the town of Sanford, Florida. In Occoquan you can take a walking tour of a beautifully restored 18th-century community known for its antiques and handcrafts. We also offer a special hotel rate at the Comfort Inn in Alexandria, Virginia, just 15 minutes from Lorton. In Sanford, while you're waiting for the train you can relax at Fort Mellon Park on Lake Monroe. Take an extra day and cruise down the St. John's River aboard the Rivership *Romance*. The famous Central Florida Zoo is nearby. And of course, after check-in, you can relax in our Lounge.

Lounge Car

So this year, go ahead and take your car on vacation with you, aboard Amtrak's **Auto Train**. It sure beats driving. Coming and going.

---

This page from a 1988 brochure explains the advantages of one of Amtrak's most unique operations—the *Auto Train*. The concept is simple and popular: You drive your car to the station, where it is loaded onto a rail auto carrier. Then, you check yourself into a Superliner car in the front half of the same train. After a relaxing overnight trip, your car is unloaded and you drive off to enjoy your vacation. *Auto Train* started as an independent (non-Amtrak) service with two routes into its Florida (Sanford, near Orlando) terminal, from Washington, D.C., and from Louisville, Ky. The Midwest service didn't make it, but the East Coast service was taken over by Amtrak, and it has flourished. Travelers find it an easy alternative to driving 900 miles on hectic Interstate 95.

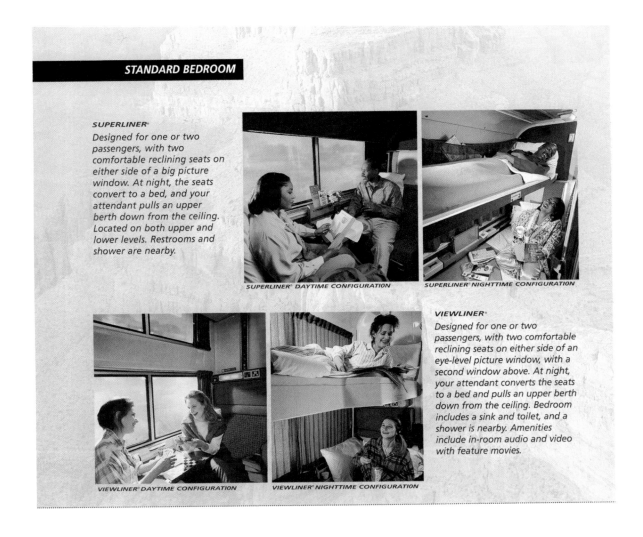

**STANDARD BEDROOM**

**SUPERLINER®**
Designed for one or two passengers, with two comfortable reclining seats on either side of a big picture window. At night, the seats convert to a bed, and your attendant pulls an upper berth down from the ceiling. Located on both upper and lower levels. Restrooms and shower are nearby.

SUPERLINER® DAYTIME CONFIGURATION

SUPERLINER® NIGHTTIME CONFIGURATION

**VIEWLINER®**
Designed for one or two passengers, with two comfortable reclining seats on either side of an eye-level picture window, with a second window above. At night, your attendant converts the seats to a bed and pulls an upper berth down from the ceiling. Bedroom includes a sink and toilet, and a shower is nearby. Amenities include in-room audio and video with feature movies.

VIEWLINER® DAYTIME CONFIGURATION

VIEWLINER® NIGHTTIME CONFIGURATION

DIMENSIONS:
3'6" x 6'6" (1.1m x 2m)

LOWER BERTH:
2'4" x 6'6" (72cm x 2m)

UPPER BERTH WITH STEPS:
2'0" x 6'2" (61cm x 1.9m)
Capacity for 2 small tote bags

SUPERLINER® STANDARD BEDROOM

DIMENSIONS:
3'6" x 6'8" (1.1m x 2m)

LOWER BERTH:
2'4" x 6'6" (72cm x 2m)

UPPER BERTH WITH STEPS:
2'4" x 6'2" (72cm x 1.9m)
Capacity for 2 small suitcases
and garment bag

VIEWLINER® STANDARD BEDROOM

These three pages from a 1999 brochure shows Amtrak's variety of private-room accommodations for the 21st Century, everything from a standard bedroom with room for one or two passengers to a handi-capped-accessible bedroom. Each page compares the amenities available in Superliner cars with those in Viewliner cars. The Viewliners are newer one-level cars featuring a second-tier window, which give a spacious feel. They are generally utilized on East Coast long-distance routes with height restrictions that precludes use of the Superliners, including the *Crescent, Lake Shore Limited, Silver Service* (New York-Florida) and the *Twilight Shoreliner.*

## DELUXE BEDROOM

**SUPERLINER®**

Upper-level bedrooms, superior comfort for two adults. Sofa and armchair convert to a wide lower berth and comfortable upper berth. Private sink and vanity and a fully enclosed private shower and toilet. Two Deluxe Bedrooms can be combined for a Deluxe Suite accommodating four people.

SUPERLINER® DAYTIME CONFIGURATION     SUPERLINER® NIGHTTIME CONFIGURATION

**VIEWLINER®**

Superior comfort for two adults. Sofa and armchair convert to a wide lower berth and comfortable upper berth. Private sink and vanity and a fully enclosed private shower and toilet. Amenities include in-room audio and video with feature movies. Two Deluxe Bedrooms can be combined for a Deluxe Suite accommodating four people.

VIEWLINER® DAYTIME CONFIGURATION     VIEWLINER® NIGHTTIME CONFIGURATION

©Amtrak 1999

**DIMENSIONS:**
6'6" x 7'6" (2m x 2.3m)

**LOWER BERTH:**
3'4" x 6'3" (1m x 1.9m)

**UPPER BERTH WITH LADDER:**
2'4" x 6'2" (72cm x 1.9m)
*Capacity for 2 suitcases*

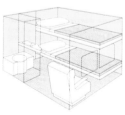

SUPERLINER® DELUXE BEDROOM

**DIMENSIONS:**
6'8" x 7'1" (2m x 2.2m)

**LOWER BERTH:**
3'4" x 6'0" (1m x 1.8m)

**UPPER BERTH WITH LADDER:**
2'4" x 6'2" (72cm x 1.9m)
*Capacity for 2 suitcases*

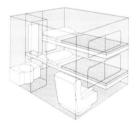

VIEWLINER® DELUXE BEDROOM

## FAMILY BEDROOM

### SUPERLINER®

The Family Bedroom occupies the entire width of the lower level at one end of the car, with private windows on both sides. At night, your attendant converts the long sofa and two seats to a wide lower berth and adult-sized upper berth, plus upper and lower child-size berths. Restrooms and shower are a few steps away.

*SUPERLINER® DAYTIME CONFIGURATION*    *SUPERLINER® NIGHTTIME CONFIGURATION*

*VIEWLINER® DAYTIME CONFIGURATION*    *VIEWLINER® NIGHTTIME CONFIGURATION*

### BEDROOM SUITES
#### VIEWLINER®

Two Deluxe Bedrooms can be combined to create a spacious suite for four, with two sofas and two armchairs converting to wide lower berths and comfortable upper berths, two enclosed showers, sinks and toilets. Amenities include in-room audio and video with feature movies.

#### SUPERLINER®

Combine two Deluxe Bedrooms to make a suite for four.

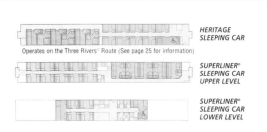

**HERITAGE SLEEPING CAR**

Operates on the Three Rivers℠ Route (See page 25 for information)

**SUPERLINER® SLEEPING CAR UPPER LEVEL**

**SUPERLINER® SLEEPING CAR LOWER LEVEL**

**VIEWLINER® SLEEPING CAR**

**DIMENSIONS:**
*5'2" x 9'5" (1.6m x 2.9m)*

**2 ADULT BERTHS WITH LADDER:**
*UPPER BERTH - 2'4" x 6'2" (72cm x 1.9m)*
*LOWER BERTH - 3'4" x 6'3" (1m x 1.9m)*

**2 CHILD BERTHS:**
*UPPER BERTH - 2'0" x 4'7" (61cm x 1.4m)*
*LOWER BERTH - 2'3" x 4'9" (69cm x 1.5m)*

*Capacity for 2-3 suitcases*

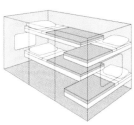

*SUPERLINER® FAMILY BEDROOM*

OVERLEAF: An Amtrak promotional map showing the extent of North American rail passenger service in November 1999. Routes included on the map include trains operated by VIA Rail Canada and Amtrak Thruway connecting bus service.

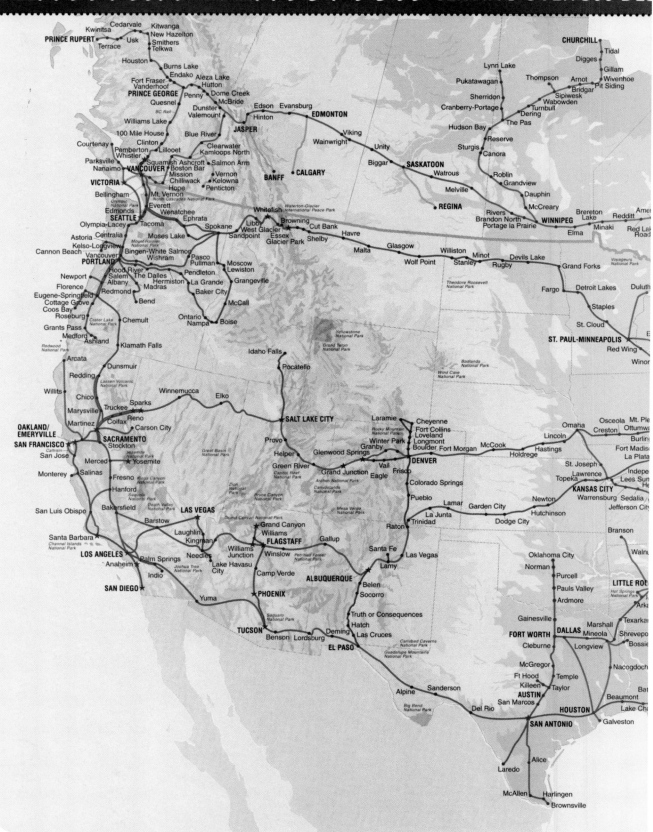

# Amtrak® America SERVING OVER 500 DES

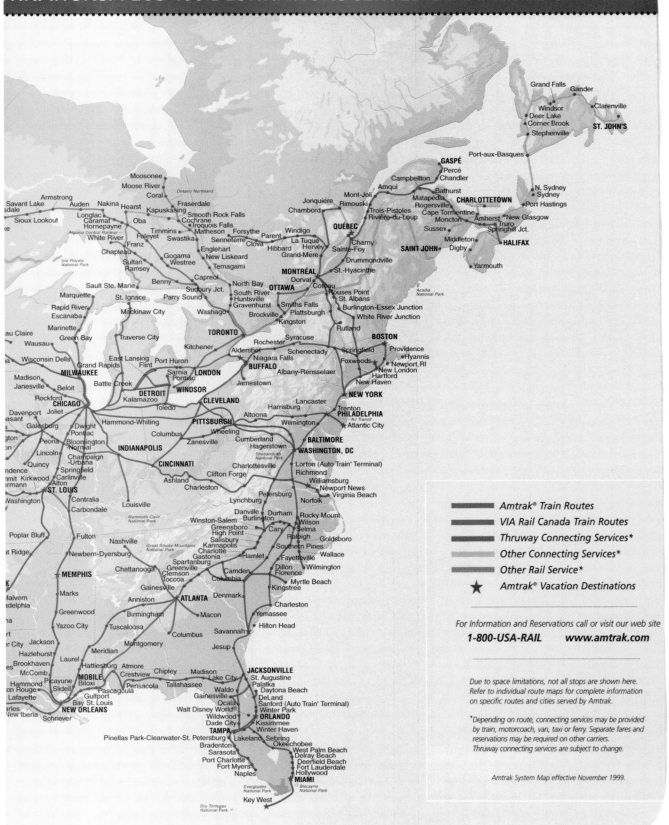

| | |
|---|---|
| ▬▬▬ | Amtrak® Train Routes |
| ▬▬▬ | VIA Rail Canada Train Routes |
| ▬▬▬ | Thruway Connecting Services* |
| ▬▬▬ | Other Connecting Services* |
| ▬▬▬ | Other Rail Service* |
| ★ | Amtrak® Vacation Destinations |

For Information and Reservations call or visit our web site
**1-800-USA-RAIL     www.amtrak.com**

Due to space limitations, not all stops are shown here.
Refer to individual route maps for complete information
on specific routes and cities served by Amtrak.

*Depending on route, connecting services may be provided
by train, motorcoach, van, taxi or ferry. Separate fares and
reservations may be required on other carriers.
Thruway connecting services are subject to change.

Amtrak System Map effective November 1999.

**ACCESSIBLE BEDROOM**

SUPERLINER® DAYTIME CONFIGURATION

SUPERLINER® NIGHTTIME CONFIGURATION

**SUPERLINER®**
*Designed for passengers with mobility impairments, with ample space for a wheelchair. Accessible Bedrooms occupy the entire width of the lower level at one end of the car with two facing, reclining seats and upper and lower berths. Sink, vanity and toilet accessible by wheelchair, separated from the room by a privacy curtain. Food and beverage service is available to the room.*

**VIEWLINER®**
*A Deluxe Bedroom equipped for passengers with mobility impairments, including ample space for a wheelchair. Reclining seat and upper and lower berth. Enclosed shower, sink and toilet are accessible by wheelchair. Food and beverage service available to the room. Amenities include in-room audio and video with feature movies.*

VIEWLINER® DAYTIME CONFIGURATION

VIEWLINER® WHEELCHAIR ACCESSIBILITY

©Amtrak 1999

**DIMENSIONS:**
6'9" x 9'5" (2m x 2.9m)

**LOWER BERTH:**
2'4" x 6'6" (72cm x 2m)

**UPPER BERTH WITH STEPS:**
2'0" x 6'2" (61cm x 1.9m)
*Capacity for 2 suitcases*

SUPERLINER® ACCESSIBLE BEDROOM ♿

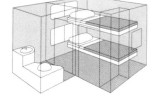

**DIMENSIONS:**
6'8" x 7'1" (2m x 2.2m)

**LOWER BERTH:**
3'4" x 6'0" (1m x 1.8m)

**UPPER BERTH WITH STEPS:**
2'4" x 6'2" (72cm x 1.9m)
*Capacity for 2 small suitcases and garment bag*

VIEWLINER® ACCESSIBLE BEDROOM ♿

Being that Amtrak is a government-subsidized business, and thanks to the Americans With Disabilities Act, Amtrak has taken great pains to develop and promote handicap-accessible facilities, including the accessible Superliner and Viewliner bedrooms described here. The Superliner room is located on the first level of the two-level cars. Both types of rooms offer a restroom with space for a wheelchair and food/beverage service to the room.

**AMTRAK® ANNOUNCES THE NEXT WAVE IN TRAIN TRAVEL**

*The new Pacific Surfliner arrives in 2000.*

**There's a lot happening at Amtrak® this year**. *Changes to make your journey more comfortable, exciting and enjoyable, wherever you want to go. In the West, we're adding new equipment, upgrading existing services and creating strategic alliances that will help make a truly seamless journey. So what's new where you're going?*

*In the summer of 2000, the San Diegans route between San Diego and San Luis Obispo will become the* **Pacific Surfliner**. *The Pacific Surfliner reflects the spirit of Southern California with all-new, state-of-the-art equipment, improved food service, plus many on-board amenities unique to the region.*

*pacific* **Surfliner**

High-speed rail is yet to hit the West Coast, but California has experienced a passenger rail revival in the last decade. The latest new service is Amtrak's *Pacific Surfliner* (formerly called the *San Diegan*), which made its debut in 2000 featuring new, comfortable bilevel cars and 11 daily round-trips between Los Angeles and San Diego. In addition to typical California amenities such as bicycle and surfboard racks, the trains also offer Pacific Business Class accommodations including power for laptops and Railfone service.

On November 16, 2000, the U.S. finally joined the high-speed rail world with the debut of Amtrak's new *Acela* service between Boston, New York and Washington, D.C. "Acela" combines the words "acceleration" and "excellence" and by all accounts Amtrak's new trains are offering both. While nowhere near the speediest trains in the world, the Acelas travel at up to 150 mph, a far cry from the 79 mph speed limit on most Amtrak routes. Running time for express service between D.C. and New York is only two hours, 28 minutes and between New York and Boston is only three hours, 18 minutes. The 20 trainsets, built by Bombardier and ALSTOM, utilize computerized tilting technology that allow fast, smooth operation on the curve-heavy route.

# All Aboard for All America!

## 9,000 Miles for $90

That headline means just what it says.

You can step aboard a railroad train in your home town—and put as much as nine thousand miles of America behind you before you return—all for the price of $90, if you ride in comfortable air-conditioned day coaches—or $135.00 (plus $45 for one or two persons in a lower berth)—if you travel in spacious Pullmans.

You can take sixty days to do it—go by any established route—stop off wherever you wish.

See with your own eyes the grandeur of this land you live in—there's no other nation like it in the world.

So think of the things you'd like to see—the New York World's Fair—the Golden Gate exposition —the multicolored canyons carved by western rivers and the man-made canyons of Manhattan— elm-shaded villages of New England and sun-drenched pueblos of the southwest—the unspoiled natural wonders of the great National Parks and the sophistication of storied cities you've read about—the shores of the Atlantic, Pacific, the Gulf of Mexico, and those inland seas, the Great Lakes —the land of Dixie and the great Northwest—the towering Rockies and the forest-clad ranges of the East—landmarks hallowed in your nation's history—and landmarks of a civilization so old it has been forgotten.

All these and more can be included in a vacation which starts the moment you step aboard a train.

It's the kind of vacation you've always dreamed of taking—and now the American railroads are ready to make it come true.

And in addition to the fascinating places you will see, you'll find new interest and luxury in today's trains, with their modern roomy coach and Pullman equipment—smart styling—ever faster schedules —and air-conditioned comfort and cleanliness.

Better talk it over with your local ticket agent now. He will help you take full advantage of this golden opportunity.

### ASSOCIATION OF AMERICAN RAILROADS WASHINGTON, D. C.

*"1940—Travel America Year"*

Talk about bargains. Just $90 paid for up to 9,000 miles of railroad travel (by coach) in 1940—only a penny per mile. The Association of American Railroads, sponsor of this ad and several which follow, has been the rail industry's primary public relations agent and lobbyist for many years. (May 1940)

# RAILROADS ARE READY

## A factual report to the American people

What if the country is called upon to meet a real emergency this year—or next? How will our rail transportation system meet its responsibilities? How does the American railroad performance of 1941 compare with that during the World War?

A thoughtful public, facing a dangerous world situation coolly and realistically, is entitled to ask such questions—and equally entitled to honest answers. Here they are:

*Bigger locomotives pull more freight.* Unqualified statements that railroads have fewer locomotives and cars than in 1917 are meaningless. Today's locomotives average half again more powerful. Today's better freight cars hold a fifth more and travel 64% faster.

*It can't happen again!* In 1917 ports and terminals were congested and transportation was slowed down because freight cars were used not to move goods but to store them. On just one order, 40 miles of cars clogged the tracks for weeks until a shipyard got ready to unload them. That won't happen again because close teamwork by the railroads, shippers and government agencies now keeps cars moving and gets them unloaded promptly.

*Housing a million men.* For the new army camps, the railroads delivered nearly two billion board feet of lumber — 75,000 carloads—in 6 recent months. Work was never held up because of any railroad failure to deliver materials. Cars were loaded and unloaded promptly by shippers and contractors. There was not the least interruption of regular rail traffic.

★ ★ ★

| 1920 | 1939 |
|---|---|
| 14,877 TON MILES PER FREIGHT TRAIN HOUR | 32,150 TON MILES PER FREIGHT TRAIN HOUR |

*Railroad efficiency more than doubled.* That is the net result of larger engines and cars, longer trains, faster schedules, better signals, streamlined yards and greatly improved operating methods. In the peak year of 1929, the railroads hauled 8¾ million more carloads of freight than they did in 1918 although they had 60,000 fewer cars and 5,000 fewer locomotives.

**Whatever the demand — America's railroads, despite the hard times of recent years, are keeping fully prepared to meet the nation's transportation needs.**

# ASSOCIATION OF AMERICAN RAILROADS, WASHINGTON, D.C.

P.S. PERFECT SHIPPING   A national campaign each APRIL to promote good packing, secure loading and careful handling of ALL shipments— sponsored by Shippers Advisory Boards. Avoid loss and damage. We can't afford to waste our national resources.

The handwriting was on the wall and America was preparing for the inevitable conflict. As for America's railroads, this would be their finest hour, as traffic greatly increased during the four-year emergency. In March 1941, the Association of American Railroads hastened to assure the public that the railroads were ready.

# TANKERS THE SUBS *CAN'T* SINK

**M**ORE than *34 million gallons of oil* a day are rolling into the East in tank cars.

That's *70 times* the amount the railroads usually have been called upon to transport — well over half the total needs, hauled in tankers the subs can't sink.

To handle this new assignment takes the full time of 1,400 locomotives, when there are a dozen other uses for every locomotive in the war program as a whole. But it's a job that has to be done, so the railroads are doing it, as a part of their bigger job of hauling 1¼ million tons of freight a mile every minute round the clock.

Behind this record oil movement is a story of the American brand of cooperation: by the companies that ship the oil — by the companies that own the tank cars — by the Federal Petroleum Cooperator — by the Office of Defense Transportation.

That's why this particular story of what the railroads are doing is a good example of what it takes to keep America working and fighting.

ASSOCIATION OF
## AMERICAN RAILROADS
UNITED FOR VICTORY
WASHINGTON, D.C.

With a scene of passing a long train of tank cars, the Association of American Railroads published this reminder, in December 1942, that railroad freight shipments were safe from enemy attack, at least on the North American continent. By the 1950s, there were some 152,000 tank cars in use on American railroads, 143,000 of them owned by private companies.

# Battle Stations

**A**merica is at battle stations all over the world—in North Africa, in the South Pacific, in Northern Europe, in Burma and India, on the islands, on the sea, in the air.

And railroad trains are at battle stations right here at home—wherever one loads troops, or picks up raw materials, or hauls the finished goods of war, or does any one of a thousand necessary wartime tasks.

Railroad men and railroad trains are working harder today than ever before—carrying one - and - a - half times the tonnage of freight and more than double the volume of military passenger travel they carried in the first World War.

For America, waging war on the gigantic scale that spells eventual victory, depends now more than ever upon the mass transportation service of its railroads.

ASSOCIATION OF

# AMERICAN RAILROADS

**ALL UNITED FOR VICTORY**

Under the floodlights, troops assemble at a small-town station. (June 1943)

# THROUGH THE DARKEST HOUR

*The railroads are part and parcel of the vital service of supply on which fighting men depend. They know first-hand the darkness of the hour before the dawn. • They follow the progress of the war by the nature and urgency of the burdens they carry—burdens that never lighten through the whole 24 hours of the day. • So through sunshine and shadow, railroad men serve the needs of war. Short on help, short on time, they know the value of every hour and every car. They know that a fighting nation counts on them to deliver the goods that Victory is made of—and doggedly, devotedly, they are sticking to that job. • Some day the dark hour will be behind us. Then our nation will look back on the courage and the will with which we faced it and judge our fiber as a people. • The railroads are working now so that when that day dawns they can, in clear knowledge of a job faithfully discharged, look forward with confidence to finer things to come.*

**ASSOCIATION OF**
# AMERICAN RAILROADS
**ALL UNITED FOR VICTORY**

BUY MORE WAR BONDS

This dramatic study in black and white, like the New Haven Railroad's famous "Kid in Upper 4," is one of World War II's most unforgettable railroad advertisements. Those who painted these scenes and created such memorable prose were certainly masters of their craft. (August 1944)

*The train to* **California** *that gives so much for so little!*

Imagine a delicious breakfast for 25c, luncheon for 50c, dinner for 35c!

Here's the very spirit of happy economy travel on the Santa Fe *Scout*, and one of its most delightful dollar-saving features —delicious Fred Harvey dining car meals for only 90c a day!

*The* **Santa Fe** *Scout*

The trimly uniformed courier-nurse on the *Scout* gives mothers a helping hand with their babies and children, and assists all other passengers requiring her free and friendly service.

There's comfort and beauty in the *Scout's* gleaming stainless steel chair cars, with their deeply cushioned adjustable seats, individual lights, broad windows, spacious dressing rooms!

## The Famous Santa Fe Economy Train That Makes it Easy and Pleasant to Save Travel-Dollars on Your California Trip

Let's talk *Scout* fares first. *You can't obtain lower rail fares on any other transcontinental road or train!*

● One-way fare, between Chicago and Los Angeles, San Diego, or San Francisco, in Scout chair cars (no berth required), $39.50; round-trip (over 4450 miles) only $65. One-way fare, in Scout sleeping cars, $49.90; round-trip fare, only $74. Berth charges extra.

Scout meals? They're delightful, generous, served by Fred Harvey. Seven regular meals on the Scout, between Chicago and Los Angeles, need cost you but $2.05! Special children's menus, too.

Scout patrons write constantly of their appreciation of the alert helpfulness of the Courier-Nurse; the friendly courtesy of the train crew; the cheery special car for women and children, and the air-conditioned comfort of this popular train.

The natural color photos shown here will tell you the story of the daily Scout like nothing else can—and enable you to

see for yourself why this fine, swift Santa Fe train can give you so much for so little on your transcontinental journey this summer.

**Grand Canyon ● Yosemite Park Golden Gate Exposition**

Santa Fe is the only railroad entering Grand Canyon National Park. So be sure to spend a day or so enjoying the indescribable grandeur of this year-round wonderland when you travel to or from California on the Scout.

Then, too, via Santa Fe, you can easily include in your western trip the sunny beaches of Southern California; Yosemite's majestic waterfalls, lakes, and big trees in the high Sierras; and San Francisco's beautiful Golden Gate Exposition, opening May 25th, 1940.

● If you buy a California round-trip ticket via Santa Fe both ways, from Chicago or other Eastern points, you may include San Diego, Los Angeles and San Francisco *at no extra ticket cost!*

Sleep tight, little man, in your snowy *Scout* bed, while the long miles slip smoothly away! In *Scout* sleeping cars, rail fares and berth charges are only about half those in standard Pullmans!

The *Scout's* modern lounge car, with its beautiful cocktail bar, is for the especial pleasure of sleeping car passengers.

**FREE** *New Booklet with Natural Color Photos of the Scout*

### And here's Santa Fe's famous day-saving dollar-saving streamliner

## *El Capitan*

**The West's only all-chair-car transcontinental streamliner**

This gay *economy* stainless steel flyer, carrying ultra-modern chair cars, Fred Harvey diner, and lounge car, whisks between Chicago and Los Angeles in just 39¾ hours! One way fare, only $39.50, plus $5 extra fare; round-trip $65, plus $10 extra fare ● Mail coupon for free booklet.

T. B. Gallaher, P.T.M., Santa Fe System Lines
1360 Railway Exchange, Chicago, Illinois.
Please send me *free* the new Scout booklet containing natural color photos; El Capitan booklet; and fares from

to

Name

Address

Atchison, Topeka & Santa was probably best known for its fleet of first-rate passenger trains. In the Chicago-Los Angeles corridor the venerable *Super Chief* was the glamour train, but Santa Fe offered other service. The *Scout*, for example, offered fast and comfortable value-priced service, including seven meals from the famous Fred Harvey folks for only $2.05. And, if you weren't satisfied with the service, this April 1940 ad notes that an upgrade to the all-coach, extra fare *El Capitan* only cost $5 each way.

# WORKING *for* VICTORY ON THE SANTA FE

### Making New Ones Out of Old Ones

Many a veteran Santa Fe gondola, already marked for retirement, has had to take a new lease on life.

Battered, broken and ready to quit, these hard-worked cars no longer had the strength to hold their loads.

Somehow, these "old boys" just had to be kept rolling!

So Santa Fe shopmen got busy. They took old steel ends from broken-down box cars, and rebuilt the old gondolas with steel sides, and a new, steel-reinforced floor— *all made from old, used materials.*

Now, these rebuilt old gondolas are proudly hauling coal and ore to the mills, war material to Army camps, tanks and guns to waiting ships—doing their part in binding an entire nation together into one unified war effort.

### Here's How It's Done

Old steel box car ends are cut in half, and the two halves, "A" and "B", reassembled and riveted to the frames of the old gondolas. Old steel beams are used to reinforce new floors in place of the original wooden beams. The running gear is completely overhauled.

**"Back the Attack with War Bonds"**

RECLAIMED FROM HERE

RE-USED HERE

## SANTA FE SYSTEM LINES

*Serving the Southwest and California*

ONE OF AMERICA'S RAILROADS — <u>ALL</u> UNITED FOR VICTORY

What must a railroad do when there's a wartime steel shortage and new steel gondola cars are desperately needed? Santa Fe had a clever answer: recycling. By combining parts from old, worn-out boxcars, as well as from old, battered gondolas, it was able to produce rebuilt gondolas to serve in the war effort. (November 1943)

# Women at Work
## *for*
## a Railroad at War

*Another chapter in the story "Working for Victory on the Santa Fe"*

America needs millions of women to take over war jobs . . . to stay with those jobs . . . to help speed the day when our fighting men will return victorious!

Santa Fe women are answering this call all along the line.

Right now thousands of Santa Fe women are doing war-vital work to "keep 'em rolling." Many of them are pitching into "unglamorous" jobs . . . greasing engines, operating turntables, wielding a shovel, cleaning roller bearings, working in blacksmith and sheet metal shops. They take pride in their work, too!

Many of them have husbands, sweethearts, brothers or sons in the armed forces. Many came to work to replace a relative who had been called into service. Others took jobs because they knew womanpower must step in when manpower goes to war.

☆ We of the Santa Fe salute these women who know that what they are doing is vital to Victory!

*"Back the Attack with War Bonds"*

## SANTA FE SYSTEM LINES
### *Serving the Southwest and California*
#### ONE OF AMERICA'S RAILROADS — ALL UNITED FOR VICTORY

During World War II, women stepped in readily and filled the gap left by the many able-bodied men who were drafted or enlisted into the service. And after the wars, many women remained in the work force. (December 1943)

Every inch the Chief

Yes, *Little Chief*, our Chief measures up to the name!
For it is the all-Pullman, extra-fare, transcontinental streamliner (along with the daily Super Chief) that is famous among discriminating travelers for smooth-riding speed, roomy comfort, and delicious Fred Harvey meals.

The Chief provides daily service between Chicago and Los Angeles, Chicago and Phoenix, Chicago and San Diego.
In conjunction with the New York Central 20th Century Limited, the Pennsylvania Broadway Limited, and Baltimore & Ohio Capitol Limited, it provides daily Pullman service between New York and Los Angeles, and between Washington and Los Angeles without changing cars.

**SANTA FE SYSTEM LINES...** Serving the West and Southwest
T. B. Gallaher, General Passenger Traffic Manager, Chicago 4

**Santa Fe**

Santa Fe's glorious "warbonnet" passenger scheme is arguably the best-loved paint scheme ever applied to a diesel locomotive. The design was a perfect fit for the railroad's Desert Southwest/Indian Country personality, but it actually came out of GM's Electro-Motive Division. The design was created exclusively for Santa Fe's first two E-units, delivered in May 1937. The warbonnet soon became synonymous with the railroad's illustrious *Super Chief*, the subject of this May 1948 ad.

# You Go by the Clock

## on the Santa Fe

—— not by the weather

Why worry about the weather?

You leave on schedule on the Santa Fe . . . get the benefits of Santa Fe's on-time performance record . . . arrive safely, relaxed and refreshed.

You board the Santa Fe at a station downtown, not out in the sticks . . . you get privacy, room to roam around, solid comfort, good sleep.

You see people and places of the romantic Southwest at eye level . . . you select food you like from a Fred Harvey menu and eat it at a table, rather than from a one-choice tray.

Figure it out. You'll go Santa Fe — *all the way!*

**Santa Fe**

Ride great trains through a great country

R. T. Anderson, General Passenger Traffic Manager, Santa Fe System Lines, Chicago 4

# Privacy as you like it

## on the Santa Fe

—— Room to Roam, too!

It's a private world of your own — your room on one of Santa Fe's great trains, whether it's a de luxe suite or economical roomette.

When you feel like roaming, there's a lounge car for friendly relaxation . . . and at mealtime, you choose from a Fred Harvey menu and eat from a table, instead of a one-choice tray.

You board the Santa Fe downtown, not out in the sticks. You leave on schedule in any weather . . . see scenery and places en route at eye level . . . arrive safely, relaxed, refreshed.

Yes, figure it out. You'll go Santa Fe — *all the way!*

**Santa Fe**

Ride great trains through a great country

R. T. Anderson, General Passenger Traffic Manager, Santa Fe System Lines, Chicago 4

This pair of ads, similar in style, were introduced one month apart (May and June 1950). Both emphasize common advertising themes of the era—safe, reliable travel in bad weather and privacy as compared to other forms of transportation—again a reaction to plane, car and even bus competition. If "Room to Roam" sounds familiar, revisit the 1947 Pennsy ad on page 170; the same tagline is in use.

*Tops in fun! Tops in travel!*

# New "Big Domes" on Santa Fe

For a new adventure on a trip to or from California, step aboard Santa Fe's new "Big Dome" lounge car on *El Capitan* or the beautiful new *San Francisco Chief*.

You'll agree it's the world's most beautiful railroad car! Topside, big picture windows and angled sofa seats give you a full panoramic view wherever you sit. And there's a convenient refreshment lounge right in the Dome.

The lower level features a cocktail lounge with unique Indian decor. A spot that is colorful, intimate and where you'll visit with friends, meet new and interesting people.

Low cost "stretch-out" seat chair car service on both these trains. Also, de luxe Pullmans on the *San Francisco Chief*. Delicious Fred Harvey meals served on both trains, planned to fit your budget.

On *your* trip between Chicago and Los Angeles or Chicago and San Francisco, enjoy this exciting new way to travel— go Santa Fe!

**Take the family along!** Phone your travel agent or any Santa Fe ticket office and let them show you how much our Family Fares can really reduce your travel costs.

In June 1954, in an era when many railroads were dropping trains, the Santa Fe introduced the *San Francisco Chief*, the railroad's first Chicago-Bay Area service. And though the train was new, most of the equipment was cobbled together from castoffs from other trains—except for the "Big Domes." Santa Fe took delivery of 14 of these massive full-length dome-lounges from Budd in 1954 and they were an immediate hit. The cars were initially assigned to both the *San Francisco Chief* and the *El Capitan*. (November 1954 ad)

NEWEST EVENT ON AMERICA'S NEW RAILROAD

New Hi-

## New Luxury Service for Coach-Fare Travel Chicago - Los Angeles

*Goes into operation in midsummer*

The instant you see it, you'll know this train is different. It's *two stories* high—designed to provide smoother rides, more room, and better panoramic views of Southwestern scenery. "Upstairs"—well above the clickety-clack of the rails—are foam-rubber reclining seats with full-length legrests, big picture windows, dining room, and full-length lounge. "Downstairs" are luggage racks and washrooms.

Courier Nurse service. Indian Guide, westbound across New Mexico. Fred Harvey meals. You'll be riding high, wide and handsome in this new all-coach *El Capitan!* Extra fare $5.00, Chicago—Los Angeles. Watch your local newspapers for the date it goes into service.

R. T. Anderson, General Passenger Traffic Manager, Chicago.

Budd's stunning, new Hi-Level cars were first tested on the Santa Fe in 1954. Then, in 1956, the railroad took delivery of 47 more (coaches, lounges and diners) and fully re-equipped the *El Capitan*. The extra-tall cars offered seating on the upper level and storage, restrooms and equipment on the lower level. The public loved the cars because they offered a better view and a quieter ride. The railroad loved the cars because they carried more passengers than a conventional car. AT&SF drew up plans to

**Hi-Level El Capitan**

**Every seat at "BIG DOME" height**

**Santa Fe**

**You dine penthouse-style.** Soft music, magnificent views, and, of course, tempting Fred Harvey dishes—all high above the noise and distraction of the kitchen below.

purchase Hi-Level sleepers for the *Super Chief*, but they never materialized. Instead, in 1963-64, Santa Fe bought 24 more Hi-Level coaches for use on the *San Francisco Chief*. The cars' long-term impact was significant. They lasted into the Amtrak era and, more importantly, inspired Amtrak's own Superliners, which are today's standard long-distance cars.

AMERICA'S NEW RAILROAD

*Center of fun on the world's most glamorous train*

## Up where the view begins
### —the Pleasure Dome of the Super Chief

It's such a wonderful place to see the Southwest—mile after magnificent mile of it. The glassed-in Pleasure Dome of the *Super Chief!*

Take the couple in the picture (the whole train has them spotted as newlyweds). Right now, he's being persuaded to come up to the dome and take in the Indian Country.

Then cocktails in the Lower Lounge and dinner at 7:30. They have reservations in the Turquoise Room, the *Super*'s famous private dining room.

But there's more to riding the Super Chief than resort-type excitement.

There's the restful and the roomy comfort of the bedrooms and suites, the delicious Fred Harvey meals, and all the luxurious little extras you find only on the Super Chief.

On *your* trip West . . . or East . . . between Chicago and Los Angeles, why not take the Super Chief? It's extra fare—but worth it!

Santa Fe

WHEN YOU GET THERE
...RENT A CAR

With the introduction of the Pleasure Dome in 1951, the Santa Fe was able to hold onto its claim that the *Super Chief* was the world's most glamorous train. The Pleasure Dome actually had three levels, including a small cocktail lounge below the dome, plus another lounge on the main level. In addition to a great view, the dome features comfortable, individual, rotating chairs. The car's best-known feature was a luxurious private dining room, the Turquoise Room, which offered cozy seating for 12 and some of the best meals available on rails—or anywhere. (October 1955 ad)

Jets of steam, racing at 2000 miles per hour through a turbine no larger than an office desk, provide 6500 horsepower for this Pennsylvania Railroad giant, the first direct drive steam turbine locomotive to be produced in the United States.

Built by Baldwin with turbines and gears made by Westinghouse, it represents an adventure in steam locomotive construction, opening the way to desired higher speeds and greater operating efficiency.

It is natural that Baldwin, a leader in locomotive development for more than a century, should have pioneered in this radically new type of steam locomotive.

But this is not the whole story. Baldwin hydraulic machinery, testing equipment, ship propellers, diesel engines and other products are serving industry in a hundred useful ways.

**SOMETHING NEW IN LOCOMOTIVES**

**POWERED LIKE A BATTLESHIP**

**BALDWIN**

*The Baldwin Locomotive Works, Philadelphia, Pennsylvania:* Locomotive & Ordnance Division; Baldwin Southwark Division; Cramp Brass & Iron Foundries Division; Standard Steel Works Division; The Whitcomb Locomotive Co.; The Pelton Water Wheel Co.; The Midvale Co.

BALDWIN SERVES THE NATION | WHICH THE RAILROADS HELPED TO BUILD

Baldwin's famous "S-2" direct-drive 6-8-6 steam turbine locomotive, built in 1944 for the Pennsylvania Railroad, is seen in a March 1945, advertisement. The S-2 created a flurry of excitement for a time, and in 1946, Lionel offered a realistic O-gauge miniature of this, in cast metal. This model train was one of the earliest to puff real smoke, created from an aspirin-like pill inserted into the smokestack. As for the real S-2s locomotive, they were removed from service in 1949.

This image, from a May 1946 Baldwin ad, shows an artist's rendition of one of the most unique locomotives ever built—the DR-12-8-1500/2, better known as the "Centipede." During World War II, Baldwin failed in its attempts to design a single-unit 6,000 h.p. passenger diesel, but retained elements of that plan in building 14 of the two-engine 3,000 h.p. Centipedes for Seaboard Air Line—at the time the largest and most-powerful diesel available. Pennsy and National Railways of Mexico also bought Centipedes, but the huge locomotives—91 feet long with a weight of 600,000 pounds—never really caught on.

# 90 degrees outside 75 degrees inside

COOL · CLEAN AIR · QUIET

# ANNOUNCING...
## first Air-Conditioned Train in Railroad History

THE COLUMBIAN runs between New York and Washington. Take it some hot day this summer. A stifling, collar-wilting day. The air in the car will be as fresh and cool as a sparkling day in fall. Engineers call it "Conditioned air." The newest theatres have it. The Columbian is the only train in the world that has it throughout. Cool, clean air that is neither too dry nor too moist—air that is in every way ideal to breathe, and kept so by our method of automatic control.

First, all dust, cinders, and smoke are filtered from the air. Then it is given just the right amount of humidity. Finally, the air is artificially cooled and is gently and evenly circulated so that the car never gets stuffy nor drafty.

Because of closed windows and rubberized trucks, outside noise is muffled, the car is relatively quiet, and dust, smoke and cinders cannot enter.

In winter the same equipment cleans the air, maintains it at the right temperature and proper humidity—better air than most people have in their homes.

Added to the other comforts of this fine train, and to our smooth roadbed, "Conditioned air" makes the ride between Washington, Baltimore, Philadelphia and New York unusually pleasant and comfortable. And the motor coach ride between train-side at Jersey City and New York and Brooklyn, with a few minutes crossing the breeze-swept Hudson, is a delightful and convenient way to enter or leave New York.

Mr. W. B. Calloway, Baltimore & Ohio Railroad, Baltimore, Md., will mail on request a descriptive folder which tells all about this outstanding advance in railroad comfort.

70,000 OF US INVITE YOU TO RIDE ON OUR RAILROAD

# BALTIMORE & OHIO

*New York . . Philadelphia . . Baltimore . . Washington . . Pittsburgh . . Cleveland . . Detroit . . Chicago . . Cincinnati . . Louisville . . St. Louis . . and intermediate points*

The first run of Baltimore & Ohio's completely air-conditioned *Columbian* was on May 24, 1931, between Washington, D.C., and Jersey City, N.J. This was the first train to carry air-conditioning throughout, and it was a historical first—a prelude to the streamlined years. This advertisement appeared in June 1931.

# WITH PROFIT...AT *2¢* A MILE?

To OPERATE profitably — with fares at 2c a mile — *while still maintaining their magnificent record for efficiency and safety*, railroads must have more passenger traffic and operating costs must be cut.

Several of the great railroads of the country have already found the solution to the problem in light-weight trains of stainless steel, Budd-built by the exclusive "Shotweld" process.

Budd-built trains of the Burlington Railroad have already shown, in over a million miles of practical service, that operating costs may be reduced as much as 40%. The record of availability for four Budd-built trains, running on regular schedules, summer and winter, has been 97%. The cost per train-mile up to June first, 1936, was 31c as against 69c for comparable standard heavy-weight trains.

Records of other railroads confirm the Burlington's experience.

Budd-built trains are not an evolution of old forms. They combine in a new form a multiplicity of new engineering principles and proved inventions. Basic is the elimination of bulky dead-weight by the use of non-corrosive stainless steel — with an elastic strength four times greater than ordinary steel.

Tremendous savings in weight and space, in wear and tear, in fuel consumption and operating costs — make it possible for Budd-built trains to provide spacious and luxurious accommodation with every modern convenience, *and yet operate profitably with fares at 2c a mile!* These trains are materially increasing passenger traffic.

• • •

*"The Conquest of Weight,"* an important brochure on Budd methods of construction, will be mailed on request.

## EDW. G. BUDD MANUFACTURING COMPANY
### PHILADELPHIA AND DETROIT
**BUDD METHODS SAFELY ELIMINATE DEAD-WEIGHT**

A September 1936 advertisement touting the *Burlington Zephyr* was sponsored by its builder, E.G. Budd Manufacturing Company. Budd claimed its stainless steel streamliner was America's first, because it was in service while Pullman-Standard's Union Pacific M-10000 was still on display at the Chicago World's Fair. Budd's real rival in the transportation business was not P-S, but the automobile. Despite claims about "increasing passenger traffic" the new technology never was able to stop railroad ridership declines that started in the 1920s.

# "THERE GOES THE NEW TRAIN!"

EVERY DAY at five o'clock it hums by at eighty miles an hour. Sleek and gleaming, this train of stainless steel brings a fresh thrill to the countryside. Millions, seeing it, sense a new impulse that has come to the rails. For this swift, smooth thing of beauty is not just another train. It is the embodiment of the new principle that is bringing about the revolution in all forms of transportation.

The old-fashioned idea that safe construction can only be obtained by massiveness was first disproved by auto-motive engineers and the designers of modern aircraft. Metallurgists opened up endless possibilities by producing new alloys, incomparably stronger than the traditional forms of steel and iron. Most notable is stainless steel — beautiful, non-corrosive, possessing four times the elastic strength of ordinary steel.

With stainless steel, Budd builds trains that have already traveled more than a million miles in practical and profitable operation — bringing new life and increasing popularity to railroad travel.

And they operate profitably with fares at 2c a mile!

Budd methods safely eliminate dead-weight in more efficient transport units and industrial structures. Budd develops a wide variety of stainless-steel products. Among these are railway cars, marine and bridge structures, airplanes, motor truck, bus and trailer bodies.

• • •

*"The Conquest of Weight,"* an important brochure on Budd methods of construction, will be mailed on request.

## EDW. G. BUDD MANUFACTURING COMPANY

PHILADELPHIA AND DETROIT

BUDD METHODS SAFELY ELIMINATE DEAD-WEIGHT

The Budd Company was rightfully proud of its role in the development of streamlined trains. In this 1936 scene, the *Burlington Zephyr* rushes by a wayside station like a beautiful streak of stainless steel. This train, introduced in 1934, was one of the several that American boys would own in miniature; American Flyer offered it during the mid-1930s in cast aluminum—and superbly detailed for its time.

## LINKING THE TWO GREATEST CITIES OF THE EAST...

### WITH LIGHT-WEIGHT, STREAMLINED SERVICE

NINETY MILES separate Philadelphia from New York. Not far, as we moderns measure distance. But young Ben Franklin, trudging southward to seek his fortune, took a week for the journey.

Footsore soldiers . . . saddle-weary patriots . . . founders of the new nation, jolting across Jersey in their slow-wheeled coaches . . . how well they knew those ninety miles!

Travel between New York and Philadelphia has been improved many times through the years, but never more dramatically than today. *For a light-weight, streamlined, high-speed train now links the two great cities with a new kind of travel-comfort!*

The Reading Company can well be proud of this most modern of trains. Its five Budd-built, light-weight, stainless-steel cars are pulled by a streamlined steam locomotive. From headlight to observation lounge it is a thing of gleaming beauty . . . swift . . . smooth-riding . . . luxuriously appointed.

Styled by Paul Cret, the new Reading streamliner has all the innovations that are attracting travelers to other Budd-built trains on railroads from Maine to the Pacific. There is a separate smoking lounge in each of the four 56-passenger cars. The fifth is a dining-car containing both a 24-passenger dining-room and a 27-passenger cocktail lounge. The train operates on a fast schedule of two round trips daily.

For the first time the Middle Atlantic States can enjoy the advantages of Budd's truly light-weight train construction. Budd builds these cars of stainless steel, which has four times the elastic strength of ordinary steel — twice that of other alloys. Welded by the exclusive Budd SHOTWELD process, they weigh from forty to fifty per cent less than conventional equipment, yet they are fully as strong and safe.

Wherever Budd trains are in service, they have brought new pleasure and new comfort to rail travel . . . along with new revenue to railroad managements.

*Originator of ALL STEEL bodies for automobiles, now used almost universally, the Edw. G. Budd Manufacturing Company has pioneered modern methods in the design and fabrication of steel products.*

## EDW. G. BUDD MANUFACTURING COMPANY
### PHILADELPHIA          DETROIT
#### BUDD METHODS SAFELY ELIMINATE DEAD-WEIGHT

Two views display Reading's steam-powered, stainless-steel *Crusader*, with cars built by Budd. For the utmost pleasure and comfort of all aboard, each of the four coaches had a separate smoking lounge. A combination diner and lounge car was also included. (From advertisements appearing December 1937 and August 1938)

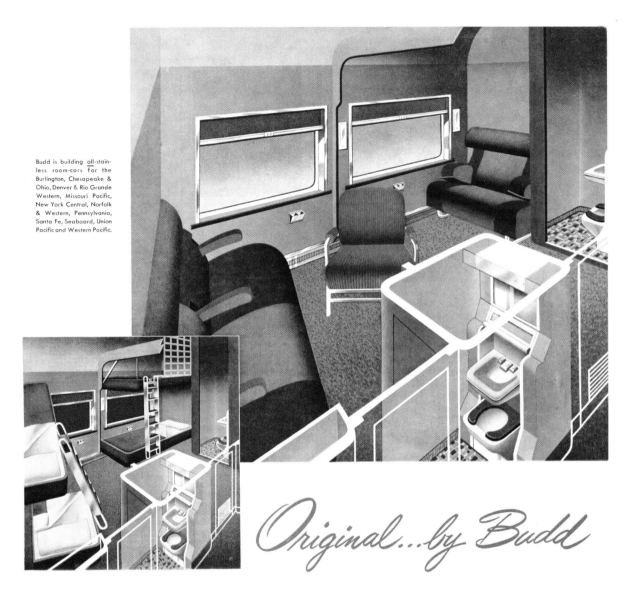

*Original...by Budd*

Too often to be mere coincidence, basic improvements in railway passenger transportation originate with Budd. The most recent is this new sleeping car, now in service.

Just as the Pioneer Zephyr, built by Budd for the Burlington Lines in 1934, created the era of lightweight, streamlined trains, these new sleeper accommodations make previous design obsolete.

Illustrated are two double-bedrooms which have been combined into a Master Drawing Room, simply by folding back the panel which separates them. You can readily see how imaginative space-engineer-ing has provided roominess, comfort and privacy. Seats for six by day; beds for four by night. Full-width, picture windows. Enclosed toilet facilities.

As was inevitable, an improvement of such obvious desirability is becoming the new standard for all sleepers. Many railroads are specifying it for their new room-car equipment, realizing that without it a car would be old before it ever carried a passenger. This post-war Budd sleeping car, of all-stainless steel construction, typifies the interest, effort and action Budd continuously devotes to more enjoyable and safer rail travel. The Budd Company, Philadelphia.

This ad offers a detailed view into a postwar "Master Drawing Room" expandable compartment. When connected as a suite, this accommodation offered to a single family, or a group, the luxury of two bathrooms. Notice that the wash basin swings up and dumps its contents into a shaft when access to the toilet is desired. These May 1948 views were provided by the Budd Company.

Chessie cars of the C & O with The Greenbrier, White Sulphur Springs, in the background.

## The New Chessie Cars on the C & O...

Beautiful new, all-stainless steel railway cars, built by Budd, are now in service on several trains of the Chesapeake and Ohio Railway.

They take you over routes rich in scenic loveliness, including the storied beauty of the Blue Ridge and Appalachian Mountains. And never have you had such opportunity to enjoy it—viewing it from the first Vista-Dome cars to go in service on any eastern railroad.

New ideas for your comfort and pleasure too numerous to catalogue, sparkle throughout these sleek and gleaming cars. An enclosed children's nursery. Spacious private rooms. A theater. Snack bars. Music at your finger tips.

Beneath their beauty, luxury and imaginative design stands the solid fact of their all-stainless steel construction. From foundation center-sill to shining roof rail, from end-post to end-post through all their frames and girders, these cars are built of this amazing, silver-hued metal, strongest ever used in railroad car construction. Cars of stainless steel structure are built for America's railroads exclusively by Budd. The Budd Company, Philadelphia.

An October 1948 Budd ad announces Chesapeake & Ohio service that never came to pass. The railroad's visionary *Chessie* trains, built by Budd, were to include amenities never before seen on railroads: luggage lockers, children's playrooms, movies and much more. Unfortunately, financial problems derailed the plans and C&O was forced to sell all but a handful of the 46 new cars purchased for the trains before they ever entered service.

Regional carrier Wabash was the last railroad to streamline in the competitive Chicago-St. Louis market, but many would argue that it ended up with the best train. Built by Budd (sponsor of this February 1950 ad), the streamlined *Blue Bird* sported four Vista-Domes in its six-car trainset. The train made a single round trip between the two cities daily, heading north in the morning and departing the Windy City in the late afternoon.

## California Takes To The Santa Fe's RDC's

THERE'S a fine highway between Los Angeles and San Diego. And the airlines provide many schedules. You'd think these conditions were hardly favorable to railway passenger business. But, a year ago the Santa Fe put two Budd RDC's on the run and substantially increased their traffic.

With RDC available, the railroads are facing their passenger carrying problems with a new spirit. An aggressive spirit. They've found that RDC can make money in services formerly daubed with red ink. And they've found that the comfort and convenience of fast, frequent RDC schedules are bringing passengers back to the rails.

A railroad official recently termed Budd RDC "one of the greatest advancements in modern railroading". More and more people are coming to agree with him. Railroad people, by buying RDC's. Traveling people, by riding in them. The Budd Company, Philadelphia, Detroit, Gary.

### PIONEERS IN BETTER TRANSPORTATION

Budd's self-propelled "RDC" (rail diesel car) was introduced in 1949 and expected to immediately revolutionize passenger service on shorter routes. The RDC effectively cut operational costs by eliminating the conventional locomotive and most of the train crew. Several railroads, including Santa Fe (featured in this June 1953 ad), New York Central, B&O, C&NW and others ordered RDCs and 342 eventually operated in North America. The trains were good performers, but many commuters were too busy driving their cars to take much notice of the new equipment and the concept was only moderately successful.

## CUSTOM-MADE TRAINS

Here are three completely different trains. The Pennsylvania's low-slung, lightweight tubular train. The New Haven's new train, in which every car propels itself. The Santa Fe's Hi-Level cars in the new El Capitan. All go in service this year.

Common to all of them, however, is the strength and safety of their stainless steel construction, found in all railway cars built by Budd.

Each has been built to meet a special need. For the Pennsylvania, lighter weight. For the New Haven, faster schedules . . . speeds up to 110 miles an hour. For the Santa Fe, to provide a better view with better riding comfort and transport more passengers with fewer cars. They demonstrate the ability of Budd to envision needs and apply imaginative engineering to meeting them.

The Budd Company, Philadelphia 32.

This May 1956 ad shows off three exotic Budd-built products from that era. From top to bottom: Pennsy's lightweight, low-slung *Keystone*, an eight-car "tubular train" that spawned the relatively successful Pioneer III commuter cars; New Haven's *Hot Rod*, in reality six modified RDCs coupled together to look like a conventional train; and the Santa Fe Hi-Levels, which set the standard for contemporary passenger car construction.

# NOW! VISTA-DOME CARS
## ON THE SCENIC ROUTE BETWEEN CHICAGO and SAN FRANCISCO
# AMERICA'S NO. 1 TRAVEL TREAT

**See the snow-capped Colorado Rockies and spectacular Feather River Canyon from a Vista-Dome during magic daylight hours**

**NEW FASTER SCHEDULE!**
*Effective May 30*

| | | |
|---|---|---|
| Lv. | Chicago (CT) | 1:30 P.M. |
| Ar. | Denver (MT) | 8:20 A.M. |
| Lv. | Denver (MT) | 9:00 A.M. |
| | *Colorado Rockies* | |
| Ar. | Salt Lake City (MT) | 11:50 P.M. |
| Lv. | Salt Lake City (MT) | 11:59 P.M. |
| | *Feather River Canyon* | |
| Ar. | San Francisco (PT) | 9:05 P.M. |

Vista-Dome coaches this summer on the Diesel-powered Exposition Flyer between Chicago, Omaha, Denver, Salt Lake City and San Francisco... the Scenic Way Across America! The matchless scenery of this route inspired inventive genius to conceive the amazing Vista-Dome! Yours to enjoy at no extra fare! *Through daily Pullman between New York and San Francisco.*

IN SERVICE LATER THIS YEAR — THE CALIFORNIA ZEPHYR FEATURING VISTA-DOME CARS

**Burlington Route**

**RIO GRANDE** ROYAL GORGE MOFFAT TUNNEL "SCENIC LINE OF THE WORLD"

**WESTERN PACIFIC** FEATHER RIVER ROUTE

*A. COTSWORTH, Jr.*
Passenger Traffic Manager
Burlington Route · Chicago

*H. F. ENO*
Passenger Traffic Manager
Rio Grande Route · Denver

*JOSEPH G. WHEELER*
General Passenger Agent
Western Pacific · San Francisco

The *Exposition Flyer* was the first Chicago-San Francisco train operated jointly by Burlington, Rio Grande and Western Pacific. Introduced as a steam-powered, heavyweight train in 1939, it clocked in at 60 hours. Despite a schedule 20 hours longer than competing UP trains, the *Flyer* and its scenic route was a hit with sightseers. This May 1948 ad announces the arrival of Vista Domes and foretells the 1949 conversion of the train into the storied *California Zephyr*.

A cutaway view in an April 1949 ad displays Vista-Dome luxury on the new *California Zephyr.* Burlington converted a stainless-steel coach to the first Vista-Dome car in 1945. In December 1947 CB&Q's *Twin Cities Zephyr* became the first train to feature the domes in regular service. Five of the train's seven cars were Budd-built Vista-Domes. Going further back in history, the first passenger coach with three built-on sightseeing domes was patented by T.J. McBride of Winnipeg, Canada. His design went unused, but following a similar train of thought, in 1904 and 1906 Canadian Pacific built four wooden, open-ended passenger cars with a caboose-like cupola at either end.

DAILY BETWEEN CHICAGO • DENVER • SALT LAKE CITY • SAN FRANCISCO

*The* **VISTA-DOME** *California Zephyr*

EXTRA COMFORT • EXTRA PLEASURE • NO EXTRA FARE

## *Now* YOU CAN <u>Look</u> WHERE YOU'RE GOING

Look ahead...look up...look down...*look everywhere*...while you glide in luxurious comfort through the magnificent Colorado Rockies and Feather River Canyon in daylight hours...Utah and Nevada, by starlight or moonlight. It's a thrilling, eye-opening experience. Your choice of low-cost VISTA-DOME reclining chair-cars or new-type Pullman accommodations, drawing rooms, bed rooms, roomettes, and sections. Through sleepers daily between New York City and San Francisco.

*Make Reservations Now!*

**NEW, FASTER DAILY SCHEDULES**

| WESTBOUND (Read Down) | | EASTBOUND (Read Up) |
|---|---|---|
| 3:30 PM Lv | . . Chicago . . . . | Ar 1:30 PM |
| 11:59 PM Lv | . . Omaha . . . . | Ar 4:55 AM |
| 1:14 AM Lv | . . Lincoln . . . . | Ar 3:40 AM |
| 8:40 AM Lv | . . Denver . . . . | Ar 7:00 PM |
| | **Colorado Rockies** | |
| 1:53 PM Lv | . . Glenwood Springs . | Lv 1:35 PM |
| 10:25 PM Lv | . . Salt Lake City . . | Lv 5:40 AM |
| 7:00-11:00 AM | *Feather River Canyon* | 2:00-6:00 PM |
| 12:28 PM Lv | . . Sacramento . . . | Lv 12:50 PM |
| 1:34 PM Ar | . . Stockton . . . | Lv 11:53 AM |
| 4:00 PM Ar | . . Oakland . . . . | Lv 9:44 AM |
| 4:50 PM Ar | . . San Francisco . . | Lv 9:00 AM |

**Luxurious** comfort at money-saving fares in new VISTA-DOME chair coaches.

**Feminine** as a boudoir is the women's lounge. Men's lounges equally complete.

**Enjoy delicious meals** and personalized service in one of the California Zephyr's beautiful diners.

## BURLINGTON • RIO GRANDE • WESTERN PACIFIC

Scenery was the main selling point of the new *California Zephyr*, though the lightweight equipment allowed the three operating railroads to lop nine hours off the old *Exposition Flyer* schedule. This ad appeared in June 1949, just three months after the train's debut.

look **up...**

look **down...**

look **all around!**

Roomy, restful coaches

Congenial companionship

Delicious meals

Thoughtful service

RIDE THE VISTA-DOME *California Zephyr*

SAN FRANCISCO · SALT LAKE CITY · DENVER · CHICAGO

Magnificent mountain vistas you can really see! Snow-capped splendors in California's Feather River Canyon and the colorful Colorado Rockies during daylight hours. The most *enjoyable* ride between California and Chicago.

Vista-Domes for all passengers. Private rooms, lowers, uppers and reserved reclining coach seats. Through sleeping cars daily, between San Francisco and New York. Make reservations at any railroad ticket office or travel bureau.

**THE MOST TALKED-ABOUT TRAIN IN THE COUNTRY**

No additional rail fare from most California points to Chicago via San Francisco

EXTRA COMFORT
EXTRA PLEASURE

no extra
fare !

| **WESTERN PACIFIC** | **RIO GRANDE** | **BURLINGTON** |
|---|---|---|
| Jos. G. Wheeler | H. F. Eno | A. Cotsworth, Jr. |
| Passenger Traffic Mgr. | Passenger Traffic Mgr. | Passenger Traffic Mgr. |
| San Francisco, Calif. | Denver, Colorado | Chicago, Illinois |

Scenic splendor like the Feather River Canyon made the *California Zephyr* popular with tourists. Western Pacific followed the river for 100 miles as its tracks crossed the Sierra via Beckwourth Pass. The route, today a Union Pacific main line, is less direct than SP's (also now UP's) Donner Pass line, but it is 2,000 feet lower in elevation and less prone to the deep winter snows that plague the Donner line.

look **up**...
look **down**...
look **all around!**

**A**board the California Zephyr, the *only* Vista-Dome stream-liner between Chicago and San Francisco, you enjoy an unobstructed, panoramic view of the most magnificent mountain scenery in the U.S.A. This train is designed and scheduled for sightseeing! You travel through the heart of the Colorado Rockies and California's Feather River Canyon *during daylight hours!*

**Luxurious private rooms and berths**...three Vista-Dome chair coaches (seats reserved)...Vista-Dome buffet lounge car...dining car...Vista-Dome observation lounge car...through Pullman daily between New York and San Francisco. **No extra fare!**

VISTA-DOME *California Zephyr*

CHICAGO · DENVER · SALT LAKE CITY · SAN FRANCISCO

*Include Southern California via San Francisco without added rail fare!*

◄ FOR FREE ILLUSTRATED BOOKLET AND COMPLETE INFORMATION ON THE CALIFORNIA ZEPHYR, WRITE:

| **BURLINGTON** | **RIO GRANDE** | **WESTERN PACIFIC** |
|---|---|---|
| J. J. Alms | H. F. Eno | Jos. G. Wheeler |
| Gen. Passenger Traffic Mgr. | Passenger Traffic Mgr. | Passenger Traffic Mgr. |
| Chicago, Illinois | Denver, Colorado | San Francisco, Calif. |

RIDE THE VISTA-DOME
*California Zephyr*
**THROUGH WINTER WONDERLANDS TO SUNNY CALIFORNIA**

**Designed and scheduled** for sightseeing, the California Zephyr (only Vista-Dome streamliner between Chicago-Denver-Salt Lake City-San Francisco) gives you thrilling daylight views of the Colorado Rockies and Feather River Canyon.

**Five Vista-Domes.** Delightful meals. Luxurious private rooms. Comfortable berths. Thrifty de luxe chair coaches. Congenial buffet lounge and observation lounge. No extra fare.

(Daily through Pullman, New York-San Francisco)

*Include Southern California via San Francisco without added rail fare!*

FREE ILLUSTRATED BOOKLET

California Zephyr Travel Bureau, Dept. 53H
101 West Adams Street, Chicago 3, Illinois
Please send colorful free booklet and information about a trip aboard the California Zephyr.

Print Name_____
Address_____
City & State_____Zone_____

**BURLINGTON · RIO GRANDE · WESTERN PACIFIC**

Whatever the season, the scenery was great from the *California Zephyr* Vista-Domes. These 1953 ads (April, at left, November, at right) noted the beauty of the route west of Denver, including daytime views of the Colorado Rockies and California's Feather River Canyon. The original *Zephyr* ceased a little more than a year before the advent of Amtrak, a victim of the 1970 Burlington Northern merger. Amtrak eventually resurrected the *California Zephyr* name and the train runs today, albeit on an ex-Southern Pacific, now Union Pacific, routing over Donner Pass—a spectacular and historic rail line in its own right.

# 5 *Vista-Domes*

## ...SCENERY UNLIMITED!

Only the *Vista-Dome CALIFORNIA ZEPHYR* gives you so much to see, so much to do.

*You look up, look down, look all around* as you enjoy day-long views of California's famous Feather River Canyon, the High Sierra and the colorful Colorado Rockies.

*You have room to roam*...from your luxurious Pullman or spacious chair coach to the congenial Vista-Dome buffet-lounge, the Vista-Dome observation-lounge, the distinctive dining car and all the rest of this wonderful train.

And only the CALIFORNIA ZEPHYR is designed and scheduled for sight-seeing. No extra fare!

(Daily through Pullman between San Francisco and New York)

*No additional rail fare from most California points to Chicago via San Francisco.*

**Ask about low-cost FAMILY FARE PLAN**

**WESTERN PACIFIC**
**RIO GRANDE · BURLINGTON**

*Through the Colorado Rockies*

THE VISTA-DOME
*California Zephyr*

**SAN FRANCISCO**
**SALT LAKE CITY**
**DENVER · CHICAGO**

**Free Illustrated Booklet**

California Zephyr
Travel Bureau, Dept. 541 S
526 Mission St., San Francisco 5, Calif.

Please send colorful free booklet and information about a trip aboard the California Zephyr.

Print Name_____

Address_____

City & State_____ Zone____

Five Vista-Domes and "scenery unlimited" were trumpeted to potential patrons in this January 1954 ad, but read the smaller print and you'll see one of the keys to the *California Zephyr's* tremendous success: the "low-cost FAMILY FARE PLAN." The train was more-relaxed and fun to ride than Union Pacific's stuffy, upscale *City* trains, and tended to attract greater numbers of family vacationers.

# 5 VISTA-DOMES
## ...Scenery Unlimited!

Only the Vista-Dome *CALIFORNIA ZEPHYR* gives you so much to see, so much to do.

You look up, look down, look all around as you enjoy day-long views of California's famous Feather River Canyon, the High Sierra and the colorful Colorado Rockies.

You have room to roam... from your luxurious Pullman or spacious chair coach to the congenial Vista-Dome buffet-lounge, the Vista-Dome observation-lounge, the distinctive dining car and all the rest of this wonderful train.

And only the CALIFORNIA ZEPHYR is designed and scheduled for sight-seeing. No extra fare!

(Daily through Pullman between San Francisco and New York)

No additional rail fare from most California points to Chicago via San Francisco.

**WESTERN PACIFIC**
**RIO GRANDE · BURLINGTON**

*Through the Colorado Rockies*

## THE VISTA-DOME
### California Zephyr

**SAN FRANCISCO**
**SALT LAKE CITY**
**DENVER · CHICAGO**

### Free Illustrated Booklet

California Zephyr
Travel Bureau, Dept. 547 S
526 Mission St., San Francisco 5, Calif.

Please send colorful free booklet and information about a trip aboard the California Zephyr.

Print Name _____

Address _____

City & State _____ Zone _____

A later version (October 1956) of the *California Zephyr* ad seen on page 61 shows that while the artwork may have changed slightly the message remained the same. And why not? The *Zephyr* was one of the most popular trains of its era.

As late as February 1961, the *California Zephyr* was still profitable and its host railroads were introducing innovations such as the San Francisco Cable Car Room buffet-lounge car. Within a few years of
this ad, rising labor costs and declining ridership marked the beginning of the end. WP tried to drop
out in 1966, but was rebuffed by public outcry and the Interstate Commerce Commission until March
22, 1970, when the last true *Zephyrs* reached their destinations.

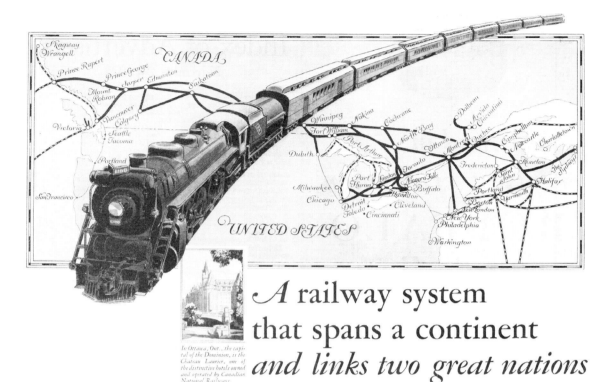

In Ottawa, Ont., the capital of the Dominion, is the Chateau Laurier, one of the distinctive hotels owned and operated by Canadian National Railways

# A railway system that spans a continent and links two great nations

NEW YORK and Montreal; Chicago and Toronto; Duluth and Winnipeg lie south and north of the International Line. But they are not foreign ground to the citizens of either the United States or Canada. Language, race and customs and the luxurious trains of Canadian National Railways link them together and make them neighbors.

Canadian National's 22,681 miles of track provide through train service between the great centers of population and industry in both countries and to every part of Canada. Crossing the border gives no more trouble than traveling from one point to another within either country. No passports are required.

Wherever you wish to go in Canada—whether to the playgrounds of the Maritime Provinces, Historic Quebec, the lake and forest regions of Ontario, the great prairie provinces, the mighty Canadian Rockies, to the Pacific Coast and Alaska—Canadian National will take you, speedily, comfortably and over a route replete with magnificent scenery.

But Canadian National is more than a railroad. It operates year-'round hotels and summer resorts throughout Canada. It provides freight, express and telegraph service throughout the Dominion with connections to all parts of the world. Canadian National Steamships carry Canada's ensign over the seven seas. Eleven Canadian National radio stations broadcast from coast to coast.

For information on Canada's natural resources and business opportunities, for tickets and accommodations, call at, write or telephone the nearest Canadian National office.

# CANADIAN NATIONAL

### The Largest Railway System in America

A pair of Canadian National advertisements (November and December, 1928) emphasize the transcontinental scope of this railroad: coast-to-coast without changing trains. With 22,681 miles of track, CN advertised that in 1928, it was the largest railway system on the American continent.

# "OPERATOR, *Get me London*"

*..imagine this..on a train traveling 50 miles an hour!*

A BUSINESS man was traveling between Toronto and Montreal on Canadian National's famous International Limited. To the train radio operator, he said, "Please get me London on the 'phone."

In fifteen minutes he was talking with his family in England, while traveling 50 miles an hour.

On only two trains in the world today—both Canadian National—is this miracle of two-way telephone service possible. Developed by Canadian National engineers, it is an instance of the progressive spirit that is bringing countless other new luxuries and conveniences to travelers over this, the largest railroad in America.

Observation cars, where the sun streams through vita-glass windows . . . radio at your chair . . . oil-electric locomotives . . . the fastest service between Montreal and the Middle West . . . two transcontinental services without changing cars. These are a few of the achievements which have made Canadian National one of the foremost transportation systems of the world.

Come to Canada this year. For helpful information get in touch with the nearest Canadian National office.

*This famous Canadian National Hotel — CHATEAU LAURIER—is part of the cosmopolitan and colorful background of Ottawa, capital city of the Dominion.*

# CANADIAN NATIONAL
### *The Largest Railway System in America*

OFFICES

| | | | |
|---|---|---|---|
| BOSTON<br>186 Tremont St. | DETROIT<br>1523 Washington Blvd. | NEW YORK<br>673 Fifth Avenue | ST. LOUIS<br>314 No. Broadway |
| BUFFALO<br>420 Main St. | DULUTH<br>430 W. Superior St. | PHILADELPHIA<br>1422 Chestnut St. | ST. PAUL<br>83 East Fifth Street |
| CHICAGO<br>4 So. Michigan Ave. | KANSAS CITY<br>705 Walnut St. | PITTSBURGH<br>355 Fifth Ave. | SAN FRANCISCO<br>648 Market St. |
| CINCINNATI<br>49 E. Fourth St. | LOS ANGELES<br>607 So. Grand Ave. | PORTLAND, ME.<br>Grand Trunk Ry. Sta. | SEATTLE<br>1329 Fourth Ave. |
| CLEVELAND<br>925 Euclid Ave. | MINNEAPOLIS<br>634 Marquette Ave. | PORTLAND, ORE.<br>302 Yamhill St. | WASHINGTON, D.C<br>901 — 15th St., N. W |

Railroad luxury had attained great heights, even in the pre-streamlined era. This advertisement, published during the summer of 1931, guaranteed telephone service available en route on two Canadian National trains. As for calls from Canada to England ("Operator, get me London"), a fifteen-minute wait for a connection was not unusual in 1931, because there was no such thing as long-distance direct dialing. Service was generally primitive compared to more recent standards — yet long-distance phone calls cost much more then.

**To make your vacation in Canada even more wonderful...**

Canadian National makes

# RECORD PURCHASE

## of new passenger equipment!

**This record purchase** marks the beginning of a new era in Canadian train travel. These modern new passenger cars offer a complete choice of accommodations...are designed to provide the utmost in comfort, in convenience, in beauty. Every day more and more of these cars are joining Canadian National's fleet of famous "name" trains traveling the length and breadth of Canada. By midsummer, they will all be in service, helping to make your Canadian *National* vacation more wonderful than ever.

Ask about Canada's Top Maple Leaf Vacations or let CANADIAN NATIONAL RAILWAYS experts package a tour for you to include side trips and stopovers. *Canadian National offices in principal U. S. cities. In Canada, Passenger Department, 360 McGill St., Montreal. Or see your Travel Agent.*

**CANADIAN NATIONAL RAILWAYS**

THE ONLY RAILWAY SERVING ALL 10 PROVINCES OF CANADA

Canadian National advertises a "record purchase" of new, streamlined passenger equipment in March 1954. The $59 million investment included 218 coaches from Canadian Car & Foundry and 141 sleeping, dining and parlor cars from Pullman-Standard. This purchase allowed CN, in 1954, to re-equip all mainline trains with lightweight, streamlined cars. Ironically, the ad features a row of colorful new locomotives—not cars—against a stylized backdrop of snow-capped cliffs.

*Picture Window....*
*by Canadian Pacific*

*Down by the sea on Canada's East Coast*

That window beside your seat on a Canadian Pacific train . . . it's a travelogue in technicolor. It's a window on natural grandeur . . . on horizon-spreading farm lands . . . on industrial vigor. It's a moving panorama of a great land . . . a land you ought to see . . . an uncrowded land of fun—and courtesy.

And it's the way to travel in Canada . . . the comfort way . . . the friendly way . . . the way tens of thousands of Americans have caught their first glimpse of a vigorous, interest-packed country.

Soon Canadian Pacific will bring you even finer travel luxury . . . in new, deluxe editions of Canadian Pacific's famous trains.

For information about vacations in any part of Canada consult any Canadian Pacific Railway office or your own agent.

*Canadian Pacific*

**SPANS THE WORLD**

Mealtime is always a most pleasant hour on the train. Memorable northeast-coast scenery is viewed from a Canadian Pacific diner in this August 1946 advertisement. Incidentally, CP, like the Pennsylvania Railroad, was one of few lines to paint its pre-streamlined passenger cars deep red instead of the usual Pullman green color.

THE UNEXCELLED GRANDEUR of the Canadian Rockies is in full view above, behind and all around you when you ride THE CANADIAN's luxurious Scenic Domes on the Banff and

## Canadian Pacific presents Canada's spectacular panorama from the

Imagine yourself in this setting—aboard this train.

Literally surrounded by natural splendor you speed across Canada in ultra-modern luxury. For 2,881 breathtaking miles you ride in royal comfort, command service unsurpassed in rail travel whether you go coach, tourist or first class.

You dine graciously in a Deluxe Dining Room Car or take your meals informally in the Skyline Coffee Shop. You sip refreshments in an intimate Mural Lounge or relax in a roomy and beautifully appointed Observation Lounge.

Aboard spacious coaches (on which all seats are reserved) you ride comfortably in reclining armchairs with full-length leg rests and adjustable head rests. And each car on THE CANADIAN has its own unique décor, its own restful charm delightfully enhanced by the unobtrusive tones of transcribed music.

In daily service between Montreal and Vancouver and Toronto and Vancouver, THE CANADIAN offers you the longest dome ride in the world, carries you comfortably across Canada under smooth diesel power.

Plan your trip now. THE CANADIAN's tremendously successful maiden year of operation has created volumes of excited comment. Service aboard THE CANADIAN

Traveling luxury combines with majestic scenery in the March 1956 ad for Canadian Pacific's new dome-equipped *Canadian*. The train traveled nearly coast-to-coast across Canada, passing through the spectacular Canadian Rockies—some would argue, the most-scenic route traversed by any North

Lake Louise route. In both this scene and the one below, the setting is the beautiful Bow River Valley, famous the world over for its unspoiled magnificence.

## Scenic Domes of The Canadian

Now take your trip of a lifetime via Banff and Lake Louise aboard Canada's only stainless steel Scenic Dome Streamliner.

has been extolled by thousands, and their enthusiasm presages an even greater demand for accommodations this year. Make your reservations early to be certain of a glorious trip for whatever season you choose.

You can get complete details on THE CANADIAN'S fast new schedule and its numerous accommodations from your local agent of Canadian Pacific in principal cities in the U.S. or Canada right now.

**Special for Camera Fans:** If you plan to shoot color, you're advised to equip your camera with a No. CC30-R filter to compensate for the glareproof tint in the glass of THE CANADIAN'S Scenic Domes. Detailed photographic tips are available on the train.

Route of THE CANADIAN

American passenger train. Canada's first stainless steel, scenic dome streamliner, the *Canadian* entered daily service on April 24, 1955, following delivery of 17 new cars from Budd—enough to outfit 18 complete trainsets.

*Canadian Pacific… by Land …across Canada*

## Now see Canadian Pacific's spectacular Banff-Lake Louise Route from the Scenic Domes of "The Canadian"

Treat yourself to the world's longest, most spectacular Scenic Dome ride as "The Canadian" winds through the Canadian Rockies on its transcontinental route. From high in the Scenic Domes of Canada's only stainless-steel Scenic Dome streamliner you'll thrill to the breath-taking view of Canada's unspoiled natural beauty. And aboard "The Canadian" you'll find the accommodations superb, the service unexcelled. You may travel tourist or first class—coach seats reserved at no extra fare.

See your travel agent for information about "The Canadian" —in daily service throughout the year between Montreal or Toronto, and Vancouver.

◀ Mile-high in the Canadian Rockies, Banff Springs is famous the world over for its scenic surroundings, complete outdoor recreation facilities. Both Banff and nearby Lake Louise are on the route of "The Canadian."

### *Canadian Pacific*

*World's Greatest Travel System*

RAILWAYS · STEAMSHIPS · AIRLINES
HOTELS · COMMUNICATIONS · EXPRESS

CP's sleek Canadian arrives at the Banff depot and happy travelers debark in anticipation of fun, excitement and an ever-unforgettable holiday. Banff and Lake Louise remain world-famous *Canadian* travel destinations, thanks in no small part to Canadian Pacific's many years of aggressively marketing the Canadian and its scenic route through the Rockies.

See more of magnificent Canada from Canadian Pacific's ultra-modern Scenic Dome trains

Aboard "The Canadian" and "The Dominion," in daily service throughout the year between Montreal-Toronto and Vancouver, you will find a happy combination of spacious comfort and gracious service.

Widely spaced coach seats have full-length head and leg rests. (And no matter which class you travel on "The Canadian," all seats are reserved at no extra cost!) Enjoy superb cuisine. But most important: you see some of the world's most magnificent scenery from the scenic domes!

En route, you may want to stop off at Banff and Lake Louise. Nestled mile-high in the Canadian Rockies, these luxurious mountain retreats are world-famous for their spectacular surroundings and gracious hospitality.

On land with scenic dome streamliners and renowned hotels, as on the seas with White Empress luxury liners and in the air with jet-prop airliners, Canadian Pacific offers a world of unsurpassed transportation service.

**RELAX IN SPACIOUS COMFORT ALONG THE WORLD'S LONGEST, MOST SPECTACULAR SCENIC DOME ROUTE, VIA BANFF AND LAKE LOUISE!**

"The Canadian," luxurious scenic dome streamliner, takes you in comfort through the heart of the mighty Canadian Rockies.

*Canadian Pacific* — *World's Most Complete Transportation System*

RAILWAYS · STEAMSHIPS · AIRLINES · HOTELS · COMMUNICATIONS · EXPRESS · TRUCKING · PIGGYBACK

Passengers take in another awesome view of the Canadian Rockies from a Canadian Pacific dome car in a May 1959 ad. The dome-equipped trainsets were standard equipment for CP's flagship *Canadian* and sister transcontinental train, *The Dominion*.

# See spectacular Canada from high-up scenic domes

Canadian Pacific, the world's most complete transportation system, invites you to ride through the Canadian Rockies in scenic-dome luxury aboard *The Canadian*.

The scenery literally surrounds you when you cross Canada in the high glass-topped domes of *The Canadian* on the Banff-Lake Louise route.

The natural beauty of the Canadian Rockies is indeed spectacular. And Canadian Pacific provides roomy coaches, tourist or first-class accommodations, superb cuisine, truly gracious service.

A stopover at the luxurious Banff Springs Hotel or the Chateau Lake Louise—just two of the world-renowned Canadian Pacific hotels—will make a memorable holiday for a traveler or his whole family.

In fact, when you go by Canadian Pacific, the facilities of the world's largest transportation system and seventy-five years of experience are at your service—for over 85,000 route miles of integrated travel and transportation services by land, sea, and air!

You enjoy the Canadian Rockies scenery at breath-takingly close range from the dome cars of *The Canadian*.

## Canadian Pacific

THE WORLD'S MOST COMPLETE TRANSPORTATION SYSTEM

Railways · Steamships · Airlines · Hotels · Express · Communications · Trucking · Piggyback

Even five years after their delivery, Canadian Pacific was touting the domes in this May 1960 ad. Thanks to its scenic route and the service provided to remote areas, the *Canadian* was a mainstay on the CP up to, and even after, the dawn of the government-sponsored VIA Rail era.

Sleep like a Kitten on ~ CHESAPEAKE and OHIO LINES

THE GEORGE WASHINGTON ♡ THE SPORTSMAN ♡ THE F.F.V. ♡ THE FINEST FLEET OF AIR CONDITIONED TRAINS IN THE WORLD

To You from America's Sleepheart

"A-L-L A-B-O-A-R-D The George Washington!" ST. LOUIS - Union Station; CHICAGO - 12th Street Central Station; INDIANAPOLIS - Union Station; LOUISVILLE - Central Station; CINCINNATI - Union Terminal; WASHINGTON - Union Station; PHILADELPHIA - Pennsylvania R. R. Stations; NEW YORK - Pennsylvania Station.

A February 1936 Valentine greeting comes from Chessie, the famous sleeping kitten trademark of the Chesapeake & Ohio. The slogan: Sleep like a kitten. Interestingly, C&O's original, non-railroad predecessor company was founded in 1785 by George Washington. Thus, it was fitting for C&O to name a train after him. The *George Washington*, inaugurated in April 1932 to commemorate the bicentennial of the first president's birth, was one of the last deluxe heavyweight trains. Its main section provided overnight service between the nation's capital and Cincinnati.

# *"North Western"* ENLARGES ITS GREAT *"400"* FLEET

## BUILT BY PULLMAN STANDARD

*The "400" Fleet operates between Chicago and Milwaukee, St. Paul-Minneapolis, Wisconsin, southern Minnesota, and the Upper Peninsula of Michigan*

Fast, luxurious, dependable, the *"400"*s have won distinction among the great trains of America. You, the millions who have patronized the *"400"*s, have given them a service record which has few equals—both in passenger volume and operating results. Now come the first postwar additions to this busy, popular fleet —new Pullman-Standard-built cars, to provide greater capacity for overflow demand; to give further enjoyment and the best in service to travelers along the *"Route of the 400s."*

The high qualities in the latest of the *"400"* series are the result of years of collaboration between Pullman-Standard and the Chicago and North Western System—both pioneers in progressive passenger car development. Pullman-Standard built the first lightweight, streamlined cars *for any railroad.* The North Western, likewise, has a long record of successful operation of this new equipment. Since 1933, we have built 141 lightweight cars for this railroad, or for its joint operation with Union Pacific and Southern Pacific.

Watch for Pullman-Standard's *"Trains of Today!"* For the *safest* and *finest* in modern rail transportation travel on trains which feature Pullman-Standard-built cars.

A composite of February and August 1946 ads tout Chicago & North Western's *400* fleet of trains. Launched initially in 1935 to compete with Milwaukee's *Hiawathas* and CB&Q's *Zephyrs* in the Chicago-Twin Cities corridor, the trains were named because they could make the 400-mile trip in roughly 400 minutes. The service was successful enough that by the 1950s, North Western had a whole fleet of *400s* providing service across the Upper Midwest.

Werner B. Schmidt

# ELECTRIFIED!

You can not know how much electric power has brought to modern railway travel until you ride on the *electrified* Chicago, Milwaukee & St. Paul between Chicago and Puget Sound. Here, for 650 scenic miles, the mightiest locomotives in the world translate the fluid force of mountain torrents into the silent, smooth and smokeless flight of "The Olympian" train. Not a jar or jolt interrupts the even pace maintained up grade and down. No soot or cinders obscure the inspiring scene. Within the incomparable "Olympian" train itself there is completest travel ease—observation-club car, ladies' lounge, luxurious sleeping cars, dining car serving delicious "Milwaukee" meals—all attended with the polite service of "Milwaukee" employes.

*The only line operating transcontinental trains by electric power*

*The only line owning and operating its own sleeping cars between Chicago and Seattle and Tacoma*

*The only line operating over its own rails all the way between Chicago and Puget Sound*

*The shortest line from Chicago to Seattle and Tacoma and the Orient*

GEORGE B. HAYNES, General Passenger Agent, 726 Union Station Building, Chicago

## CHICAGO, MILWAUKEE & ST. PAUL RAILWAY

1521-480          TO PUGET SOUND—ELECTRIFIED

*The 2000-mile transcontinental unit of the Chicago, Milwaukee & St. Paul Railway, part of a perfectly equipped railroad system of more than 11,000 miles*

Artist Werner Schmidt captures the size, weight and might of a Milwaukee Road "St. Paul type" electric locomotive in this illustration used in a September 1925 ad. The Milwaukee's Pacific Extension to Seattle and Tacoma was completed in 1909 and six years later 656 miles of the route in Montana, Idaho and Washington was electrified. Financial problems—meaning not enough cash to maintain the electrical equipment—finally brought down the catenary in 1974. O-gauge and Standard-gauge replicas of these "St. Pauls" were introduced by Lionel in the late 1920s, and are now treasured collectors' pieces.

**FAMOUS TRAINS**

*The Olympian*

Chicago {Spokane-Seattle-Tacoma}

*The Pioneer Limited*

Chicago · St. Paul · Minneapolis

*The Columbian*

Chicago {Yellowstone-Spokane} Twin Cities {Seattle · Tacoma}

*The Southwest Limited*

Chicago {Excelsior Springs-Milwaukee {Kansas City}

*The Arrow*

Chicago {Des Moines · Omaha-Milwaukee {Sioux City}

## DINNER *by Rector*

*Mr. George Rector, Director of The Milwaukee Road's Department of Cuisine.*

Everybody knows of George Rector!

Readers of The Saturday Evening Post followed him weekly through the delightful chapters of "The Girl from Rector's" and "A Cook's Tour."

Countless Americans—and distinguished persons from other lands—have happy recollections of his reign at Rector's, for years the brightest spot on brilliant Broadway. His fame is world-wide; his skill and genius hailed wherever the mastery of cuisine is concerned.

Now—on the famous trains of The Milwaukee Road—folks are marveling at the delicious food and exquisite service of Rector.

A departure in dining car service —the acquisition of the master hand to direct cuisine. Yet not surprising on The Milwaukee Road, where the dining cars command the best to be had.

Thus, "Dinner by Rector" takes its place on the lengthening list of Milwaukee Road achievements—660 miles of electrification, silent roller bearings, club cars moderne, coil spring mattresses, and a host of other features contributing to the comfort and pleasure of our patrons.

*For copy of booklet or detailed information on any subject concerning this railroad, address The Milwaukee Road, Room 884 R, Union Station, Chicago*

## The MILWAUKEE ROAD

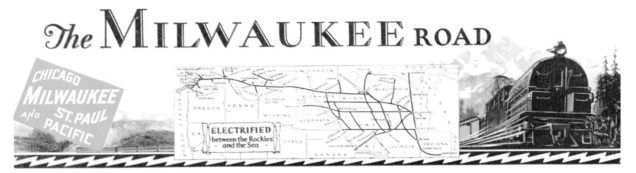

**CHICAGO MILWAUKEE AND ST. PAUL PACIFIC**

**ELECTRIFIED** between the Rockies and the Sea

Renowned New York and Chicago restauranteur George Rector was hired—and touted in this December 1928 ad—by the Milwaukee Road as Director of Cuisine. Milwaukee's elegant, pre-streamlined dining cars offered excellent food and service, but its flagship trains ran in competitive markets out of Chicago to the Twin Cities, Omaha, Kansas City and Seattle. The Rector name had strong appeal with the upscale clientele that still used trains as their primary mode of long-distance transportation in the 1920s.

# *What's the Olympian "in the hole" for, Bill?*

CONDUCTOR BILL can't talk about his railroad orders in wartime—even to such an old friend of the line as Monty Miller, foreman of the Angle D ranch.

It may be the famous, electrified Olympian has gone "in the hole"—which is railroadese for waiting on a side track—because it's more important for a military train to have right of way.

Station agents, conductors, brakemen, and other railroad men don't like to appear unobliging—but they've pledged themselves for the duration to give no information to anyone about unusual train movements.

That's in the interest of national security. An idle word dropped about a troop train—or a supply train's schedule and destination—might reach enemy ears and lead to an attack on a convoy days and even weeks afterward.

For the most part, passengers realize this situation. They too, keep mum about war traffic they see on the railroad.

If the Olympian, the Hiawathas, the Pioneer Limited or other heavily traveled trains happen to be delayed, there is little complaining among passengers. For this understanding attitude, we of The Milwaukee Road are deeply grateful.

Supporting the war effort was a common advertising theme during World War II and, apparently fair payback for minor inconveniences. As this August 1944 ad announces, Milwaukee's *Olympian* and other premier trains would sometimes be put "in the hole" (in a siding) to allow a troop or military shipment train to pass unimpeded. In truth, the war was a boon for the railroads in every way, and represented the final heyday of rail travel in the U.S.

To a legendary
name is added
a great record of
achievement...

## The Hiawathas

THE Milwaukee Road points pridefully to the record of its great fleet of HIAWATHAS. Improved again and again since the original was placed in service, these Speedliners were so soundly conceived and built that they have scarcely been marked by the huge traffic of the war years. Today's HIAWATHAS are still tops in comfort, beauty, speed—and in patronage. Milwaukee Road trains now in the making will provide luxury and beauty that will lift passenger travel to a new high. Your vacation or business trips will pay dividends in comfort if you ride on one of the HIAWATHAS.

F. N. Hicks, Passenger Traffic Manager, Chicago 6, Ill.

HIAWATHAS SERVE CHICAGO · MILWAUKEE · NORTHERN WISCONSIN · MINNEAPOLIS
ST. PAUL · CEDAR RAPIDS · DUBUQUE · DES MOINES · OMAHA · SIOUX CITY · SIOUX FALLS

## THE MILWAUKEE ROAD

Milwaukee Road's streamlined *Hiawatha* equipment was built by the railroad's own shop forces and made its debut in 1934. It was a rousing success. The first *Hiawathas* were pulled by handsome stream-shrouded Atlantic-type (4-4-2) steam locomotives that attained test speeds of 128 mph in 1935. In regular service the pace was more restrained, but still fast. In 1938 the 4-4-2s were supplemented by streamlined 4-6-4s, and Alco DL-109 diesels were added in 1941—the latter shown side-by-side with steam power in this July 1946 ad.

# CHICAGO-PACIFIC NORTHWEST

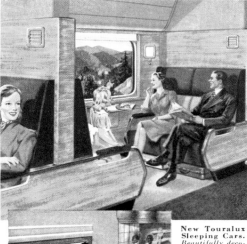

Since 1935 the famous HIAWATHA fleet has been making transportation records in the Midwest. Now this Speedliner service is being extended with the OLYMPIAN HIAWATHAS providing a 45 hour schedule between Chicago and Puget Sound.

Ten of the cars in each twelve car train will be brand new and brilliantly different, designed to make your travel hours on this scenic route more delightful than ever before. Some of the features of these postwar cars are illustrated here.

Ready for service this Fall on the OLYMPIAN HIAWATHAS will be new all-room sleeping cars with the distinctive Sky Top Lounge. This spacious observation room will permit crest-to-canyon views of the Rocky, Bitter Root and Cascade Mountains. Pending delivery of these cars, bedrooms, compartments and drawing rooms will be available in standard sleeping cars.

**New Touralux Sleeping Cars.** *Beautifully decorated and luxuriously appointed, these brand new cars offer accommodations at rates far below standard fares. Nothing like this ever before!*

**New Tip Top Grill** *(at left) with restaurant section, curved bar and cocktail lounge is open to all passengers. A gay and colorful car with radio and recorded music.*

### *Faster Schedule . . . No Extra Fare . . . In Service June 29th*

Enjoy the restful silence and riding ease of the diesel-powered OLYMPIAN HIAWATHAS as you speed through the Northwest wonderland. Asleep or awake, vacationing or on business, you'll find these Milwaukee Road Speedliners fulfill your ideal of postwar rail travel. Presenting fresh ideas in decorations and arrangements, they offer a complete range of luxurious accommodations.

| Westbound | | Eastbound | |
|---|---|---|---|
| Lv. Chicago | 1:30 pm | Lv. Tacoma | 1:30 pm |
| Lv. Milwaukee | 2:45 pm | Lv. Seattle | 2:45 pm |
| Lv. La Crosse | 5:33 pm | Lv. Spokane | 10:15 pm |
| Lv. St. Paul | 7:45 pm | Lv. Missoula | 5:50 am |
| Lv. Minneapolis | 8:30 pm | Lv. Butte | 8:38 am |
| Ar. Aberdeen | 1:10 am | Lv. Three Forks | 10:28 am |
| Ar. Three Forks | 1:57 pm | *(Yellowstone)* | |
| *(Yellowstone)* | | Lv. Aberdeen | 1:45 am |
| Ar. Butte | 3:48 pm | Ar. Minneapolis | 6:45 am |
| Ar. Missoula | 6:18 pm | Ar. St. Paul | 7:25 am |
| Ar. Spokane | 11:50 pm | Ar. La Crosse | 9:38 am |
| Ar. Seattle | 8:30 am | Ar. Milwaukee | 12:30 pm |
| Ar. Tacoma | 9:45 am | Ar. Chicago | 1:45 pm |

*For reservations, ask your local railroad agent or write*
*F. N. Hicks, Passenger Traffic Manager, Union Station, Chicago 6, Ill.*

**New Improved Hiawatha Coaches** *are specially designed for restful cross-country cruising. Foam rubber reclining chairs, fluorescent lighting, spacious lounges with separate lavatory and smoking areas.*

# THE MILWAUKEE ROAD
## Your Friendly Host to the Pacific Coast

By the time of this August 1947 ad, diesels locomotives had gained a strong foothold in the Milwaukee Road, though steam power remained in service until the mid-1950s and the Pacific Extension was partially electrified until 1974. Glimpses inside and outside of the newest *Hiawatha* equipment, new Fairbanks-Morse diesels and the debut of a faster Chicago-Seattle/Tacoma schedule highlight this postwar marketing pitch.

## "Gee, Daddy, they had a private car just for us ladies"

That's right, young lady. There is a combination Touralux-coach with 8 berth sections and 24 reserved coach seats *exclusively for women and children* on The Milwaukee Road's OLYMPIAN HIAWATHA.

The tastefully decorated Touralux sleeping cars have individually lighted and air conditioned berths. Yet berth cost and fare on a round trip between Chicago and Seattle is about $37 less than in standard sleepers.

You can ride in comfortable, reclining chair coaches like the one pictured below, at left, for less than 2c a mile . . . round trip between Chicago and Seattle only $76.20 plus tax.

While the OLYMPIAN HIAWATHA offers these unique advantages for the thrifty, it also provides de luxe Pullman accommodations. No matter what your choice, you enjoy fine food, friendly service and a fast schedule of 45 hours between Chicago and the Pacific north coast over a gloriously scenic route.

Railroad tickets are the ideal Christmas gift. Prepaid tickets may be arranged through your local railroad agent, or write: F. N. Hicks, Passenger Traffic Manager, 708 Union Station, Chicago 6, Ill.

*OLYMPIAN*
## Hiawatha
*Daily service between*

CHICAGO · MILWAUKEE · TWIN CITIES · MILES CITY · BUTTE SPOKANE · SEATTLE · TACOMA

### THE MILWAUKEE ROAD

Chicago, Milwaukee, St. Paul and Pacific Railroad

*Left*—Reclining chairs padded with foam rubber, footrests, fluorescent lighting, big luggage racks and spacious lounge rooms are features of the big, orange colored coaches on the OLYMPIAN HIAWATHA.

*Right*—This view of the women's Touralux car shows the exceptionally comfortable daytime seats. Lower berths are higher, wider and longer than before and there is a charming lounge.

Times have clearly changed in the last half-century. This October 1947 advertisement promotes the *Olympian Hiawatha's* women-and-children only combination Touralux coach. Compare the lower right illustration with the upper-right illustration on page 79—roughly the same scene, but the man has been replaced by a woman.

## *It's a Hiawatha Year!*

*Hiawatha Routes*

**THE MILWAUKEE ROAD**

The distinctive, glass-roofed Skytop Lounge shown in the illustration is a new type of observation room for trackside to mountain top scenic views. Skytop Lounges are carried on the Morning and Afternoon Twin Cities HIAWATHAS and soon will appear on the Olympian HIAWATHA. These cars typify the advanced styling of other Speedlined equipment included in The Milwaukee Road's extensive car building program.

New cars now on the rails have permitted the presentation of improved and new Hiawathas now operating nine thousand miles a day. Additional new cars, scheduled for early delivery, will result in the further amplification of Hiawatha service.

All the new cars embody the latest design and engineering improvements to make your travel hours even more pleasant on "the friendly Railroad of the friendly West". H. Sengstacken, Passenger Traffic Manager, 708 Union Station, Chicago 6, Illinois.

In spring 1948 the Milwaukee Road's *Morning Hiawatha* and *Afternoon Hiawatha* (plying the route between Chicago and the Twin Cities) acquired new streamlined equipment "from end to end." The distinctive Skytop parlor-observation car was a product of the Milwaukee Shops and famed industrial designer Brooks Stevens (who also designed the Studebaker and Oscar Meyer's Weinermobile).

Milwaukee Road's distinctive Skytop Lounges were such a hit that the road ordered more of the glass-paneled cars. This May 1949 ad touts latest incarnation of Brook Stevens' vision: Pullman-Standard-built bedroom-observation cars delivered in January 1949 that extended the Skytop concept to the road's streamliners to the Pacific Northwest.

## AMERICA'S FIRST SUPER DOMES

### NOW ON THE *Hiawathas*

**CHICAGO • TWIN CITIES • PACIFIC NORTHWEST**

*Delightfully new for a wonderful view.* First end-to-end domes on any railroad! The first dome cars of any type between Chicago and the Pacific Northwest!

Introducing new principles of car design, these rolling roof gardens have comfortable chairs for 68. Views unlimited! See the palisaded valley of the Mississippi . . . rugged Montana Canyon . . . the continental divide of the Rockies . . . the forested Bitter Roots by moonlight . . . the rocky pinnacles of Washington's Cascades.

The luxurious Cafe Lounge on the lower deck of the Super Dome car is the smartest club room on wheels. With its warm colors and charming decorative scheme, it is the perfect spot to listen to the radio and enjoy a beverage or a light meal. All passengers are welcome anywhere in the Dome car.

Super Dome cars are in daily service on the transcontinental Olympian HIAWATHA and on the Twin Cities HIAWATHAS. Ride with us for a thrill that is delighting thousands.

*The glass-enclosed Skytop Lounge, another unique Hiawatha feature.*

### Vacation in the PACIFIC NORTHWEST

Get extra pleasure. Ride the Super Dome over the scenic route to Yellowstone Park, Montana Rockies, Spokane for Grand Coulee Dam, Seattle and Tacoma, gateways to Alaska. See the Puget Sound country with Mt. Rainier, Olympic Peninsula and British Columbia.

For free vacation literature, write to Harry Sengstacken, Room 700, Union Station, Chicago 6.

## THE MILWAUKEE ROAD

Following the Skytop Lounge, Milwaukee Road's next passenger train innovation was the first full-length dome car—the Super Dome. Introduced in 1952, the Pullman Standard buffet lounge cars were also among the heaviest streamlined railroad cars ever built. The Milwaukee rostered 10 Super Domes; six were assigned to *Olympian Hiawatha* service and the rest were in the *Twin Cities Hiawatha* equipment pool. (March 1952 advertisement)

# The
## *pause that refreshes*
## brightens the hours
## on the
## OREGON TRAIL

WHERE once only covered wagons lumbered and squeaked—you speed like the wind on the "Portland Rose." Where once the hope beyond the horizon was water for man and beast—you lounge in a big easy chair in a club car, with tingling, ice-cold Coca-Cola at your elbow • • • Progress, bringing comfort and greater fitness for whatever's doing, brings *the pause that refreshes*. On the fastest trains, the proudest ocean liners, at the great airports—the same as along busy city streets. It's a magic moment—this pause for a delicious drink with a cool after-sense of refreshment. You relax. It rests you. And gives new zest for the hours ahead.

**THE BEST SERVED DRINK IN THE WORLD**

A pure drink of natural flavors served ice-cold in its own glass and in its own bottle: The crystal-thin Coca-Cola glass that represents the best in soda fountain service. The distinctive Coca-Cola bottle you can always identify; it is sterilized, filled and sealed air-tight without the touch of human hands, insuring purity and wholesomeness.   The Coca-Cola Company, Atlanta, Ga.

**LISTEN IN** ➤ Grantland Rice ➤ Famous Sports Champions ➤ Coca-Cola Orchestra ➤ Wednesday 10:30 to 11 p. m. Eastern Standard Time ➤ Coast-to-Coast NBC Network.

You ride lounge cars like this, with radios and soda fountains, on the magnificent "Portland Rose" (Chicago - Portland) and "Columbine" (Chicago - Denver) of the Union Pacific.

**9 MILLION A DAY**

Drink
*Coca-Cola*
Delicious and Refreshing

*It had to be good to get where it is*

Two of the greatest names in American industry—Coca-Cola and Union Pacific—joined forces for an early color ad (November 1930), but it's obvious that the soft drink manufacturer paid for the ad. The lounge car scene purports to represent two classic UP heavyweight trains, the Omaha-Denver *Columbine* and the Denver-Portland *Portland Rose*.

The famous, lightweight *Talgo*, originally field-proven in Spain, is now pioneering a new era of railroad transportation in the U. S. Prototypes of these new Talgos, as well as the original ACF-built Spanish version, were all road-tested with Consolidated Electrodynamics instruments to evaluate design features and riding comfort.

Whenever you need fast, accurate data for new-product development, product improvement, or quality control, CEC can help you. The instruments, equipment, and systems available through Consolidated will place you in command of any analytical, control, or data-processing problem. How CEC can help improve your own products, competitive position, *and profits* is told in Brochure 23—"Your Next Move for Profit and Progress." *Send for it today.*

## Most significant move in modern railroading

*FIRST ACF-TALGO in revenue operation in the U. S. is Rock Island's "Jet Rocket". Its prototypes were road-tested with CEC Recording Oscillographs. Strain gages, accelerometers, travel gages, and three-way ride recorders completed the test equipment.*

## Consolidated Electrodynamics

**CEC** *300 North Sierra Madre Villa, Pasadena, California*

NATIONWIDE COMPANY-OWNED SALES & SERVICE OFFICES

The Talgo futuristic train featured lightweight design and an exotic suspension system, but was really just another articulated streamliner. The train was developed jointly by American and Spanish engineers, and proved a success in Spain, but the design flopped here, because passengers disliked the ride and the trains suffered from frequent mechanical problems. The American Car & Foundry-built *Jet Rocket* was featured in an October 1956 ad, but lasted less than two years in Chicago-Peoria service for Rock Island before being scrapped.

THE ROYAL GORGE – COLORADO

**TO OR FROM CALIFORNIA**

SEE THE BEST OF THE WEST
ONLY THE ROYAL GORGE ROUTE
OFFERS YOU

1. The Colorado Rockies
2. The Royal Gorge
3. Feather River Canyon

It costs no more to travel the scenic way across America . . . through The Rockies not around them. Through coaches and Pullmans between St. Louis, Kansas City, Pueblo, Salt Lake City and San Francisco. Ride The Royal Gorge — the train that gives you . . . 1. The Colorado Rockies, 2. The Royal Gorge, 3. California's Feather River Canyon — all in Daylight hours. Stopovers permitted at all points enroute.

I. G. Miller, *Passenger Traffic Mgr.*
Missouri Pacific Lines, Dept. A
Missouri Pacific Building
St. Louis 3, Missouri

Please send me FREE Brochure and information about The Royal Gorge Route to and from California.

Name _____

Address _____

City _____ State _____

*I. G. MILLER*
*Passenger Traffic Mgr.*
*Missouri Pacific*

*H. F. ENO*
*Passenger Traffic Mgr.*
*Rio Grande*

*JOSEPH G. WHEELER*
*General Passenger Agent*
*Western Pacific*

Denver & Rio Grande's *Royal Gorge* provided Denver-Salt Lake City service via Pueblo, Colo., and the train's scenic namesake canyon, but as attested in this May 1948 advertisement, was a key link in transcontinental service in conjunction with Missouri Pacific and Western Pacific. Though relatively small in size, Rio Grande thrived for years as a bridge line, working with partner railroads to stand toe-to-toe with larger competitors such as Southern Pacific, Santa Fe and, especially, Union Pacific.

Passenger comfort is king on the Southern Pacific's sleek new Daylight trains. Cool, conditioned air lulls you in balmy ease. Lights were never so restful...and steady. What did the engineers choose to keep car lights and air-conditioning trouble-free on these $1,000,000 trains? They chose the newest type battery for the newest things on rails. It's the steel-alkaline battery...invented by Thomas Edison...the only kind built of steel.

Daylight cars are 1/3 lighter than ordinary cars. The Edison battery matches this modern trend —it is 1/3 lighter than any other battery. And, this remarkable "power box" lives 2 to 5 times longer. Wise industrialists depend on it...on railroads, ships, in mines and industrial trucks.

Hitching itself to a star, Edison Batteries evokes the *Daylight* name to promote its more-mundane project (which actually was used on the new 1937 SP streamliners). The eye-catching image of the *Daylight*'s trademark Lima-built 4-8-4 steam locomotive is more significant to modern rail enthusiasts. The massive locomotives (nearly 16 feet high and 65 feet long, excluding tender) were mainstay power on the railroad well into the 1950s. One—the 4449—gained fame pulling the *American Freedom Train* and operates in periodic excursion service today, still wearing its gorgeous *Daylight* colors.

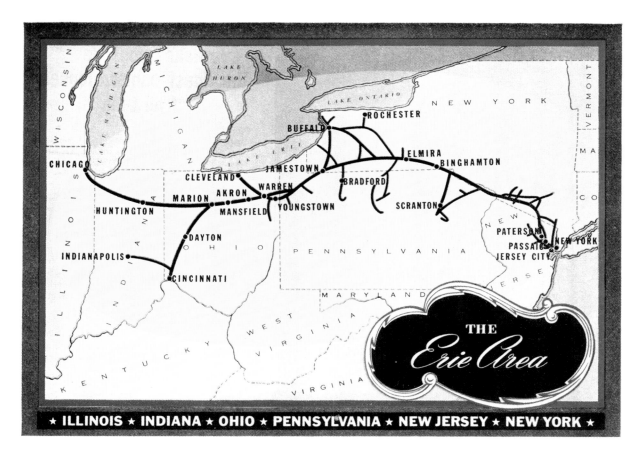

ILLINOIS ★ INDIANA ★ OHIO ★ PENNSYLVANIA ★ NEW JERSEY ★ NEW YORK ★

## Where 34% of Americans Go Shopping

Here, in the six states of New York, New Jersey, Pennsylvania, Ohio, Illinois, and Indiana, lives 34% of America's population. And in the year 1939, these people bought over 16½ billion dollars' worth of merchandise in the stores of the Erie Area—40% of the Nation's total retail sales!

Think how much *greater* that volume will be during the *postwar* period . . . not only for retail merchandise, but for homes, processed materials, industrial products of every kind.

With America's greatest markets, unlimited resources, and unexcelled rail transportation, this Industrial Heart of

America has every requirement for immediate and future development of business enterprise.

And, ready to cooperate in locating plant sites, developing supply and distribution routes, and providing safe, dependable transportation, is the Erie Railroad—serving well for over a century the Industrial Heart of America.

Your free copy of the Erie Area Industrial Map, and any special information you desire, is available free of charge or obligation. Write today to George F. Weston, Industrial Commissioner, Erie Railroad, Midland Building, Cleveland 15, Ohio.

## Erie Railroad

During World War II, 34 percent of America's population lived in the six-state region served by the Erie Railroad. What's more, the war effort depended on this nation's heavy industry, much of which was located on or near Erie routes. Railroad freight service played a key part in America's defense and railroad's worked to ensure their role wouldn't diminish after the war. In this November 1944 advertisement, complete with route map, the Erie sends out a clear invitation to new customers: build a plant along one of our lines!

## THE PARADE IS ON.. as General Motors becomes the BIGGEST BUILDER OF LOCOMOTIVES IN THE WORLD

SEVEN YEARS OF PROGRESS—*In the brief time since crowds thronged to greet this history-making stream-liner, the M-10001, as it completed the first GM Diesel-powered coast-to-coast run, General Motors has grown from a pioneer beginning to the No.1 locomotive builder in the world.*

For the past three years, more locomotives have rolled from the General Motors plant in La Grange, Ill., than from any other plant in America.

Quick to act on every chance to improve service, railroad management is buying General Motors locomotives in greater numbers than any other kind.

That includes mainline passenger locomotives of course. The lines over which they run now network the nation.

It includes switchers. More than 500 are on duty in freight yards today.

It includes freight locomotives — able to bring new speed and economy to the biggest job the railroads have to handle.

And to build these locomotives requires a factory such as the world has never seen before—a completely self-contained plant in which the results of General Motors research and technological progress combine to produce Diesel engines, electrical equipment, bodies, frames and hundreds of other parts. Here these are fabricated and brought together in finished locomotives as ready to run as the automobiles that come off the line in other General Motors factories.

**ELECTRO-MOTIVE CORPORATION**
Subsidiary of General Motors, La Grange, Ill.

**GENERAL MOTORS LOCOMOTIVES**

When this ad ran in September 1941 more than 90 percent of the diesel passenger locomotives then in service were GM-built. Founded in the early 1920s by H.L. Hamilton, Electro-Motive was at first an independent company, but later became a part of General Motors. In 1941, diesel-electric locomotives performed less than 1 percent of freight service, 7.75 percent of passenger service, and 12.01 percent of yard switching. But by 1966, diesel-electrics would perform 99 percent of all railroad service in the U.S.

# BIG TOOLS FOR A BIG JOB!

It takes an organization with long-accumulated skills to produce modern locomotives by the hundreds—to meet the most vital need for motive power in railroad history

YOU must go back more than a quarter century to find the reasons why General Motors has become the most important locomotive builder in the world.

Take, for example, the vastly more efficient power plant that drives such mighty streamliners as the one poised over the trucks above.

*It has made possible the fastest scheduled passenger runs in America.*

*It has materially reduced operating costs.*

*It has enabled every passenger train using General Motors locomotives to operate at a profit.*

These contributions to railroad transportation trace directly to more than a quarter century of research and engineering experience with internal combustion engines—and to the manufacturing "know how" gained from producing more than

29,000,000 motor vehicles. Out of this knowledge has come

*—the first standardized building of complete locomotives in one self-contained factory—including the fabrication and assembly of Diesel engines, frames and even such electrical equipment as generators, traction motors and control parts.*

Yes, it takes big tools for a big job like this. And thanks to progressive railroad management they're kept working at capacity—producing these GM locomotives for passenger, freight and switching service at a pacemaking rate.

**ELECTRO-MOTIVE CORPORATION**
Subsidiary of General Motors, La Grange, Illinois

*From General Motors' long experience in quantity production come many of the new processes and machine techniques required to build these modern locomotives in the volume it takes to meet demand today.*

## GENERAL MOTORS LOCOMOTIVES

General Motors' Electro-Motive plant at La Grange, Ill., is featured in a November 1941 ad.

# PATHFINDERS OF THE DIESEL ERA

*The original Burlington Zephyr which inaugurated a new era in American transportation history in 1934. After more than 1,650,000 miles it still is assigned to its daily round trip of 465 miles between Lincoln and McCook, Nebraska.*

*Latest of the illustrious descendants of the original Zephyr—one of the sixteen 5400-horsepower General Motors Freight Locomotives being put into wartime service by the Burlington Lines.*

IT is just ten years since the famous Burlington Zephyr introduced new ideas in railroad travel. It was the world's first Diesel-powered streamlined train. Its power plant was General Motors Diesel. Today hundreds of General Motors Diesel Locomotives are hauling passengers and freight on 75 American railroads. They operate many millions of miles annually with astounding dependability and economy. Day by day additional GM Locomotives are entering that honored field of more than one million miles of operation. Every day brings new records of performance. And this performance, highlighted by its invaluable contribution to the astonishing war record of the railroads, is providing a glimpse of the greater day of railroading which lies ahead.

*Keep America Strong*
**BUY WAR BONDS**

**GM**
GENERAL MOTORS
**DIESEL POWER**

**LOCOMOTIVES . . . . . . . ELECTRO-MOTIVE DIVISION, La Grange, Ill.**

**ENGINES . . 150 to 2000 H.P. . . CLEVELAND DIESEL ENGINE DIVISION, Cleveland, Ohio**

**ENGINES . . . . 15 to 250 H.P. . . . . . . DETROIT DIESEL ENGINE DIVISION, Detroit, Mich.**

This May 1944 advertisement was sponsored by General Motors, which dominated the first four decades of diesel locomotive manufacturing. Here, the "then and now" scenes compare the original (then) 10-year-old *Burlington Zephyr* with one of GM's latest locomotive offerings, the FT, shown in its as-marketed four-unit, 5,000 hp. configuration. In actuality, the FT was four separate 1,350 hp locomotives—two cabbed A-units and two cabless B-units—and railroads mixed them and matched them to meet their varying horsepower needs.

## "ON TIME"

When this man chalks up "On time" on the train-arrivals board, he makes more than a simple report.

It means that businessmen meet their dates. Through travelers make their connections. Homecomers meet those who wait, when expected. On freight it means that materials and products get to their destination promptly.

Thus the amazing record of General Motors Diesel locomotives for being "On time" is tremendously important to millions — besides setting standards hitherto thought impossible.

Records of large railroads show that for all purposes, passenger and freight, General Motors Diesels have met schedules 97% of *the time*, exclusive of non-locomotive tie-ups.

In addition to ushering in this new era of prompt railroading — in addition to making faster running time possible — General Motors Diesels also show remarkable operating and maintenance economies.

This means that General Motors Diesels magnificently pay their way. Their savings can help to speed revitalization of lines and advance the luxuries of streamlined transportation which they originally inspired. From this everyone concerned can reap newer and greater benefits.

*"Better trains follow better locomotives"*

**GM** GENERAL MOTORS **DIESEL POWER**

# ELECTRO-MOTIVE DIVISION

LA GRANGE, ILL.

GENERAL MOTORS

The traditional "train-arrivals" chalkboard is the centerpiece of a March 1947 advertisement by GM's Electro-Motive Division. This example of vintage railroadiana has long since been replaced by computer screens.

A luxurious compartment on the
TWENTIETH CENTURY LIMITED

*For more than two years, this famous train on the New York Central has been powered by a General Motors locomotive on its daily run, 929 miles each way, between Harmon, N. Y. and Chicago. Also powered by GM Diesels are the Central's Knickerbocker and Southwestern, between Harmon and St. Louis.*

## "There's something really good about this morning!"

She feels as rested and relaxed this morning as she would had she slept in her own bed at home.

There are two reasons:

Modern trains follow modern locomotives. Since General Motors Diesel locomotives were introduced thirteen years ago, modernization of passenger equipment has made dramatic strides. But the locomotive itself deserves part of the credit. The flow of power in a GM Diesel locomotive is so smooth

that you ride through the night without jerks at starting and stopping. You glide to a stop — start so smoothly that you would need to watch the landscape to know when your train starts to roll.

That is one of the many reasons why experienced travelers choose the trains with GM power up ahead.

And you can ride through the night—on a transcontinental journey—without a single change of locomotives.

And the savings in operating costs have enabled the railroads to provide extra comforts for passengers.

Fact is, the entire economy of the nation benefits as the railroads approach closer and closer to complete dieselization—the traveling public, shippers, investors and the railroads themselves.

*"Better trains follow better locomotives"*

## ELECTRO-MOTIVE DIVISION

LA GRANGE, ILL.

GENERAL MOTORS

**GM** GENERAL MOTORS

**DIESEL POWER**

In addition to its massive investment in lightweight passenger equipment after the war, New York Central embarked on dieselization in earnest. As this July 1947 EMD ad attests, the Central was one of many roads that invested in the 2,000 h.p. E7 passenger diesel. Between the model's debut in 1945 and its end of production in 1949, 428 E7As and 82 E7Bs entered service, making it one of the most popular passenger locomotives ever built.

Observation-lounge car on the famous
**PANAMA LIMITED**
This luxurious Illinois Central train is powered by a General Motors Diesel locomotive on its daily 16½-hour run, 921 miles each way between Chicago and New Orleans. Also powered by GM Diesels are the I.C.'s other famous trains—City of New Orleans, City of Miami, Green Diamond, Daylight, Night Diamond, Land O'Corn and Miss Lou.

## *"Ninety-five? I thought we were doing about sixty!"*

Unless you count the mileposts as they flash by, you can hardly believe the distance the Panama Limited is covering with a General Motors Diesel locomotive up at the head of the train.

The flow of power is so smooth that you get from here to there almost before you know it, at a hundred miles an hour a lot of the time.

The Panama Limited is just one example of how GM Diesel locomotives have stepped up schedules on American railroads.

Throughout the country, there are at least 96 different runs made from start to stop at 60 miles or more — a total of more than 7,320 daily scheduled miles. There are more than 23 non-stop runs of 102 to 325 miles in length covered at averages of 60 to 80 miles an hour.

This stepping up of schedules is one of the benefits which GM Diesel locomotives have brought to more than 150 famous name trains on more than a score of railroads — and that is just about all of the Diesel-powered crack trains in the United

States. And in addition, these GM Diesel locomotives are so reliable that some railroads report as high as 97% "on time" arrivals.

No wonder more and more of the crack trains of the nation are being powered by these General Motors locomotives.

In the thirteen years since they first made their bow, they have helped the railroads reduce operating costs — and increased passenger traffic, because they made train travel such a pleasure.

*"Better trains follow better locomotives"*

## ELECTRO-MOTIVE DIVISION

GENERAL MOTORS

LA GRANGE, ILL.

**GM** GENERAL MOTORS

**DIESEL POWER**

Illinois Central's colorful *Panama Limited* is the focus of this EMD ad from August 1947, during an era when railroads were doggedly trying to attract the attention of postwar travelers with new innovations. The Chicago-New Orleans *Panama Limited* was no exception. This upscale, all-Pullman train provided luxurious comfort and even interesting amenities—dial telephones linking sleepers to the dining and lounge areas, and even speedometers to remind passenger how fast the train was traveling. And it *was* fast—speeds often approached 100 mph and with streamlined, lightweight equipment, IC ratcheted down the schedule for the 921-mile run from 20 hours to 18 hours and eventually to 16-1/2 hours by the 1950s.

# IT HAPPENS 150 TIMES A DAY IN CHICAGO

A MEASURE of the railroads' high preference for General Motors Diesel locomotives can be found in Chicago, hub of the nation's railways.

There, high-speed mainline passenger trains arrive or depart behind a General Motors Diesel 150 times every day.

Similarly an array of General Motors Diesel-powered trains arrives and departs every day at Washington, Denver, Kansas City, St. Louis, New Orleans, Seattle, Miami, Atlanta, Los Angeles, Minneapolis-St. Paul, Jacksonville, Omaha — in fact at almost every large railroad terminal in the country.

These General Motors Diesel-powered trains include more than 150 of America's most famous "name" trains—the fast flyers and streamliners that have so greatly increased railway travel.

Such overwhelming endorsement by leading railroads is based on operating experience covering more than one and one-half billion passenger train car-miles piled up behind these locomotives since General Motors pioneered the Diesel main-line locomotives in 1934.

This experience has demonstrated that General Motors Diesels maintain faster, more regular "on time" schedules, cost less to operate, require less maintenance and service and have a far longer useful life than any other type of locomotive.

All of which explains why General Motors is now the world's largest builder of locomotives, and why smart travelers say *"the best trains follow General Motors locomotives!"*

## ELECTRO-MOTIVE DIVISION

GENERAL MOTORS • LA GRANGE, ILL.

Home of the Diesel locomotive

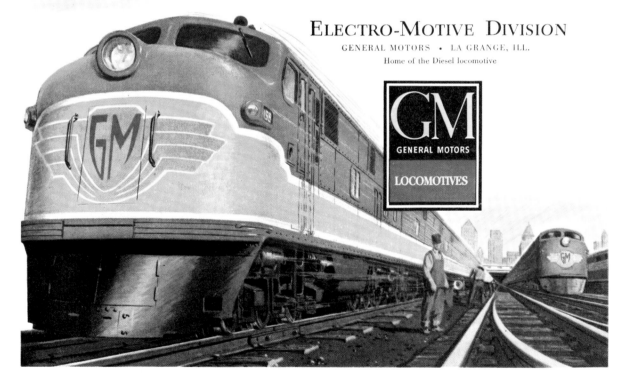

Though this E7 was GM's first-class passenger diesel when this ad ran in May 1948, within two years Electro-Motive Division would be offering the improved E8. Though it looked similar in profile, the new model offered numerous new features and performance over its predecessor, including 2,250 h.p., a power increase of 12 percent.

This view from Lookout Mountain, Chattanooga, Tenn., is typical of the scenic and historic South, through which the Southern Railway passes. Among the name trains on this railway are the Crescent Limited and the Southerner, operating daily between New York, Washington, Atlanta and New Orleans. These and other famous trains on the Southern are powered by General Motors locomotives.

## *See America First Class*

TO see America first class, here is the important thing to remember:

Pick out the trains with a General Motors Diesel locomotive up ahead.

Then, regardless of the ticket you buy, you'll travel everywhere — first class. For these General Motors locomotives give a smoother ride. Trains start and stop without annoying jolts or jerks.

You'll make your time count, too, because of faster "on-time" schedules. And you'll *see* more because no smoke or steam will mar your view.

That's why General Motors locomotives are heading 197 of the nation's fastest, finest name trains.

And why smart travelers say, "Better trains follow General Motors locomotives."

### ELECTRO-MOTIVE DIVISION

GENERAL MOTORS · LA GRANGE, ILL.

*Home of the Diesel Locomotive*

**GM** GENERAL MOTORS LOCOMOTIVES

Apple green and off-white E-units (featured in this November 1948 EMD ad) were the staple power on Southern Railway passenger trains for three decades. The railroad's flagship train was the *Crescent*, which actually used trackage owned by five different railroads in making its trek from New York to New Orleans. Southern was one of a handful of railroads that initially chose not to join Amtrak and continued to operate its *Southern Crescent* until 1979, when it relented and joined the national rail passenger system.

The colorful recreation car on The Jeffersonian, Pennsylvania Railroad all-coach streamliner, provides a luxurious game and reading lounge, a children's playroom, a miniature movie theater and a sunken buffet lounge. The Jeffersonian is in daily service between New York and St. Louis. It is powered by a General Motors locomotive.

## PLAY AS YOU GO

YOU get more fun out of the pleasures today's travel affords when your train is powered by a General Motors Diesel locomotive.

For then you travel with a new smoothness — and a new speed too. Often, on the straightaways, your train will top 100 miles an hour.

General Motors locomotives have also brought a new cleanliness to travel — no smoke and cinders to mar your appearance; no clouds of steam to mar your view.

For years General Motors locomotives have held the records for on-time arrivals.

It is easy to see why 197 of America's finest, fastest name trains are headed by General Motors power.

Easy to understand why better trains follow General Motors locomotives.

### ELECTRO-MOTIVE DIVISION

GENERAL MOTORS • LA GRANGE, ILL.

*Home of the Diesel Locomotive*

EMD E-units and the Pennsylvania Railroad *Jeffersonian* recreation car team up in a General Motors ad from December 1948. The Pennsy livery that adorned the popular diesel units shown in the ad was often mistaken for black; in truth it is Brunswick green and in conjunction with the distinctive "cat whiskers" striping ranks as one of the most popular schemes among railroad enthusiasts and modelers.

GONE are the "good old days" when a fleeting view of the glories of nature *en route* might be had through clouds of steam and smoke that streamed from the engine up ahead. All accompanied by bone-shaking jerks and jolts at stopping and starting, to say nothing of dirty hands, dirty linen and an occasional cinder in the eye.

\* \* \*

HERE now are the grand new days with such magnificent trains as these *California Zephyrs*. They are operated jointly between Chicago and San Francisco by the Burlington, the Denver & Rio Grande Western, and the Western Pacific. Vista Dome observation affords full, free vision of the scenery amid comfortable and luxurious surroundings. These crack trains are powered by General Motors Diesel locomotives.

*"Better trains follow General Motors Locomotives"*

To be sure of enjoying to the full the new and exciting features that modern railroad travel provides, there is just one thing to remember: Better trains follow General Motors locomotives.

*Vista Dome observation permits passengers on the California Zephyrs to enjoy to the full America's beautiful and impressive western country with its gorgeous mountains and broad plains.*

# ELECTRO-MOTIVE
DIVISION OF GENERAL MOTORS • LA GRANGE, ILL.

*Home of the Diesel Locomotive*

Starting in 1949, Chicago, Burlington & Quincy, Denver & Rio Grande Western and Western Pacific teamed up to operate the venerable *California Zephyr*, which carried cross-country travelers in Vista-Dome style for more than two decades. Celebrating the brand-new service, the focus of this July 1949 General Motors ad is actually a stylish trio of EMD "covered wagons"—one representative locomotive for each of the three roads that carried passengers between Chicago and San Francisco.

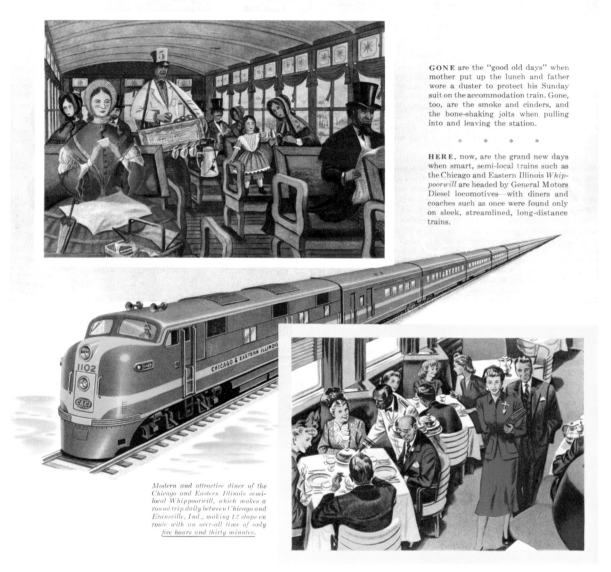

GONE are the "good old days" when mother put up the lunch and father wore a duster to protect his Sunday suit on the accommodation train. Gone, too, are the smoke and cinders, and the bone-shaking jolts when pulling into and leaving the station.

\*　　\*　　\*

HERE, now, are the grand new days when smart, semi-local trains such as the Chicago and Eastern Illinois *Whippoorwill* are headed by General Motors Diesel locomotives—with diners and coaches such as once were found only on sleek, streamlined, long-distance trains.

*Modern and attractive diner of the Chicago and Eastern Illinois semi-local Whippoorwill, which makes a round trip daily between Chicago and Evansville, Ind., making 12 stops en route with an over-all time of only five hours and thirty minutes.*

"Better Trains Follow General Motors Locomotives"

Yes, a great many better trains now follow General Motors locomotives in semi-local service as well as in long-distance service—working toward the not too distant day when *all* railroad travel will be "first class." A good thing to remember when you plan a trip *anywhere*.

## ELECTRO-MOTIVE
DIVISION OF GENERAL MOTORS ● LA GRANGE, ILL.
*Home of the Diesel Locomotive*

A "then and now" scene from one of a series of ads sponsored by GM's Electro-Motive Division in the late 1940s. The modern view depicts Chicago & Eastern Illinois' attractive-but-short-lived *Whippoorwill*, shown with an EMD E7 on the point. Though appearing to run on forever in this stylized view, the train, one of the first new postwar streamliners (delivered by Pullman-Standard in 1946), only sported seven cars. Ironically, about the time this ad was run, the train was eliminated and its equipment blended into Louisville & Nashville's *Georgian* trains running over the C&EI between St. Louis and Chicago.

The FIESTA, a luxurious diner-lounge on the new GOLDEN STATE, is one of the most picturesque passenger cars ever built. Its canopied ceiling, tiled floor, adobe bar and hand-carved furnishings are appropriately in the Mexican-Southwestern motif; for this fast streamlined train runs between Chicago and Los Angeles, and is jointly operated by the Rock Island and the Southern Pacific. The General Motors locomotive up ahead adds to the pleasure.

# *Quiet Sunday dinner — 100 miles an hour*

WHEN a train powered by a General Motors Diesel locomotive glides into — or out of — a station, there's not even a ripple in the glass of water at your elbow.

You travel with a new smoothness — and a new speed, too. Often, on the straightaways, your train may make 100 miles an hour.

General Motors locomotives have also brought a new cleanliness to travel — no soot and cinders to mar your appearance; no clouds of smoke and steam to mar your view.

They have held, for several years, the records for on-time arrivals.

That's why it is easy to see why 200 of America's finest, fastest name trains are headed by General Motors power.

Easy to understand why better trains follow General Motors locomotives.

*See the Electro-Motive Exhibit at the Chicago Railroad Fair.*

**GM** GENERAL MOTORS

**LOCOMOTIVES**

Dessert time arrives in the Fiesta Car, the diner-lounge on the *Golden State* and the *Golden Rocket*, operated jointly by Southen Pacific and Rock Island. When this September 1948, advertisement appeared, some 200 "name" trains were headed by GM-built Electro-Motive diesels.

GONE are the "good old days" when just a chance to sit or stand on the rear platform was all an "observation" car had to offer. Gone are the cinders showering from the engine up ahead that almost invariably got into grandpa's eye so he couldn't see much anyway. Gone, too, the smoke and steam that soiled lovely clothes.

\* \* \*

HERE today are such fleet, luxurious trains as the all-Pullman *Capitol Limited* operated between Washington, D. C. and Chicago by the Baltimore & Ohio Railroad. Here, too, is the smooth, cinder-free, on-time ride assured by the General Motors Diesel locomotives that power this nationally famous train.

*"Better Trains Follow General Motors Locomotives"*

*There's so much to do and so much to see in a roomy, luxurious observation car on the* Capitol Limited *that the trip seems all too short between the nation's capital and Chicago.*

Today it's easy — and getting easier every day — to choose trains powered by General Motors Diesel locomotives. Because everywhere they are bringing new smoothness, new cleanliness, new comfort to railway travel.

**ELECTRO MOTIVE**

DIVISION OF GENERAL MOTORS . . . LA GRANGE, ILL.

*Home of the Diesel Locomotive*

**GM** GENERAL MOTORS LOCOMOTIVES

This October 1949 ad for General Motors' Electro-Motive Division shows the great progress passenger trains had made between the 1850s and 1950s. "Then and now" views compare the inside of observation cars. There is also a picture of Baltimore & Ohio's all-Pullman *Capitol Limited*, which served the Washington, D.C.-Chicago run with a "cinder-free" diesel-powered train—a great selling point during the steam-to-diesel transition years.

The Texas Special, crack train operated jointly by the Frisco and the Katy lines, runs between St. Louis, Dallas and San Antonio. The mecca of liberty-loving Americans who visit San Antonio is the Alamo, cradle of Texan independence where, in 1836, originated the inspiring battle-cry, "Remember the Alamo!"

# SEE AMERICA FIRST CLASS

THERE'S one sure way to see America first class — pick out trains with a General Motors Diesel locomotive up ahead.

For these General Motors locomotives give a smoother ride. Trains start and stop without annoying jerks or jolts.

You'll make your time count for more, too, because of faster, "on-time" schedules. And you'll see more because no smoke or steam will mar your view.

That's why General Motors locomotives are heading 197 of the nation's fastest, finest trains — and that's a majority of the Diesel-powered crack trains in the United States.

You'll find, as so many other smart travelers find, that *"Better trains follow General Motors locomotives."*

## ELECTRO-MOTIVE DIVISION

GENERAL MOTORS • LA GRANGE, ILL.

*Home of the Diesel Locomotive*

**GM** GENERAL MOTORS LOCOMOTIVES

The Alamo, landmark of Texas history, is paired with the *Texas Special* for a February 1949 EMD ad. This St. Louis-San Antonio train was a joint operation of Frisco and Missouri-Kansas-Texas (M-K-T or "Katy") and wore an eye-catching red-and-silver livery chosen because passenger surveys indicated the public wanted to ride bright-colored trains! The trains were a success for a few years, but in the 1950s ridership declines started. Frisco dropped out in 1959 and Katy switched the northern terminus to Kansas City. Cutting service back to Dallas in 1964 didn't help and MKT dropped the train in 1965.

*"Better trains follow General Motors Locomotives"*

GONE long ago are the "good old days" when no one really expected to get a good night's rest on a sleeping car—and privacy was at a premium. Gone too are the odors of oil lamps, the uncertain heat of oil burning stoves, drafts, soot, cinders, and the jerky sleep-destroying stops and starts so familiar to old-time travelers.

★          ★          ★

HERE now are such fast, crack trains as the *Missouri Pacific Eagles* with luxurious private sleeping quarters that invite restful, unbroken slumber. Then, to make assurance of smooth, clean, on-time riding, these trains are powered by General Motors Diesel locomotives on their long journeys between St. Louis and Denver, and throughout the Southwest.

**GM** GENERAL MOTORS LOCOMOTIVES  Deep, refreshing sleep, free from jolts and jars and noise, is just one more proof that better trains follow General Motors locomotives. A good thing to remember when you plan your next trip—anywhere.

*A roomy, sleep-inviting bedroom on a Missouri Pacific Eagle offers the comforts of a fine home, plus the ingenious planning of America's leading car builders.*

# ELECTRO-MOTIVE DIVISION OF GENERAL MOTORS • LA GRANGE, ILL.

*Home of the Diesel Locomotive*

The *Eagle* streamliners were the pride of the Missouri Pacific, hauling passengers between St. Louis, Kansas City and Omaha starting in 1940. The first *Eagles* featured lightweight cars built by American Car & Foundry and EMD E3 diesel locomotives (the real star of this May 1949 GM ad). The concept was so successful, MoPac renamed the original trains the *Missouri River Eagles* and hatched a variety of siblings, including the *Delta Eagle* (St. Louis-Memphis/Louisiana) in 1941, the *Colorado Eagle* (St. Louis-Colorado) in 1942 and the *Texas Eagle* (St. Louis-Texas) in 1948.

*The new Southern Belle, smartly equipped streamliner of Kansas City Southern Lines, speeds daily each way over the 873 miles between Kansas City and New Orleans. Each train is powered by a General Motors Diesel locomotive.*

**GONE** are the "good old days" when passengers literally rubbed elbows in the washroom. The more daring shaved with a straight, old-fashioned razor, defying the jolts and jars of the train at starting and stopping. Smoke, steam and cinders from the engine up ahead didn't help matters, either.

**HERE** now are the grand new days. Modern passenger coaches provide every conceivable means of making railroad travel clean, restful and comfortable. On the nation's railroads, hundreds of such fine, fast trains are powered by General Motors Diesel locomotives.

*It's a pleasure to spruce up in a bright, cheery private bedroom on the Southern Belle. Plenty of room—with modern fixtures at finger-tip convenience to help you do a smooth, first-class job.*

Wherever you travel, pick a train powered by a General Motors locomotive. Then you'll really travel first class, in *less time*, and *on time*. You'll find, for your greater pleasure, that *better trains always follow General Motors locomotives.*

**ELECTRO MOTIVE** DIVISION OF GENERAL MOTORS

*La Grange, Illinois* • *Home of the Diesel Locomotive*

Kansas City Southern's colorful *Southern Belle* (known as "The Sweetheart of American Trains") is the star of this November 1949 GM ad. KCS, which still exists today as one of the last independent regional railroads, has thrived by providing a fast, reliable route from the agricultural Midwest to the oil-rich Gulf Coast. The Kansas City-New Orleans *Southern Belle* was inaugurated in 1940, then the war intervened, and the train did not debut streamliner status and regular operations until April 1949. The train operated for two more decades, making its last run in November 1969.

# Rubber "girdles" give trains their streamlined figures

*A typical example of Goodrich development in rubber*

HOW can a streamliner bend on a curve? It looks to be a rigid unit from headlight to tail-light — in fact that's what makes it streamlined. The answer is a rubber girdle between cars that gives the train flexibility, just as it gives it to the modern girl as compared to her whale-boned ancestor of the gay 90's.

But — the rubber compound which was used didn't last. Sun and air attacked it, and early streamliners were too often laid up for new rubber diaphragms. Train builders weren't satisfied — they felt that something should be done to prevent these costly delays and replacements.

Then Goodrich engineers developed an entirely new diaphragm, made of cord-reinforced rubber covered with a synthetic which resists sun and air. And the Goodrich product can be made in any color, to match the silver, red or green of the train.

The diaphragms made by Goodrich have now been in use for months with no sign of deterioration, no cost for repair or replacement. They illustrate the experience of Goodrich engineers with rubber and synthetic compounding — an experience which is always at your disposal to help you solve product or production problems and make sure you are getting maximum value from any rubber or synthetic product you buy. The B. F. Goodrich Company, Mechanical Rubber Goods Division, Akron, Ohio.

## Goodrich
ALL *products problems* IN RUBBER

The "diaphragm" is the flexible tunnel interconnecting two adjacent passenger cars. Here's an interesting message from B.F. Goodrich Co., explaining how it developed an improved version for the latest streamliners. Until 1887, all passenger coaches had been open-ended, making passage from car to car extremely hazardous while the train was in motion. From 1887 to 1893, passenger cars used "narrow vestibules" and diaphragms for greater safety, and in 1893 the Pullman Co. exhibited its new wide-vestibule "Jamestown" passenger car at the Columbian Exposition. (February 1940)

In February 1927, the exotic-sounding *Oriental Limited* was Great Northern's premier train. The train connected Chicago with Seattle and Portland, though GN truly reached out to the Orient thanks to its Great Northern Steamship Company. Though this ad touts electrification as a travel benefit, it was actually a transportation necessity. GN electrified 43 miles of track between Wenatchee and Skykomish, Washington, to avoid running steam trains through its 2.63-mile-long Cascade Tunnel. In 1929 a new, electrified 8-mile-long Cascade Tunnel opened, but in 1956 the wires came down with the debut of a ventilation system in the bore.

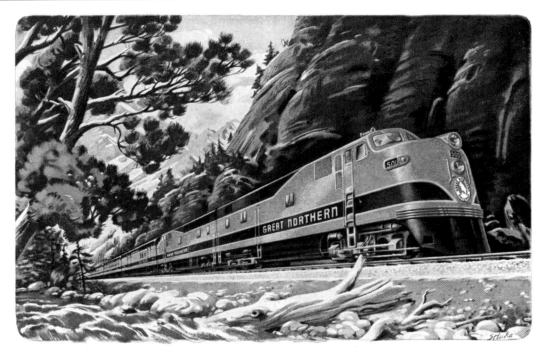

## the *New* Empire Builder
### custom-built for pleasant, faster travel

A new generation of a long-distinguished fleet of transcontinental trains—Great Northern's *New* EMPIRE BUILDERS. The *first* modern, sleeping car-coach trains built since the war, the New EMPIRE BUILDERS inaugurate the *first* streamliner service between Chicago and the Pacific Northwest on a daily 45-hour schedule. These sleek, colorful, diesel-drawn trains are custom-built for comfortable, refreshing travel. New style coaches . . . duplex roomettes . . . spacious bedrooms . . . cheerful lounges . . . gay coffee shops . . . and charming dining cars with Great Northern's famous food service. The *New* EMPIRE BUILDERS—modern trains designed for modern travelers.

*New design duplex roomettes . . . ideal for the passenger who desires complete privacy and comfort.*

*New style Day-Nite coaches . . . more room for each passenger, more comfort and convenience.*

**Serves the Best of the Great Northwest**

Post-war streamlined equipment was featured in this December 1946 ad for Great Northern's green-and-orange *Empire Builder*, which had replaced the *Oriental Limited* as the railroad's flagship train in 1929. The *Empire Builder* celebrated the nickname and legacy of the James J. Hill, the man who, starting in 1878, built the GN into one of America's great railroads. The train connected Chicago and Seattle; GN relied on corporate partner Burlington to handle duties east of Chicago. The *Empire Builder* survives today as one of Amtrak's most-popular trains.

# POST-WAR VACATION

**this
is the year
and this
the right train**

Seattle and Portland are only two nights from Chicago on Great Northern's swift, streamlined *New Empire Builder*. No extra fare.

Modern coaches with leg rests. No additional charge for reserved seats.

You enjoy privacy and restful sleep in luxurious duplex roomettes and bedrooms.

## GREAT NORTHERN'S
## *NEW EMPIRE BUILDER*

● This year visit the Pacific Northwest and California to your heart's content. Travel on the *first* and *finest* postwar transcontinental train. Diesel powered, this green and orange superliner streaks along the smoothest roadbed in the Northwest. Inside there's more color, more comfort, more convenience than you'd have thought possible before the war. Come aboard soon! Write to V. J. KENNY, Passenger Traffic Manager, Great Northern Railway, St. Paul 1, Minn.

The June 1947 advertisement offers both a colorful route map and three views of Great Northern's newly equipped *Empire Builder*. Five new streamlined trainsets were introduced in February 1947 and during the ten months that followed, 139,310 passengers traveled on this train that made a 2,211-mile jaunt between Chicago and the Pacific Northwest. And what a value—duplex roomettes cost only $2.13 more than a lower berth!

 *Great places to go...*

MOUNT RAINIER in Washington, gleaming in white-crested majesty, beckons you to one of the many fabulous vacationlands in the Pacific Northwest. This fourth highest U. S. peak, viewed from Paradise Valley, is a short, pleasant trip from Seattle.

MANY GLACIER HOTEL on Swiftcurrent Lake is in the heart of Montana's Glacier National Park. Here you can explore a mountain or valley every day . . . hike or ride through snowfields or virgin timber, fish or loaf on sunlit shores of blue, glacier-fed lakes.

*2 Great Northern Trains get you there*

ON THE EMPIRE BUILDER relax in The Ranch, where Western hospitality rules. There's no railway car like it! The Ranch is just one of the luxurious features that make Great Northern's streamlined Empire Builder newest and best to the Pacific Northwest. You go great when you go Great Northern.

ON THE WESTERN STAR, which serves Glacier National Park from June 15 to September 10, you dine like a king at modest cost. This modern streamliner offers you travel luxury and comfort both in Pullmans and in economical Day-Nite coaches. You go great when you go Great Northern.

For information on ☐ Glacier Park, ☐ Pacific Northwest, ☐ California, check, clip and mail to Great Northern Ry., Dept. H-42, St. Paul 1, Minn. Include name, address.

*Great Northern's*
EMPIRE BUILDER  *2 Great Trains*
WESTERN STAR

In 1910, Glacier National Park was founded on a million acres that were too rough and rocky for farmlands, but ideal for vacationers and tourists. The scenery was absolutely spectacular. And soon, the Great Northern Railway built the Many Glacier Hotel, seen at upper right. Great Northern's *Western Star* served Glacier National Park in the summertime; a view inside its comfortable dining car is seen at lower right. At lower left is a view inside "The Ranch," an atmospheric diner-lounge aboard the *Empire Builder*. It featured a Western motif, with pinto leather-covered seats, rustic wood-and-iron decorations everywhere, and even—for a time—a piano bar in the lounge section. (April 1952 advertisement)

*MORE LUXURY DOME SEATS FOR THE MOST SCENIC MILES ON ANY TRAIN*

# GO GREAT... GO

### 4 GREAT DOMES ON THE *EMPIRE BUILDER*

Long a pacemaker for train travel at its finest, Great Northern's distinguished Empire Builder now provides 147 topside seats in new Great Dome cars—the most dome seats on any streamliner between Chicago and Pacific Northwest cities.

There now are three luxurious Great Domes in the coach section of the Empire Builder . . . plus an exciting, colorful full-length Great Dome in the Pullman section, with America's smartest lounge on rails on the lower deck.

For a vacation trip of a lifetime . . . for business travel, step aboard the Empire Builder. There's *no extra fare* for helping yourself to a grandstand seat in the Great Domes for the *extra wonderful sightseeing* through Great Northern country.

*For information: Write P. G. Holmes, Pass. Traff. Mgr., G. N. Ry., St. Paul 1, Minn.*

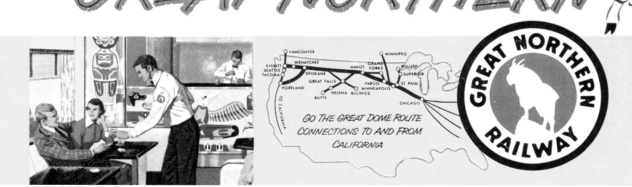

## GREAT DOMES ON THE GREAT NORTHERN

The Great Northern Railway is an engineering masterpiece blessed by some of the most wonderful scenery in America.

Its Empire Builder glides past towering Rocky Mountains in Glacier National Park . . . along jade rivers and white-capped Puget Sound . . . through the forested Cascades . . . on its super-scenic trail between Chicago, St. Paul-Minneapolis, Spokane, Seattle and Portland.

Here are sights to thrill you, watching through the enormous curved windows of the new stainless steel dome cars, built by Budd, which now distinguish the Great Northern's Empire Builder.

The Great Northern, in company with many other railroads, has made every imaginative provision to make your trip by train the most restful, the most stimulating way to travel . . . the safest and most certain way to reach your destination . . . sprinkled all over with enjoyment.

To provide this feast of travel perfection, railroads call on Budd.

Philadelphia          Detroit          Gary

One of the many beautiful railroad paintings by Leslie Ragan was featured in a Budd Company advertisement from September 1955. The illustration depicts Great Northern's beautiful *Empire Builder* and in particular, one of its brand-new Great Domes, which actually made their debut in September 1955. GN, always leader in providing great passenger service, actually borrowed the full-length dome idea from rival Milwaukee Road, which had introduced its own Super Domes in 1953. PREVIOUS PAGES: A stunning October 1955 ad for the *Empire Builder* and its Great Domes.

## The Railroad Revolution

LAST December, *Fortune* made a prophecy. In the lightweight, streamlined Diesel train, said this publication, lay the genesis of a railroad revolution.

Today—less than one year later—the revolution is in full swing. The Diesel train is fast becoming a familiar part of the American scene. And a silvery symbol of this new era in rail transportation is the New York, New Haven and Hartford's "Comet."

Slipping through space like a meteor through the sky, this new train cuts one-third off the regular time between Boston and Providence. It can travel at a speed of 110 miles an hour, and still have power in reserve.

And every mile "The Comet" clicks off is a tribute to the quality of Gulf products. For its two great Diesel units are now fueled and lubricated exclusively by Gulf.

Perhaps no single organization is better equipped to take a part in the railroad revolution than the Gulf Refining Company. Its experimental work with Diesel engines dates back many years, beginning with the marine engines in Gulf's own great fleet of tankers.

As the Diesel has lost weight and gained horsepower, special fuels and lubricants have been developed to meet each changing condition. And now Gulf scientists are working towards the day when Diesel transportation will demand still more of Gulf.

It is possible, and even probable, that the Diesel train will soon become the ordinary means of high-speed overland travel. But however fast it may develop, Gulf will be ready with the proper fuels and lubricants.

## GULF REFINING COMPANY

Burlington's *Zephyr* and Union Pacific's M-10000 ushered in the streamliner era, but close on their heels was New York, New Haven & Hartford's *Comet*, featured in a September 1935 ad. Interestingly, the train was a product of Goodyear-Zeppelin, an airship manufacturer that started looking to break away from its declining market following the crash of the U.S. Navy airship *Akron* in 1933. The three-car train carried up to 160 passengers, and starting offering speedy Providence-Boston service in June 1935. It was a success—but New Haven's bankruptcy in 1935 prevented the railroad in investing any more *Comet* siblings.

This dramatic demonstration of the worth of the Westinghouse Air Brake occurred on the trial run. As the train emerged from a tunnel, the engineer saw a balky horse on the crossing ahead. Suddenly the horse bolted and threw the driver on the tracks. The air brake stopped the train just four feet from disaster.

## When Money Talked In No Uncertain Terms

*"You can't stop a train with wind!"*

That was the answer George Westinghouse received when he pleaded with railroad men to allow him to test his air brake. He had spent all his money on its manufacture and was unable to finance a test run himself. Finally a friend, Ralph Baggaley, offered to advance the necessary money. With this financing, the trial run was made and the worth of the air brake dramatically proved.

**Money Helps To Meet The Test**

If your family should ever have to go along without you, they would be put to a severe test. How they would solve the problem of the readjustment period depends largely on your foresight now. Enough income to cover their needs for a year or more can help them meet the test by giving them the "breathing spell" necessary for making clear-headed plans. The John Hancock Readjustment Income Plan is especially designed to provide such an income, payable in equal monthly amounts or on a graduated scale.

How this plan operates is clearly illustrated in our booklet entitled "Two Lives," which takes but four minutes to read. Write for your copy, addressing Dept. S-9, John Hancock Mutual Life Insurance Co., 197 Clarendon St., Boston, Mass.

*John Hancock*
MUTUAL
LIFE INSURANCE COMPANY
OF BOSTON, MASSACHUSETTS
GUY W. COX, President

In the 19th century, the adaptation of Westinghouse air brakes brought much greater safety to America's railroads. This December 1940, advertisement was sponsored by John Hancock Life Insurance Co., a company with a vested interest in improving railroads.

Two "classic" advertisements show Lionel electric trains in November 1940 (left), and December 1954 (right). As with real railroads, in 1940 most electric trains were models of steam-powered units. But notice that in 1954, diesels were taking over.

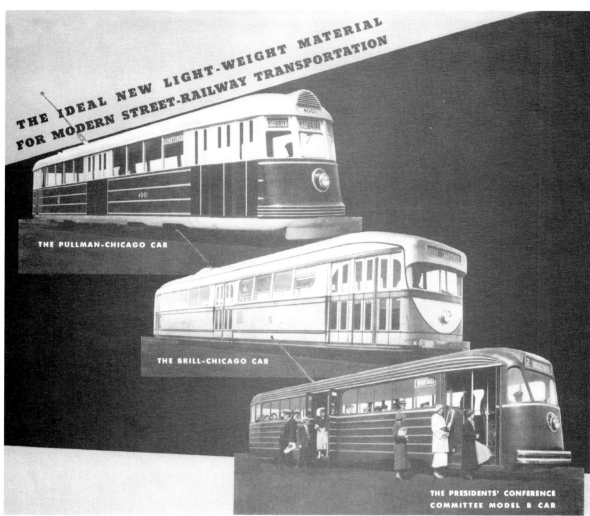

After the mid-1920s, few new streetcars (also known as trolley cars, the ancestors of today's light-rail cars) were ordered. Trolley lines began to dwindle in the face of motorbus competition. Though streetcar service was declining in the 1930s, some cities ordered streamlined equipment, hoping that would help the situation. This 1935 Masonite ad shows three basic types of streamlined streetcars.

Two of The Centuries at the new Buffalo Central Terminal at midnight — *From a painting by Walter L. Greene.*

# THE 20<sup>th</sup> CENTURY LIMITED
## leads the world's greatest fleet
### of DE LUXE FAST TRAINS

NIGHT after night the world's largest fleet of de luxe fast trains speeds over the smooth water level route of the New York Central Lines—the great central artery of travel between the Mississippi Valley and the Atlantic Seaboard.

For more than a quarter of a century the standard bearer of this service has been the *20th Century Limited*. Because of the great public preference for the *Century* between Chicago and New York, this famous train is now operated as a fleet of trains in two divisions—the first division bearing the name of the *Advance 20th Century Limited*.

As a further extension of *Century* service, with a later afternoon departure from both New York and Chicago, New York Central Lines recently inaugurated the new 20-hour de

luxe train, *The Commodore Vanderbilt*. The two *Centuries* and *The Commodore Vanderbilt* carry the great majority of men and women of affairs who travel between the two cities— and who place a high value on restful sleep en route.

This is the only route between New York and Chicago that is protected all the way by the Automatic Electric Train Stop—commended as "an outstanding contribution to safety in travel." It is the only route that finds a low-level pass through the Appalachian Mountain barrier. The broad steel highway of the New York Central lines is nearly at sea level for a thousand miles. And this, too, is the only route that takes the traveler through the Hudson River Valley, one of the most famous scenic highways of the world.

**New York Central 20-Hour Fleet**

**NEW YORK TO CHICAGO**

ADVANCE 20TH CENTURY LIMITED
Lv. New York 2:00 p.m.  Ar. Chicago 9:00 a.m.

20TH CENTURY LIMITED
Lv. New York 2:45 p.m.  Ar. Chicago 9:45 a.m.

THE COMMODORE VANDERBILT
Lv. New York 4:00 p.m.  Ar. Chicago 11:00 a.m.

THE WOLVERINE (via Michigan Central)
Lv. New York 5:00 p.m.  Ar. Chicago 12:00 noon

**CHICAGO TO NEW YORK**

FAST MAIL
Lv. Chicago 9:50 a.m.  Ar. New York 6:50 a.m.

THE WOLVERINE (via Michigan Central)
Lv. Chicago 11:00 a.m.  Ar. New York 8:00 a.m.

ADVANCE 20TH CENTURY LIMITED
Lv. Chicago 12:00 noon  Ar. New York 9:00 a.m.

20TH CENTURY LIMITED
Lv. Chicago 12:40 p.m.  Ar. New York 9:40 a.m.

THE COMMODORE VANDERBILT
Lv. Chicago 2:00 p.m.  Ar. New York 11:00 a.m.

# NEW YORK CENTRAL LINES

TWENTIETH CENTURY LIMITED: *Chicago, New York, New England*  —  SOUTHWESTERN LIMITED: *St. Louis, New York, New England*

Eastbound and westbound trains of New York Central's *20th Century Limited* meet at midnight at the new terminal in Buffalo, N.Y., in this December 1929 scene. Note that safety was an important factor to the traveling public and the Central took great pains to promote its Automatic Electric Train Stop, which helped prevent rear-end collisions. Safety issues were far from the greatest threat to railroads; the lone plane in the night sky foretold of competition from airlines, then in their infancy, that would change the way Americans traveled.

IT PAYS TO RIDE THE CENTURY

THE ENGINE OF THE "CENTURY"

## TO THE MOTHER OF A *Lucky Little Lady*

Your daughter does not know what high spirited adventure is a journey on the most distinguished of the world's fine trains. She doesn't know that when she stepped aboard the 20th Century Limited, many thousand experts, most of them unseen, assumed responsibility for all her comforts, for her pleasure and her safety.

Through the years she will remember *this* of all the journeys she will ever take. As the wheels of the Century begin to roll, traveling becomes a glamorous event.

The spacious observation car shall be her thrilling palace on wheels. She shall dine like a queen, on her favorite foods, skilfully conjured by the Century's chef. As she retires, the Century maid shall attend her needs.

All through the night she shall feel at home; at ease in her clean and hushed, air-conditioned, window-sealed compartment. She shall enjoy a deep night's rest—there are no ups and downs on the Water Level Route—no mountains to be crossed. And, oblivious to icy winds, or snow or sleet or fog, she shall be as safe as though she were at home—guarded by the most advanced and scientific safety system in the world.

Tomorrow morning, strictly on the minute, she shall step from this luxurious hotel-on-wheels, with enthusiastic tales for all her friends—about her swift and magic journey on America's most widely-famed conveyance — the train that makes a trip a rich and unforgetable experience.

### New York—Chicago in 16½ Hours

| | |
|---|---|
| Lv. New York (E.S.T.) | 5:30 P. M. |
| Lv. Boston (E.S.T.) | 3:00 P. M. |
| Ar. Chicago (C.S.T.) | 9:00 A. M. |
| Lv. Chicago (C.S.T.) | 3:30 P. M. |
| Ar. New York (E.S.T.) | 9:00 A. M. |
| Ar. Boston (E.S.T.) | 11:25 A. M. |

In New York Central's Great Steel Fleet are scores of famous trains that simplify and glorify a journey. Day or night, there is a New York Central train that gets you to New York or Boston, Chicago or St. Louis, in hotel-like comfort, relieved of all the strain and hazards of the highway. And at the present greatly-lowered fares — 2 cents a mile in deep-seated coaches and 3 cents a mile in Pullmans, plus the new low Pullman charge—everyone can now afford to travel this easiest of all the ways to go. Next time you go out of town ask the nearest New York Central agent how little it costs to get there.

## NEW YORK CENTRAL  SYSTEM

*The Water Level Route...You Can Sleep*

This New York Central ad from February 1937 represented some of the last pre-streamliner advertising for the *20th Century Limited*. At this time, the Chicago-New York train clocked in at 16-1/2 hours over the Central's 961-mile Water Level Route. The thrill of standing on the open platform still had appeal, but streamlined equipment was the future. The inset (likely a view of a stream-shrouded Pacific pulling the *Mercury*, NYC's first streamlined train) hints of things to come.

# NEW 20TH CENTURY LIMITED

**More than the world's newest train —it's a new mode of transportation!**

For over a generation, the "Century" has been known as the world's greatest train. But in the course of a few short months the "Century" has outdone itself:..has given you an entirely new and advanced mode of travel.

Sleek, streamlined beauty that she is, the "Century" gives you a dinner fit for a king, an evening of restful pleasure and a perfect sleep in quiet, air-conditioned privacy ...and brings you into New York or Chicago on the dot of nine. No jar or bump mars your rest, for special alloy steel springs and tightlock couplers cushion the fleeting miles. And with all this smooth speed ...your restful enjoyment is sharpened by knowing that you're riding the road that holds the coveted Harriman Safety Medal.

Your first trip on the *new* "Century" will open your eyes to what advanced rail travel can be. Everything is *new*, you'll find, except two things: The *fare*, which is unchanged. And the *roadbed*...which has long been the pride of the Water Level Route. Like thousands of other travelers, you'll say, *"more than ever, it PAYS to ride the 'Century'!"*

The First "Luxury Liner on Wheels!"

**NEW YORK — CHICAGO
16 HOURS**

| | |
|---|---|
| Leave New York | 6:00 P.M. |
| Arrive Chicago | 9:00 A.M. |
| Leave Chicago | 4:00 P.M. |
| Arrive New York | 9:00 A.M. |

SCENIC LOUNGE...rounded and full-visioned so you can enjoy the scenic splendor of the Water Level Route! Leather settees face the windows!

**NEW YORK CENTRAL**
THE WATER LEVEL ROUTE ...YOU CAN SLEEP

CAFE CENTURY...like a smart restaurant! It even has semi-private dining alcoves. Food by famous Century chefs.

BAR LOUNGE CAR...Like the cocktail lounge of a fashionable hotel. Spacious, restful, luxurious. Unique lens lighting system.

A ROOMETTE...Rest and read in daytime privacy ...at night, a private bedroom...Clothes closet; complete toilet. Costs the same as a regular section.

Many argue that the 1938 *20th Century Limited* was the epitome of streamlined trains. New York Central turned to famed industrial design Henry Dreyfuss to style its flagship, inside and out, and the results were stunning. Probably the most memorable component of the new train was its Alco-built J Class Hudson (4-6-4) steam locomotives, only 10 of which were built for the Central.

# *Your arrival is an event!*

## And your trip on board the "Century" truly an "Overnight Vacation"

IT'S *you* they're waiting to greet, those eager strangers pressed against the ropes. They do not know you in person, but the respect in their eyes is a salute that stamps you as a person of distinction.

Yet your arrival on the Century was but a happy climax to a complete overnight vacation. Your accommodation was spacious, private, yet homelike in its solid comfort. Your fellow passengers proved to be *your* kind of people. You dined like a king and your meal was royally served. Later, listening to the latest popular recorded music in the Cafe Century, you marveled to think that you really were on a train.

*And how you slept last night!* A deep, sweet slumber, undisturbed by jolt or jar! For you traveled the famous Water Level Route—the smooth mountainless roadbed from East to West.

This morning you understood why crowds always gather to greet the Century's arrivals. And, yourself rested and relaxed, you understood too why travel-wise America has long agreed *"It Pays to Ride the Century."*

**Convenient Schedule • New York—Chicago**
*Grand Central Terminal          La Salle St. Station*
Lv. New York . 6:00 P.M.   Lv. Chicago . . 4:00 P.M.
Ar. Chicago . . 9:00 A.M.   Ar. New York . 9:00 A.M.
*(Daylight Saving Time Shown)*

THE *20ᵀᴴ Century Limited*

NEW YORK **CENTRAL** SYSTEM

The Water Level Route
—You Can Sleep

The Dreyfuss-designed *20th Century Limited* was the ultimate expression of railroad elegance, but it probably made its mark more through understatement rather than gawdiness. The designer used the term "cleanlining" to describe the smooth, sophisticated look that the cars exuded. And the public loved the results. As this August 1941 suggests (actually, exaggerates) everyone could feel like a celebrity on the Water Level Route.

*The Cradle that never rocks!*

*Neither jolt nor jar mars the sweet serenity
of their slumber on the 20th Century Limited*

STRANGE, is it not, that with so many eye-opening wonders on board the 20th Century Limited, the most wonderful of all occurs the instant your eyelids close?

Forgotten, then, is the glowing excitement on the world's most famous train. Forgotten, too, the first breathless moment in the scenic Observation Lounge, the banquet that was your dinner, and your evening of enjoyment in the Cafe Century. Almost before your head

nestles on the pillow, you are asleep.

Far ahead in the locomotive, the engineer pilots the train smoothly. Watchers and signalmen all along the route guard your swift passage. A courteous train crew is at your instant call. They are representatives of the 120,000 men and women of New York Central—120,000 men and women who are, as it were, united to guard your slumber and add to your comfort.

So you speed over the famous Water

Level Route—the *only* water-level route between East and West. Tomorrow, completely rested and on time regardless of the weather, you will discover what the travel-wise have long known —that morning on the Century is always *good* morning!

· · ·

*Overnight New York—Chicago*
*Between Grand Central Terminal and La Salle St. Station*
Lv. New York . 6:00 P. M.   Ar. Chicago   9:00 A. M.
Lv. Chicago . . 4:00 P. M.   Ar. New York  9:00 A. M.

*Ride* THE 20ᵀᴴ CENTURY LIMITED

NEW YORK CENTRAL SYSTEM
THE WATER LEVEL ROUTE—YOU CAN SLEEP

Just one month before the attack on Pearl Harbor, a mother and daughter slumber in comfort as the *20th Century Limited* speeds them along in the moonlight between New York and Chicago. New York Central's Water Level route between the two cities was actually 43 miles longer than arch-rival Pennsvania Railroad's competing line. Yet, the two railroads offered identical trip times—the NYC route having avoided the slow climb over the Alleghenies.

NEW YORK'S IMMORTALS WATCH A WONDROUS RE-BIRTH

*Alexander Hamilton, Washington Irving, Peter Stuyvesant, DeWitt Clinton, Robert Fulton, Henry Hudson loom above the famous Highlands of the Hudson River*

# FAMOUS *Empire State Express* BECOMES WORLD'S NEWEST AND FINEST STREAMLINER

*The sheer beauty, comfort and gaiety of atmosphere of the new "Empire" diner set a new mode in travel luxury. In this environment, you will doubly enjoy the far-famed New York Central "table."*

*Here in the Observation Lounge you may check the speed-ometer as the train glides along . . . or listen to the radio . . . or play cards . . . or just relax as you watch the beautiful Hudson River and Mohawk Valley unfold.*

## New York Central again makes transportation history!

Fifty years ago a new era in transportation began with the historic first run of the Empire State Express. Pulled by the famous locomotive "999", it was the world's fastest long-distance train!

Now, in its Golden Anniversary year, the "Empire" is making history again for New York Central . . . and for the nation. Here is really a new way of travel—new in luxury—new in all its appointments—new in the relaxation and pleasure it offers you!

The 120,000 men and women of New York Central are the real creators of this train. It reflects all the little things they have learned about pleasing you . . . historic murals and fluorescent lighting beautify its spacious parlor cars and coaches . . . its tavern car is like a distinguished club . . . its observation lounge a miracle of modern design.

The new "Empire" will soon begin daily service over the most beautiful and historic route in America.

NEW YORK · BUFFALO · CLEVELAND · DETROIT

*New York Central*

THE SCENIC WATER LEVEL ROUTE

NEW YORK CENTRAL SYSTEM

After the debut of the new *20th Century Limited*, New York Central waited three years to debut another streamlined train, the New York-Cleveland *Empire State Express*. The train boasted new Budd-built lightweight cars and stream-shrouded steam locomotives. Unfortunately, bad timing undermined the debut of the new train—it was inaugurated on December 7, 1941, as America forgot about train travel and focused on the war launched by that day's attack on Pearl Harbor.

# Wartime Guide to Grand Central

STEP FROM the busy heart of New York into the cathedral-like beauty of Grand Central Terminal . . . and watch the smooth flow of wartime America on the move.

Beneath this high, blue-vaulted ceiling now pass some 54,000,000 travelers a year. Boys on their way to war . . . watched to the train gates by bravely smiling parents. Workers journeying to strange new war jobs in faraway cities. Business leaders speeding to win new war production battles.

Together they form part of the greatest military and civilian traffic that America's railroads have ever carried. A tremendous task, vital to Victory, and rich in promise for the future.

Out of this experience will be born the finer rail transport of tomorrow . . . when Grand Central Terminal will echo to the footsteps and laughter of a free, victorious people bound on swift errands of peace.

**❶ 14,800 QUESTIONS AN HOUR**

During a busy wartime hour, Terminal information men answer 14,800 questions. To save holding up ticket lines, get information *in advance* at this booth or by telephone.

**❷ GRAND CENTRAL SERVICE FLAG**

This flag honors 21,314 New York Central employees. Thousands of other Central workers have sons and daughters in uniform . . . an added drive behind this railroad's war effort.

**❸ TICKET OFFICE 90% BUSIER**

New York Central has added extra windows and personnel to meet the war rush. Even so, war-wise travelers prefer to buy tickets during quieter mid-morning and early evening hours.

**❹ SERVICE MEN'S LOUNGE**

Busiest on weekends when thousands travel on furlough. To give them room on weekend trains, plan trips you *must* make for *mid-week*.

**❺ 54,000,000 PASSENGERS A YEAR**

A record number of essential wartime passengers now flows through Grand Central train gates. Fighters, workers, Government and industrial leaders . . . bound on vital errands along the "Warpath of the United Nations."

**❻ BAGGAGE CHECKING COUNTER**

Some 150,000 pieces of baggage a month are now checked through Grand Central. People have learned to travel light, checking larger luggage, carrying only *one small grip* on crowded trains.

**❼ TROOPS ON THE MOVE**

Today, half the nation's Pullmans and 30% of its coaches are needed to move 2,000,000 troops per month. One more reason railroads can't always provide the accommodations you want.

**GRAND CENTRAL TERMINAL**

*Gateway to all New York's Attractions*

Arrive at Grand Central Terminal, 42nd St. and Park Ave. . . in the midst of New York's finest hotels. Fast, frequent subway trains to the Fair Grounds; close to Radio City; two blocks to Fifth Avenue shops . . . nearby are theatres, night-clubs, restaurants . . the finest of the city's attractions.

**❽ THE COMMUTER'S STATION**

Grand Central Terminal's Lower Level is principally the commuter's station. Now in war time it is busier than ever because thousands of former automobile travelers must be carried by train.

**❾ MAIN WAITING ROOM**

Here someone (perhaps a soldier on furlough) may have to wait over for a later train if *you* fail to cancel an unwanted reservation. These days, cancel reservations the *minute* your plans change.

**FREE GUIDE TO GRAND CENTRAL**

Packed with stories, pictures and a large fascinating detailed cutaway view that takes you behind the scenes of this great Terminal in war time. Write Passenger Dept., Room 1261J, 466 Lexington Ave., New York, N. Y.

## New York Central

ONE OF AMERICA'S RAILROADS — ALL UNITED FOR VICTORY

BUY MORE
WAR BONDS
AND STAMPS

For years, New York's Grand Central has been the world's most famous railroad terminal. Trains reached its lower recesses by tunneling under Park Avenue in downtown Manhattan. They moved slowly and mysteriously through a dim subterranean world bejeweled by multicolored signal lights along the way. The interior view is from July 1943, the exterior view, top right, is from June 1939. In the Golden Age of Radio, millions listened to a dramatic series entitled "Grand Central Station"—wonderful publicity for the railroads. The majestic NYC landmark has recently been restored. It's considered a national treasure.

# What life is like on a troop train...

## speeding over the Water Level Route

This is "Main 100"... identified on New York Central orders only by its code number. Speeding toward a secret destination, it's one of the vast fleet of trains that now move 2,000,000 troops a month over the rails of America. Picture the thousands of Pullmans and coaches this task requires. You'll see then why car space for civilian travel is limited ... why Americans are urged to make only essential trips. *"Main 100" must have the right of way!*

**FIELD KITCHEN.** Mess Sergeant sets up kitchen in baggage car to serve 3 or 4 troop cars. That's what many baggage cars are doing. So please *travel light!*

**MESS CALL.** Men eat at their seats. On some trains they file up to kitchen to be served; on others, food is brought to them. Meals are tops ... one reason *your* home and *our* diners are rationed.

**FIRST AID.** Army Surgeon installs his "field hospital" in a washroom. His prompt care for minor ills keeps our fighters fit.

**G.H.Q. ON WHEELS.** From his drawing room "headquarters," Train Commander orders all details of this traveling Army camp ... of which he alone knows the destination.

**RAILROAD LIAISON.** New York Central "Train Escort" goes along to aid Train Commander with transportation, extra supplies, mail, special stops and other matters.

**PREPARING FOR TAPS.** At time set by Train Commander (later than in camp) Porter makes up berths ... as carefully as he would for the most generous Pullman passenger.

**V MAIL.** Men write many letters, hoping for answers. To guard secrecy, none may be mailed except through the Train Escort at points designated by the Train Commander.

**39 MEN TO A CAR.** Two men sleep in lower berth, one in upper. Even so, troop moves now use half the Pullmans, a third of the coaches ... one reason *you* may find space hard to get.

**SEEING AMERICA.** Troops spend much time at windows. Averaging six moves during training, they see the Hudson River and Great Lakes this trip ... perhaps California next.

# New York Central

### BUY MORE WAR BONDS

## ONE OF AMERICA'S RAILROADS — ALL UNITED FOR VICTORY

In September 1943, troop trains were becoming an increasingly common sight on America's railroads. The New York Central gives civilian readers a little peek inside.

# Wartime Housekeeping on Wheels

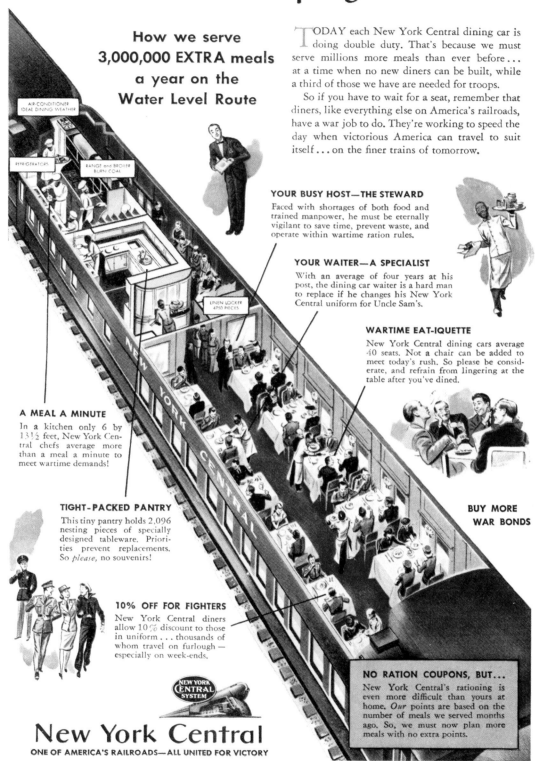

## How we serve 3,000,000 EXTRA meals a year on the Water Level Route

TODAY each New York Central dining car is doing double duty. That's because we must serve millions more meals than ever before... at a time when no new diners can be built, while a third of those we have are needed for troops.

So if you have to wait for a seat, remember that diners, like everything else on America's railroads, have a war job to do. They're working to speed the day when victorious America can travel to suit itself... on the finer trains of tomorrow.

**AIR-CONDITIONER**
IDEAL DINING WEATHER

**REFRIGERATORS**

**RANGE and BROILER**
BURN COAL

**LINEN LOCKER**
4750 PIECES

**YOUR BUSY HOST—THE STEWARD**
Faced with shortages of both food and trained manpower, he must be eternally vigilant to save time, prevent waste, and operate within wartime ration rules.

**YOUR WAITER—A SPECIALIST**
With an average of four years at his post, the dining car waiter is a hard man to replace if he changes his New York Central uniform for Uncle Sam's.

**WARTIME EAT-IQUETTE**
New York Central dining cars average 40 seats. Not a chair can be added to meet today's rush. So please be considerate, and refrain from lingering at the table after you've dined.

**A MEAL A MINUTE**
In a kitchen only 6 by 13½ feet, New York Central chefs average more than a meal a minute to meet wartime demands!

**TIGHT-PACKED PANTRY**
This tiny pantry holds 2,096 nesting pieces of specially designed tableware. Priorities prevent replacements. So *please*, no souvenirs!

**10% OFF FOR FIGHTERS**
New York Central diners allow 10% discount to those in uniform... thousands of whom travel on furlough — especially on week-ends.

**BUY MORE WAR BONDS**

**NO RATION COUPONS, BUT...**
New York Central's rationing is even more difficult than yours at home. *Our* points are based on the number of meals we served months ago. So, we must now plan more meals with no extra points.

**NEW YORK CENTRAL SYSTEM**

# New York Central
ONE OF AMERICA'S RAILROADS—ALL UNITED FOR VICTORY

New York Central takes you on a tour of a dining car. The good service continues, but with certain restrictions because of wartime. This is another of New York Central's cutaway views, published in November 1943.

# Modern "MOHAWKS" on the Warpath

**New Dual-Purpose Locomotives Speed War Traffic on the Water Level Route**

THERE'S a full-throated roar from her stubby stack as "Mohawk 3112" swings into the straightaway with a string of troop-filled Pullmans in tow. There's an answering roar from her twin locomotive, eastbound with a mile-long train of war freight.

Two engines of a kind. Two of New York Central's versatile "Mohawks"... with their big, six-foot drivers ... able to haul heavy freight on the Water Level Route or speed the 20th Century Limited through on schedule.

Made possible by an almost gradeless right of way, "Mohawks" are the newest among the vast fleet of specially-designed steam, electric and Diesel locomotives that wear the New York Central emblem. And their instant adaptability to freight or passenger service means much to efficient wartime operation on this east-west link in America's vital railroad supply line.

Today, thundering through ancient valleys where Mohawk braves once fought, these modern "Mohawks" too are on the warpath. And even as they speed the Victory traffic... their efficient performance is guiding New York Central designers who are already shaping the still finer locomotives of tomorrow.

**MODERN MOTIVE POWER**
This latest New York Central locomotive weighs only 198½ tons. Yet, it develops 5,400 horsepower ... ample to haul heavy freight on the *Water Level Route*.

LEVER OPENS FIREBOX DOORS

STOKER CONTROLS

WHISTLE VALVE

AIR BRAKES

POWER-OPERATED REVERSE GEAR

SIX-FOOT DRIVERS

15,500-GALLON WATER TANK

**WATER WITHOUT A WAIT.** From these 1800-foot track "pans"... water is scooped up into the tender on the run. Signal tells enginemen when to lower scoop.

**"GREEN OVER GREEN."** The fireman shouts his readings of each signal to the engineer as a double safety check. It's also part of his training as a future engineer.

**AN EXPERT HAND ON THROTTLE.** Though New York Central engineers average 20 years' experience, each must pass frequent tests for physical fitness and knowledge of operating rules.

**NO MORE SHOVELING.** This automatic stoker feeds the fire efficiently at the twist of the fireman's wrist. By working valves, he can "blow" coal to any part of the firebox.

**600 MILES ON A TENDERFUL.** Today's "Mohawk" can pull a passenger train 600 miles on one tender of coal. It gets a third more power per ton than engines of World War I.

**AUTOMATIC TRAIN CONTROL.** Electric control on right of tender would automatically stop the train if a caution or red signal were passed ... one of many modern safety devices on every "Mohawk."

## New York Central
### One of America's Railroads All United for Victory

**NEW YORK CENTRAL SYSTEM**

**LET YOUR DOLLARS FIGHT INFANTILE PARALYSIS**

Diesel locomotives exploded in popularity during the post-war years, but steam still ruled the rails on the New York Central —and on most other railroads — during the World War II emergency. Another of a series of several fascinating educational ads of the mid-1940s, sponsored by New York Central, gives magazine readers inside information on the operations of a major line. (February 1944)

An ad explains the "nerve center" of the railroad in the signal tower. This was in April 1944, many years before the era of computerized operations.

"Neither snow, nor rain, nor heat, nor gloom of night stays these couriers from the swift completion of their appointed rounds."

Herodotus

# Traveling on a POSTAGE STAMP

**How 3 billion pieces of wartime mail a year speed over the Water Level Route**

NOT ONE of the passengers aboard the 20th Century Limited ever sets foot here. This car is reserved for wartime travelers of a different kind . . . tiny V-mail . . . important business letters . . . registered envelopes packed with war contracts and blueprints . . . all part of the three billion pieces of mail that speed each year over New York Central.

Hour after hour, as the Century bores through the night, deft-fingered postal clerks sort this cargo of "preferential mail." And tomorrow, on arrival, the pouches and sacks will be ready for immediate forwarding or delivery.

Winter or summer, through storm or fair weather, these "post offices on wheels" provide lowest cost transportation for 96% of the nation's vast mail tonnage. A vital war service of American railroads today. A service that will be still swifter and more efficient aboard the finer, faster trains of tomorrow.

**WASH ROOM AND LOCKERS**

**PIGEON-HOLES**

**LAST BAG ABOARD!**
Just before the Century pulls out, several bags of last-minute mail are collected from the mail room in the station. Many business firms regularly send messengers to the station with important mail for overnight delivery between New York and Chicago, as well as intermediate points.

**OVERHEAD PAPER BOXES**

**MILE-A-MINUTE SORTING**
Pouches with mail from all parts of the United States and many foreign countries are dumped on this table for sorting. Here, highly trained clerks work through the night as their car speeds east or west over New York Central's Water Level Route.

**WAITING "OPENMOUTHED"**
These racks hold bags open. Clerks become expert at tossing mail into the openmouthed sacks as they sort it.

**CHECKING MAIL BAGS**

**CINDER SHIELD**

**TRAVELING MAIL BOX**
This letter chute permits passengers to put letters directly aboard the post-office car at stops along the way.

**MAGNIFYING V-MAIL**
Clerks often read photographically-reduced V-mail addresses under a lens. These tiny envelopes get speed preference and regularly ride the Century. Soldier mail moves in vast volume, but even more would be welcomed by service men far from home.

**DOOR TO BAGGAGE AND EXPRESS COMPARTMENT**

**"GUARDING THE REDS"**
Registered letters, called "reds," are carefully guarded and recorded. Every clerk carries a gun. Pouches are locked in the presence of a second clerk who signs as witness. And a special padlock records exactly how many times each pouch is opened.

**BUY MORE WAR BONDS**

**"PICKER-UPPER"**
On most through trains, this Catcher Arm is swung out to snatch mail bags from mail cranes at way stations . . . providing fast mail service for even small towns.

**NEW YORK CENTRAL SYSTEM**

# New York Central
## ONE OF AMERICA'S RAILROADS—ALL UNITED FOR VICTORY

Back in the 1940s, much of America's surface mail was carried by train. First class postage rate was only three cents an ounce (and it cost extra to send a letter or package via Air Mail). Here's a look inside the Railway Post Office car that headed up the *20th Century Limited*. Mail was processed en route, and the speed and dependability of this train eventually led to the placement of special mailboxes in the business districts of terminal cities on the New York Central route designated for the collection of *20th Century Limited*-transported letters—a tribute to an illustrious train. (This ad appeared in May and July of 1944.)

Another of New York Central's interesting cut-away views shows the interior of a ward car on a hospital train. Had you traveled by rail during World War II, you might occasionally have passed one of these hospital trains along the way. But how could a delicate surgical operation be performed aboard a moving train? They weren't. If it was necessary, in an emergency, to use the operating room (seen at upper left), the train would first be stopped on a sidetrack. (July 1944 advertisement)

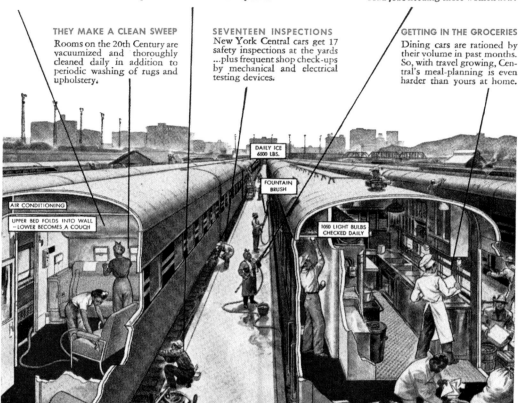

**EXTRA BEDS TO MAKE IN WARTIME**
In peacetime, multiple-berth rooms were often taken by single occupants. Now, many business associates patriotically arrange to share such accommodations to save war-vital train space.

**SAFETY FIRST, LAST, ALWAYS!**
Brakes are thoroughly tested twice at the yard, and again at the station before the train starts its run. No shortage of manpower interferes with that strict safety rule.

**WOMEN AT WORK**
With 25,600 New York Central men in uniform, thousands of women help keep wartime traffic moving. Car service is among the many railroad jobs needing more women *now*.

**THEY MAKE A CLEAN SWEEP**
Rooms on the 20th Century are vacuumized and thoroughly cleaned daily in addition to periodic washing of rugs and upholstery.

**SEVENTEEN INSPECTIONS**
New York Central cars get 17 safety inspections at the yards ...plus frequent shop check-ups by mechanical and electrical testing devices.

**GETTING IN THE GROCERIES**
Dining cars are rationed by their volume in past months. So, with travel growing, Central's meal-planning is even harder than yours at home.

# Housekeeping headaches of the "CENTURY"

**Travel Volume up ... Manpower down ... and the 20th Century Limited plus 800 other New York Central trains to service every day!**

HALF AN HOUR AGO, some 200 wartime passengers stepped off the 20th Century Limited. Already a switch engine has hustled the empty train out to the yards. And now New York Central service crews swarm over it.

Hammers clink against steel. Fountain brushes spurt against windows. Electric trucks hustle about with fresh ice and linen and groceries.

War adds both urgency and difficulty to the daily servicing of more than 800 New York Central trains. Travel has doubled. Supplies are scarce. And manpower is even scarcer.

But essentials still get 100% attention. And shorthandedness has even taught new short cuts, new methods that will mean greater efficiency when Victory frees America's railroads to bring you the finer travel of tomorrow.

> **NEW FREE BOOKLET** with fascinating, cutaway pictures that take you into a locomotive cab, troop train, caboose, hospital car, Grand Central Terminal, and other places "BEHIND THE SCENES OF A RAILROAD AT WAR." Write to New York Central, Room 1221E, 466 Lexington Ave., New York 17, N.Y.

**BUY MORE WAR BONDS**

# New York Central
ONE OF AMERICA'S RAILROADS—ALL UNITED FOR VICTORY

These behind-the-scenes views of the New York Central seemed to be making a hit with magazine readers, so a free booklet collection of them was made available to the public. Note the offer at lower right. (September 1944)

# BLACK MAGIC! 95,000,000 tons of it a year

## travel over New York Central

SOMEWHERE, American airborne troops attack. Their thousands of Nylon parachutes, mushrooming in the dawn sky, were made from . . . *coal!*

Somewhere, a girl war worker directs the hissing spark of an electric welder. Back of that spark is a dynamo, turned by the power of . . . *coal!*

Somewhere, a trainload of war materiel rushes to keep a secret appointment with a convoy. It is sped on its way by the driving force of . . . *coal!*

If ever there was black magic, it's the modern magic locked in a lump of coal. And New York Central is proud to have this fighting fuel as its largest single customer.

For this railroad acts as a giant mechanical stoker . . . picking up coal from mines and other railroads . . . and feeding the ceaseless black stream to industries and docks and coal dealers along its 11,000-mile right of way.

More than 60,000 coal cars now wear the "N.Y.C." But even that vast fleet must be reinforced with cars of other roads to handle the yearly wartime total of 95,000,000 tons.

*Today, only careful timing and organization keep coal flowing to where it is needed. Tomorrow, that war experience will pay dividends. Dividends in still more efficient fuel delivery to industries and homes of post-war "Centraland."*

### "SPURS" TO VICTORY
New York Central "spur" tracks and branches serve mines in five leading coal states. At each mine, loaded cars must be picked up daily and replaced by empties to maintain the vital flow of coal.

### STOKING THE FIRES OF WAR
One big plant may burn as much as 200 carloads of coal a day. Those cars must be delivered in endless procession from the mines to the plant siding . . . and the empties speeded back for more coal.

### "SINGLE HEADERS"
Even when coal moves in solid, 90-car trains, one engine hauls it on nearly any part of the almost gradeless *Water Level Route*. Yet, despite this natural efficiency, Central uses some 14,000,000 tons of coal a year.

### GENTLE GIANT
This giant coal dumper picks up a car and pours its 70-ton load into a ship as easily as you'd pour sugar from a spoon. Gently, too. For New York Central takes *extra* care to prevent coal breakage.

### HELP SAVE FIGHTING FUEL
Due to war demands, it's not always possible to deliver to your dealer as many cars of coal as he or we or you could wish. So please use your coal supply with care . . . help conserve America's fighting fuel.

## NEW YORK CENTRAL
ONE OF AMERICA'S RAILROADS—ALL UNITED FOR VICTORY

### ONE DAY'S COAL TRAFFIC
If all the cars of coal hauled in just *one day* by New York Central were gathered in this big lakeside yard, here's what you would see . . . 4500 cars . . . 35 solid miles of them!

BUY MORE
WAR BONDS

A dramatic salute is given to the importance of coal as an energy source that helped to win the war effort. Thirty-five solid miles of gondolas and hopper cars full of coal were hauled every day by the New York Central, as of November 1944, when this ad was published.

Meet the New York Central test engineers who help create tomorrow's finer engines

## They put Locomotives in a Test-Tube

Mile after tense mile, New York Central test engineers cling to the speeding locomotive, or watch each flicker of the instruments back in the Dynamometer Car.

They feel the pulse of the mighty cylinders. They sample the smoke-box gases. They weigh every pound of coal for the firebox and every ton of pull on the drawbar. And steadily, the data they gather is recorded on the Dynamometer Car's moving chart. For this little car with the big name is their "laboratory on wheels"... where they figuratively put 250 tons of locomotive in a test-tube to study its performance.

Today, their work helps New York Central operate more efficiently as a vital link in the wartime supply line. And tomorrow... when critical materials are again available... their records will point the way to still finer locomotives for the future.

**He Puts "Dine" in Dyn-a-mometer**
Testing a locomotive often takes weeks. So the staff lives aboard the Dynamometer Car. A New York Central dining car chef goes along to serve hearty meals.

**Locomotive Dietician**
This observer weighs out each 100 lbs. of coal fed into the fire-box. Even on New York Central's naturally efficient *Water Level Route*, ways to save fuel are constantly sought.

**Chart Keeps Pace with Train**
Gears link the wheels of the Dynamometer Car to these paper rolls. For each yard the car travels, the paper moves a fraction of an inch beneath the recording pens.

**"Scientists in Overalls"**
Dressed in overalls and protected by temporary windbreakers, these New York Central engineers check engine performance and flash their findings back to the Dynamometer Car.

**Tons on a Pen Point!**
These oil cylinders can reduce a locomotive's 500,000-lb. pull down to a tiny force that moves a pen in New York Central's Dynamometer Car.

MILEPOST SPOTTER

INTER-COMMUNICATIONS TELEPHONE

TRAIN CONDUCTOR

BERTHS FOR STAFF

KITCHEN

PLOTTING-TABLE

HE TAKES THE ENGINE'S TEMPERATURE

CHEF'S ROOM

X5006

DYNAMOMETER

**Tester in Chief**
Either the Dynamometer Engineer, or his senior assistant, directs every detail in the complex and important task of performance-testing a locomotive for New York Central.

**He Writes with 16 Pens!**
The Chart Operator watches over the 16 automatic pens that record speed, distance, pull, steam pressure and a dozen other items of performance data. He also notes on the moving chart facts phoned in by other observers.

*LET YOUR DOLLARS FIGHT INFANTILE PARALYSIS*

# NEW YORK CENTRAL
### THE WATER LEVEL ROUTE

The average railroad passenger had never heard of a dynamometer car, but it was a necessity for locomotive maintenance on the New York Central and other railroads—and good fodder for this February 1945 advertisement.

# Who's Who on the "Century"

*...calling the roll aboard the flagship
of New York Central's wartime fleet*

**Ticket Team**
New York Central and Pullman Conductors collect tickets together. Yet that's the least of their jobs. Former is responsible for operation of the train, while the latter's exacting task is to make passengers as comfortable as possible under wartime conditions.

DORMITORY FOR CREW

**"Key" Man in Wartime**
With thousands of production executives riding the Century, the Secretary is a "key" man in more ways than one. He types many a war-important letter or document. And he registers passengers so as to reach them quickly if telegrams arrive en route.

**Commissary Commander**
Your Steward holds a difficult post. He strives to maintain standards of food and service despite rationing and the fact that many experienced cooks and waiters have changed their New York Central uniforms for Uncle Sam's.

**The Press of War**
Sudden errands of war often allow little time for packing, and may last longer than expected. So the services of the Valet on the 20th Century Limited in pressing and repairing clothes are particularly helpful in these hectic days.

**Rear Guard Action**
The Rear Brakeman is the train's "rear guard." Among his duties is checking with signal tower men, station agents and other railroaders along the route. They inspect each car as it speeds past, then signal a safety report to him.

**Time for Dinner**
Today, hundreds of busy executives count their meals en route among the few they have time and freedom to enjoy. Chefs, kitchen staffs and New York Central's Commissary Department do their utmost to see that those meals *are* enjoyed.

**First Aid to First-Timers**
War has brought many "first-timers" to the railroads. Porter shows each the air-conditioning regulator, reading lights, clothes closets, disappearing bed and toilette facilities, and other new comforts that foreshadow the "Trains of Tomorrow."

THESE are the men you *see*. But up ahead, the engineer and fireman handle your train with smooth efficiency. The baggage man and mail car crew care for their important cargoes. And all along the line are dispatchers, signalmen, track maintainers, shop workers and many others . . . each helping to man New York Central's fleet of some 800 passenger trains a day.

With fellow railroaders of America, they're learning new efficiencies from the wartime task of moving the greatest traffic in history. And tomorrow, they'll apply those lessons to bring you still finer travel aboard America's post-war trains.

**BUY MORE WAR BONDS**

NEW YORK CENTRAL SYSTEM

# New York Central
### THE WATER LEVEL ROUTE

The crew and its quarters are the focus of yet another of New York Central's fascinating and educational cut-away ads from March 1945. Did you ever wonder where the train crew slept on a long-distance run? This question and many others are answered here.

# They keep a
# SUPER SERVICE STATION
## for New York Central Locomotives

THE run ends. Engineer and fireman climb down from the cab, and a "hostler" takes over. Under his expert hand, 350 tons of pulsing steel move obediently off to the roundhouse . . . that super-service station for locomotives.

Here, mechanics, electricians, pipe-fitters, specialists in many crafts work day and night . . . inspecting, repairing, lubricating and adjusting the streamlined "Hudsons" and mighty "Mohawks" of New York Central's motive power fleet.

Today, with modern machines and electrical aids, they're cutting precious hours from maintenance time . . . keeping engines longer on the job to move the vast war traffic. And tomorrow these roundhouse teams will apply their war-born efficiency to servicing the still finer locomotives now taking shape in the de-signing rooms and testing laboratories of New York Central.

**PARTS DEPARTMENT**
Roundhouse "Storekeeper" normally has thousands of engine parts on hand. They range from huge driving wheels to tiny springs for the Valve-Speed Indicator . . . a modern device that keeps a safety and efficiency record for each locomotive.

**LOOKING "UNDER THE HOOD"**
Locomotive front swings open and Inspector steps into the smokebox for examination of the interior. Rigid check-up keeps New York Central engines working efficiently despite heavy war loads.

**A GOOD TURN IN WARTIME!**
Girls operate many roundhouse turn-tables. With more than 26,000 New York Central employees in armed services, more women are needed for railroad jobs.

ELECTRIC TURNTABLE

BOILERS WASHED EVERY 30 DAYS

CRANE LIFTS ENGINE PARTS

MACHINE SHOP FOR REPAIRS

FOREMAN'S OFFICE

**"CHECK THAT WIRING!"**
On a modern New York Central steam locomotive, Electricians have many things to check . . . from the headlight to the electric Train Stop, the wonderful guardian that would halt train *automatically* if danger signal were passed.

**LUBRICATION JOB— LOCOMOTIVE SIZE!**
Roundhouse Grease Cup Fillers use lubricating guns so large they are moved about on wheels. Grease and oil are forced out by high pressure air from nearby power house.

**ELECTRIC "DETECTIVE"**
Before invisible cracks in steel can grow and cause a breakdown, Machinists locate them with an electric detector called the Mag-naflux. "An ounce of pre-vention is worth tons of cure," on New York Central.

**"CHANGE THOSE TIRES!"**
Locomotives have steel tires. When tires need changing, electric Drop Table lowers 32 tons of driving wheels and whisks them to service track . . . 50% faster than old methods of wheel removal.

FREE! NEW, ENLARGED BOOKLET, "Behind the Scenes of a Railroad at War"—13 cutaway pictures of 20th Century Limited, caboose, engine cab, troop train, mail car, hospital train, etc. Write Room 1223D, 466 Lexing-ton Ave., New York 17, N. Y.

NEW YORK CENTRAL SYSTEM

# NEW YORK CENTRAL
## THE WATER LEVEL ROUTE

**BUY MORE WAR BONDS**

A revealing view looks into the workings of a locomotive roundhouse on the New York Central. In June 1945, when this ad was published, steam was still the primary pulling power on this and most other major railroads. The post-war diesel boom dramatically changed locomotive facilities. Diesel locomo-tives, more readily bidirectional and operated in multiple-unit fashion, didn't demand turntables and the signature roundhouse facility that often accompanied them.

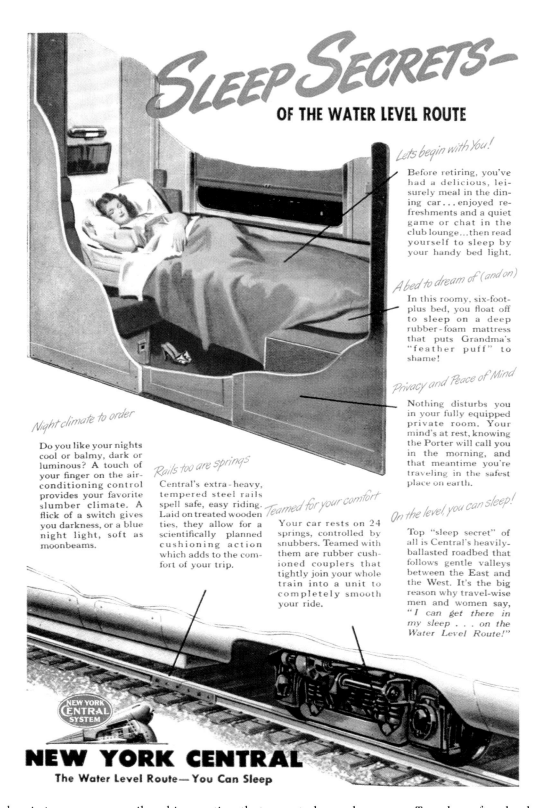

# SLEEP SECRETS—
## OF THE WATER LEVEL ROUTE

*Lets begin with You!*

Before retiring, you've had a delicious, leisurely meal in the dining car...enjoyed refreshments and a quiet game or chat in the club lounge...then read yourself to sleep by your handy bed light.

*A bed to dream of (and on)*

In this roomy, six-foot-plus bed, you float off to sleep on a deep rubber-foam mattress that puts Grandma's "feather puff" to shame!

*Privacy and Peace of Mind*

Nothing disturbs you in your fully equipped private room. Your mind's at rest, knowing the Porter will call you in the morning, and that meantime you're traveling in the safest place on earth.

*Night climate to order*

Do you like your nights cool or balmy, dark or luminous? A touch of your finger on the air-conditioning control provides your favorite slumber climate. A flick of a switch gives you darkness, or a blue night light, soft as moonbeams.

*Rails too are springs*

Central's extra-heavy, tempered steel rails spell safe, easy riding. Laid on treated wooden ties, they allow for a scientifically planned cushioning action which adds to the comfort of your trip.

*Teamed for your comfort*

Your car rests on 24 springs, controlled by snubbers. Teamed with them are rubber cushioned couplers that tightly join your whole train into a unit to completely smooth your ride.

*On the level, you can sleep!*

Top "sleep secret" of all is Central's heavily-ballasted roadbed that follows gentle valleys between the East and the West. It's the big reason why travel-wise men and women say, *"I can get there in my sleep . . . on the Water Level Route!"*

## NEW YORK CENTRAL
### The Water Level Route—You Can Sleep

The sleeping car was one railroad innovation that even today makes sense. Travelers often booked overnight passage on long-distance trains in lieu of booking a hotel room at their destination—a good use of sleep time and a way to save money. This February 1946 ad gives us a peek inside a New York Central roomette, which offered travelers a relatively comfortable night's rest—a far cry from the cramped airline seats in which today's frequent flyers are often trapped.

# The *Magic Carpet* rolls out again

IT'S CENTURY TIME! A minute ago, outside the station, you were in the heart of a great city, with hurrying crowds, blaring taxis, newsboys shouting the evening headlines. Now you're in a different world as you follow that crimson carpet down the platform of Grand Central Terminal toward the softly lighted, streamlined cars that will be your club on wheels for tonight.

### Relax by Twilight

Magically, the day's tension vanishes when you step into the Century's luxurious Observation car. Deep cushioned easy chairs invite you to relax. And outside the wide windows, the twilit beauty of the Water Level Route unrolls a background for repose.

### The Face is Familiar

Beside superb cuisine and service, there's a fascination about dinner on this favorite train of famous people. For nearby may be a lovely face you last saw in technicolor, or a distinguished one that would be news on any financial page.

### Awake Refreshed

You arrive looking and feeling your best. For all night, in the quiet privacy of your room, a spacious bed, a rubber-foam mattress, and the smooth Water Level Route have conspired to give you deep, refreshing sleep.

**NEW YORK CENTRAL SYSTEM**

## NEW YORK CENTRAL
The Water Level Route—You Can Sleep

The *only* all-room extra-fare train between New York and Chicago.

**20TH CENTURY LIMITED**

New York Central's "Magic Carpet" (actually the *20th Century Limited*) whisked passengers out of the crowded turmoil of the big city (either New York or Chicago) and into the wide-open spaces for a comfortable overnight run to their destination. (April 1946 advertisement)

**New Coach for CINDERELLA!**

**New York Central's New Cars
Play Fairy Godmother
To Travel Budgets**

*I felt like Cinderella* when I found I'd have to plan my holiday trip on a shoestring!

*But I felt like a Princess* when I saw my gleaming new air-conditioned coach, with its huge windows and smart interior done by a famous designer.

*Reserved for her Highness* is the way I felt about the wonderful, soft reclining seat reserved for me at no extra charge on this luxurious New York Central coach streamliner.

*The Lounge was Palatial.* It had a deep-cushioned divan for smoking and chatting. And there was a real dressing table with lighted mirror and all the latest fixings!

*"Look at these LOW COACH FARES!"*

| | ONE WAY (Plus Tax) | ROUND TRIP (Plus Tax) |
|---|---|---|
| CHICAGO NEW YORK | $20.02 | $30.00 |
| BOSTON DETROIT | $18.32 | $25.70 |
| ST. LOUIS CLEVELAND | $11.83 | $17.60 |
| NEW YORK CINCINNATI | $16.45 | $24.60 |

*Coming!* CARS ENOUGH FOR 52 NEW STREAMLINERS TO UNDERLINE THE *NEW* IN . . .

**NEW YORK CENTRAL**
The *Scenic* Water Level Route

NEW YORK CENTRAL SYSTEM

Following the end of World War II, on December 13, 1945, New York Central placed what was at that time the largest single order for passenger equipment—420 new cars. Accordingly, NYC was soon crowing that it had ordered five solid miles of cars! The $34 million order, when coupled with an earlier order for approximately 300 cars, gave the railroad reason to announce in this August 1946 ad that it had ordered enough cars to outfit 52 new streamliners.

## NEW POWER

to serve
new industry
on New York Central

**400,000 Postwar Horsepower!** Over half of New York Central's 145 new Diesel units are here. And the rest are on the way. Added to the fleet of efficient, new, steam "Niagaras", this means 400,000 postwar horsepower harnessed to your transportation needs when you choose a Central location.

**A Moving Force in Your Success!** World's largest postwar locomotive fleet is your assurance of smooth, fast, all-weather service. A completely dependable link between your plant and America's richest markets... leading Atlantic ports... and the varied sources of supply tapped by New York Central's 11,000-mile rail network.

**"Central" Locations to Order!** This Railroad will gladly help you find an industrial site to fit your needs among the many served by its new motive power. Contact New York Central's nearest Industrial Representative or your local freight agent. Or write Industrial Department, New York Central System, 466 Lexington Ave., New York 17, N. Y.

*Why 547 New Plants Picked "CENTRAL" Locations Last Year!*

**C**ONCENTRATED in New York Central's territory is 52% of U. S. buying power.

**E**LECTRICITY at low cost, and sources of pure water for industrial uses, are both plentiful here.

**N**EW specialized cars are adding to New York Central's modern 158,000 freight car fleet.

**T**RAVELING personnel benefits from the luxurious, all-weather service of Central's Great Steel Fleet.

**R**AIL service via Central reaches ports handling 85% of Atlantic coast foreign trade.

**A**REA produces 75% of U. S. bituminous coal and steel, plus many other materials and supplies.

**L**ABOR supply includes nearly two-thirds of America's highly skilled factory workers.

## NEW YORK CENTRAL
The Water Level Route

Though New York Central passenger trains garnered the most publicity, freight hauling was important business for the railroad, as this September 1947 ad attests. NYC was also an innovator in this arena, with services such as the express *Pacemaker* freights, which made their debut on Boston-Buffalo and New York City-Buffalo routes in 1946. Noted by their attractive, red-and-gray box cars, the *Pacemaker* fast freights were afforded similar treatment to passenger trains, operating at speeds up to 60 mph on tracks usually reserved for the passenger fleet.

# Riding the "Century" on a 3¢ Stamp

## Business letters, like business men, save <u>business time</u> aboard New York Central's great overnighters.

**1** **In New York and Chicago,** another business day ends . . . and last minute mail begins its nightly rush toward the waiting *20th Century Limiteds*. It comes in speeding mail trucks. It arrives by breathless messengers from the great business houses. In New York, it even flashes underground by pneumatic tube.

**2** **The Little Mail Rooms** at LaSalle Street Station and Grand Central Terminal seethe with action. Clerks work elbow to elbow, sorting and stamping the stream of letters. Then, just as the clock ticks off the final seconds before *Century* time, the last bulging bags rumble down the platforms and are tossed aboard.

**3** **Now Begins a Nightlong Task** for the clerks aboard the speeding mail cars of the *20th Century Limiteds*. Altogether, the 70 clerks sort or handle 1,000,000 pieces of east and westbound "preferential mail" daily. And when the twin Dieseliners glide into New York and Chicago, all mail is ready for immediate city delivery . . . or forwarding to other railroads.

**4** **And the Century is Not Alone!** The life of many cities is linked by fast overnight trains of the Great Steel Fleet. Aboard them, business letters . . . like business men . . . travel with no loss of business time. And travel, too, with complete, year-round all-weather dependability.

**FREIGHT OVERNIGHTERS, TOO!** Throughout America's richest industrial and commercial territory, New York Central provides overnight transportation, not only for men and mail, but for merchandise as well . . . one more reason for choosing a "Central" Location. For expert help in locating *your* new plant or warehouse, contact Central's nearest Industrial Representative or your local freight agent. Or write Industrial Dept., New York Central System, 466 Lexington Ave., New York 17, N. Y.

# New York Central

### The Water Level Route—You Can Sleep

Only three cents to ride the *20th Century Limited?* That's all it cost in December 1947—for one of the 1 million pieces of mail handled daily by the New York Central's fleet of Railway Post Office cars.

More new equipment had been added to the *20th Century Limited*, including this "Lookout Lounge" with its raised floor and enlarged windows, by November 1948.

# Sure as sundown

### New York Central overnighters go *weather or no!*

Skyways and highways may be storm-swept. It doesn't matter. Not to you!

Whatever city you're in or bound for on New York Central... there's an all-weather Dieseliner to take you, with an overnight vacation on the way. So step aboard and *rest assured!*

*Assured* of an air-conditioned climate and ample room to roam.

*Assured* of tempting, freshly prepared meals in the dining car ... refreshments and sociability in the lounge.

*Assured* of a perfectly appointed room...a big, soft bed...and a smooth Water Level Route, made for slumber.

*Assured* that you'll *keep* those distant dates tomorrow...with a certainty no other travel can match!

## New York Central
#### The Water Level Route — You Can Sleep

The thrill heightens as you walk to your car of the *20th Century Limited*, via the famous red carpet, deep under the heart of New York City and Grand Central Station. (September 1951 advertisement)

# "Central" Attraction!

## Mealtime magic no other travel can match

**What roadside snack** . . . what eat-at-your-seat tray . . . can compare to the fun of a meal on wheels in a streamlined New York Central diner?

Sparkling table. Attentive service. A varied and tempting menu. Every dish fresh from the stainless steel kitchen. Every course served with a big helping of scenery on the side!

Dining in comfort. Relaxing over refreshments in the lounge. Sleeping on the gentle Water Level Route. They're all part of your New York Central overnight vacation.

A vacation that gets you there *really* rested. And gets you there with *all-weather* certainty that no highway or skyway can match!

*Like Breakfast in Bed?* You can wake up to that comfort, too, on many a New York Central dreamliner. Enjoy it right in the privacy of your own hotel-room-on-wheels!

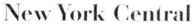 New York Central

The Water Level Route—You Can Sleep

A delicious meal in the diner is enjoyed by a mother and son. As the October 1952, advertisement states, every course is served "with a big helping of scenery on the side." Note, too, that those traveling in private rooms could, on many New York Central trains, order breakfast in bed.

# Christmas Window on the Water Level Rou[te]

**Watch New York Central trains** roll past this time of year. You'll see Christmas windows by the hundred ... bright with the most precious of all gifts. People!

Couples taking their children to see Grandmother (on money-saving Family Fares). Older folk, off to spend Christmas with married sons or daughters—enjoying every minute of New York Central comfort.

Youngsters from school or college getting a first taste of holiday fare in the dining car. Fathers, away on business, taking it easy in the club car ... sure that New York Central will get them home "weather or no."

These are the year's favorite jobs for New York Central men and women. So whether you ride with us or meet the train ... here's wishing you a MERRY CHRISTMAS!

*Give Tickets—The Gift that Brings Them Home!*
Ask any Central ticket agent how easy it is to send rail and Pullman tickets as your gift to someone you want with you at holiday time.

## New York Central
The Water Level Route—You Can Sleep

Another war, the Korean Conflict, had come and gone by December 1953 when this cheery ad appeared. Unfortunately, things were not so upbeat in the New York Central passenger department. Despite its massive post-World War II investment in new equipment, ridership was slumping and the future of the railroad's once-vaunted passenger fleet looked cloudy.

# One by one, the windows close their eyes

## ...for a wonderful Water Level Route sleep

Nighttime on New York Central. Long ago, the last, leisurely dining
car patron pushed back his chair with a contented sigh.
Only a few night owls still chat over refreshments in the club car. One by
one, shades come down and lights go out as this great hotel-on-wheels glides
along gentle, low-level valleys. The guests, in their Pullman
private rooms, drift off to slumberland ... with a downy comfort and
a deep-down sense of all-weather security no skyway or highway can match.

**GOING OUR WAY?** Throughout this area, you'll find
New York Central streamliners and dreamliners to make
your trips a daylight delight or an overnight vacation.

## New York Central
The Water Level Route—You Can Sleep

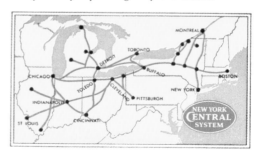

A New York Central streamliner glides toward its destination as the adjacent Hudson river shimmers in the moonlight in an inviting scene from a November 1953 ad. Yet, by this time, travelers were starting to decline the invitation in favor of other forms of transportation—competition acknowledged, ironically, in the ad's reference to "skyway or highway."

**Nature made only one** low-level route between East and Midwest. And, for a hundred years, New York Central has improved on Nature for your comfort.

Start your trip with refreshments in the lounge. Chat, read, relax as your diesel-electric dreamliner glides over a roadbed smooth as a garden path.

Later, sit at leisure over a famous New York Central dinner. Enjoy it in the diner . . . or in the privacy of your own Pullman hotel-room-on-wheels.

Bedtime is best of all! Your big, soft bed is waiting. So drift off to dreamland with a deep-down sense of all-weather security no skyway or highway can match.

For you're traveling the *naturally* gentle Water Level Route. And *on the level*, you can sleep!

**For a Headstart on Tomorrow, Go New York Central Tonight!**

20th Century Limited
Commodore Vanderbilt } CHICAGO · NEW YORK
New England States—CHICAGO · BOSTON
Southwestern Limited
The Knickerbocker } NEW YORK · ST. LOUIS
Cleveland Limited—NEW YORK · CLEVELAND
The Detroiter—NEW YORK · DETROIT
Ohio State Limited—CINCINNATI · NEW YORK
Motor City Special—DETROIT · CHICAGO
The Forest City—CLEVELAND · CHICAGO

**New York Central's Water Level Route**

Another beautiful New York Central ad touting the benefits of riding an overnight train on the Water Level Route; this one dates from February 1954. As the train list above suggests, the Central offered a tremendous variety of overnight passenger trains, but by this date demand for the service was waning. Cutbacks to the *Commodore Vanderbilt* started in 1955 and the train was history by 1960.

Appearing just days before the Christmas of 1942, this poignant message was long to be remembered. Many such wartime advertisements have become "classics" in picture and prose.

Wartime, heavy industry and steam power converge as part of a memorable advertisement that appeared in March 1944. The 2,000-mile Norfolk & Western was not among America's largest railroads during World War II, but it ranked among the most important because it served the rich Appalachian coal fields and a variety of heavy industries essential to the war effort. The N&W was a favorite of steam locomotive fans, as steam power predominated on the road through much of the 1950s, and remained in service on some West Virginia branch lines until the spring of 1960.

Like most other railroads, Norfolk & Western rushed to streamline its passenger trains in the wake of the second world war. Thanks to a fortuitous pre-war (1941) order for lightweight cars, it was able to debut a makeshift streamlined *Powhatan Arrow* in 1946 when most roads were still trying to buy new equipment. In 1949, N&W re-equipped the Norfolk-Cincinnati train with all-new cars from Pullman-Standard—service trumpeted in two ads from July and August of that year—but the railroad stuck by its signature steam locomotives, no doubt to the delight of its coal-company customers.

## NATION'S GOING-EST RAILROAD!

▷ America's newest fleet of diesel locomotives . . . 529 units with average age only 2.5 years.

▷ 81,006 modern freight cars — more per mile of line than any other major U. S. railroad.

▷ Busiest large railroad . . . greatest freight traffic density.

▷ A 30% longer railroad with merger of the Virginian into Norfolk and Western. *Wonderful new industrial sites.*

▷ New, easier grades, more interchange points with other railroads.

▷ Now a billion dollars in assets.

This is why the dynamic, new Norfolk and Western means savings in time and money to shippers!

GENERAL OFFICES • ROANOKE, VIRGINIA

The switch to diesel power came fast and furious after World War II. At the end of the war there were 39,000 steam and 4,000 diesel locomotives; by 1958 the change was nearly complete with only 2,400 steam and 27,200 diesel locomotives in service. The N&W was reportedly the last American railroad to order a new steam locomotive (in 1953), but when it started to dieselize in earnest the end came quickly. By the time of this September 1960 ad, steam was gone from the railroad.

# THIS IS THE TRAIN THAT HAS

**THE VIEW'S TERRIFIC ON NORTHERN PACIFIC!** Send now for "Northwest Adventure", free booklet of scenic trips you can take to Yellowstone, dude ranches, to or from the Pacific Northwest, California or Alaska. Write G. W. Rodine, 226 Northern Pacific Railway, St. Paul 1, Minnesota.

By July 1956, Northern Pacific's *North Coast Limited* had taken on a dramatically different look. The train was streamlined with the addition of new equipment between 1946 and 1948, but starting in 1952 even more significant changes took shape. NP hired industrial designer Raymond Loewy to give the train a facelift and the result was the memorable two-tone green paint scheme. In 1954, Budd-built

# EVERYTHING!

It is the only train between Chicago and the North Pacific Coast that offers you four Vista-Domes . . . the attention of a friendly Stewardess-Nurse . . . the fascinating Traveller's Rest buffet-lounge . . . plus truly superb meals. This train is the . . .

## VISTA-DOME
## *North Coast Limited*

### One of the world's *Extra Fine* trains!

**Friendly welcome.** Your Stewardess-Nurse makes you feel right at home on your trip.

**Luxury with a western flavor.** That's the handsome, colorful Traveller's Rest buffet-lounge.

NORTHERN PACIFIC RAILWAY

CHICAGO · TWIN CITIES · SPOKANE · PORTLAND · TACOMA · SEATTLE

Vista-Dome coaches and sleepers arrived on the property, a year in advance of competitor Great Northern adding dome service. Plus—in a nod to airlines—Stewardess-Nurses became a fixture to take levels of customer service even higher.

# NEWEST TRAIN WEST

INDEED A VERITABLE MOVING PALACE

## FOR GUESTS WHO DINE WELL

New Dining cars, as well as the most modern of Pullmans, have been created for the NORTH COAST LIMITED, for the enjoyment of travelers between Chicago and the Northern Pacific Coast.

For Western information and free vacation booklets, address E. E. Nelson, 265 N. P. Bldg., Saint Paul, Minn.

Color posters, 30x40 in., of "Rainier National Park"—see opposite page—may be secured for 25¢ in stamps.

A July 1930 glimpse into a heavyweight dining cars reveals the simple elegance of the era, but a sharp contrast to later lightweight equipment. Northern Pacific's *North Coast Limited* was the oldest train connecting Chicago (via corporate partner Burlington east of the Twin Cities) and the Pacific Northwest, service that debuted in 1890.

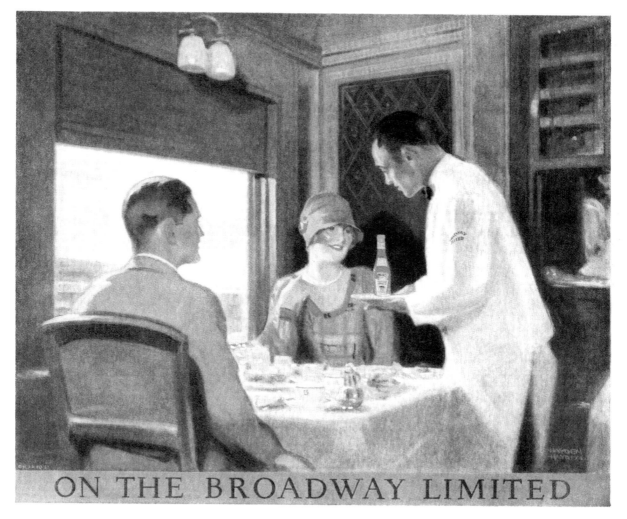

## ON THE BROADWAY LIMITED

# *The Choice of the Nation*

In its service to the American public, the Pennsylvania Railroad System serves a direct population of over fifty-two millions. It is the keystone of the nation's travel system.

In keeping with its many refinements, the Pennsylvania Railroad serves on its dining cars Heinz Tomato Ketchup and Heinz Chili Sauce. Like the Pennsylvania Railroad, the House of Heinz serves the nation—its products are the choice of those who demand the utmost in purity, cleanliness and taste in foods.

To meet the particular demands of a particular public, other great American railroads, as well as the world's leading hotels, restaurants and clubs, serve these well-known condiments.

Two Keystone State industrial powerhouses—Pennsylvania Railroad and H.J. Heinz Company (whose ketchup and chili sauce were served on Pennsy diners)—teamed up for this very early color advertisement, from February 1927. The *Broadway Limited* was PRR's flagship train between New York and Chicago and a worthy competitor to New York Central's *20th Century Limited*.

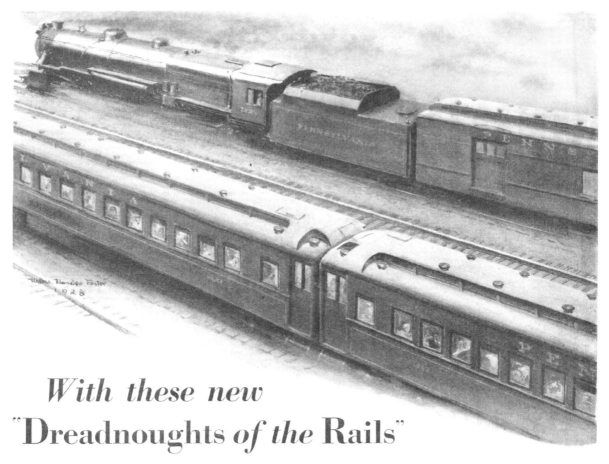

# With these new "Dreadnoughts of the Rails"

*Wooden coaches go the way of wooden ships . . . the Pennsylvania provides complete steel equipment for safer and more comfortable coach travel.*

TRAINS for a hundred cities whir down the singing rails—and every train from stem to stern of solid steel!

That will soon be the rule on the Pennsylvania — the first railroad to attain this goal.

Before the end of this year—upon delivery of an additional 320 new improved all-steel passenger cars — the Pennsylvania will eliminate completely all wooden coaches from all regular steam runs.*

$100,000,000 has been involved in the making of this immense fleet of all-steel passenger equipment train cars. At the end of this year these cars will number one-fifth of all the steel passenger cars in use in the United States.

These new *"Dreadnoughts of the Rails"* represent a distinct step forward in providing safer and more comfortable coach travel.

One-sixth of all railroad passengers in the United States travel on the Pennsylvania Railroad. To transport them, the Pennsylvania operates 3800 passenger trains daily, limited and local. Seventy-three percent of these passengers travel in the Pennsylvania's coaches.

*A few wooden coaches of the wide-vestibule type will be kept on hand for emergency service until they, too, are replaced.

### SIX SPECIAL FEATURES
*that add comfort in the latest Pennsylvania all-steel coaches:*

Roller-bearings eliminate the jars and jolts of starting and, by doing away with "hotboxes," minimize the risk of delays.

A scientifically designed system of ventilation insures a continuous flow of fresh air, at properly moderated temperatures, at all times.

High-backed seats give unusual comfort.

The most modern reflected lighting floods the cars with abundant steady illumination.

Pleasingly large washrooms are fitted with gleaming basins and mirrors, soap and towel vendors, and comfortable plush seats.

A new, attractive style of decoration gives light, bright ivory ceilings—fawn colored walls with brown trimmings—aisle strips of deep green.

# PENNSYLVANIA RAILROAD

*Carries more passengers, hauls more freight than any other railroad in America*

A November 1928 ad announces Pennsy's commitment to eliminate wooden cars from its passenger fleet. Pennsylvania Railroad pioneered the use of steel cars, building its first in 1905 and ordering 500 more by 1907. By 1909, nearly half the new passenger equipment ordered by American railroads was all-steel, and by 1914 wooden coaches were basically obsolete—though as the ad notes, wooden equipment was kept on hand even at this late date "for emergency service."

# *Inside Story*
## of the Pennsylvania
### *FLEET OF MODERNISM*

*Bar-lounge, Broadway Limited*

**Observation Cars** end in glass-enclosed luxury. Deep divans . . lounge chairs . . low tabourets . . soft lighting effects . . modern panelling . . harmonize in a setting of great beauty. **Master Rooms** (below)—on Broadway and Liberty Limiteds—the ultimate in travel luxury. Superb lounge with radio, modern appointments, twin beds . . off this, private bathroom with shower.

YOU ARE looking squarely into a new epoch in travel enjoyment . . the sumptuous new interiors of foremost Pennsylvania Railroad trains.

Eight premier trains, four in each direction, fashioned and fused into a fleet of modernism by . . the artistry of that eminent designer Raymond Loewy . . the practical knowledge of the Pullman Company . . the 92 years' experience of the Pennsylvania Railroad.

See how the old graciously bows to the new! Bar-lounge cars resplendent with divans, "conversation corners", murals, other niceties . . observation cars with the casual sophistication of smart clubs . . dining cars exciting to both eye and palate. More accommodations than ever before. Master Rooms, Roomettes, Duplexes, plus new versions of double bedrooms, drawing rooms and compartments give new comfort, new privacy. Increased length beds, individual toilet facilities — distinct innovations.

Leading the fleet is the *Broadway Limited*, transformed into a palatial all-room train . . complete privacy over the shortest route between New York and Chicago, daily in record new time . . 16 hours!

So, if your taste runs to the modern, *travel modern* . . on the railroad that provides *a Fleet of Modernism*, the Pennsylvania!

## Pennsylvania Railroad
SHORTEST ROUTE BETWEEN EAST AND WEST — HEAVIEST RAIL, FINEST ROADBED IN AMERICA. YOU CAN SLEEP *restfully*

Industrial designer Raymond Loewy had many assignments during the 1930s, but none may have been more significant than his work on Pennsylvania Railroad's Fleet of Modernism and the streamlined, Tuscan red and maroon *Broadway Limited* of 1938. The new train was clearly an answer to New York Central's Dreyfuss-designed *20th Century Limited*, but many don't realize that the competing roads actually coordinated their efforts to re-design and launch their trains. In fact, the two carriers jointly negotiated contracts with Pullman-Standard to build the new cars and with Pullman to operate sleeper service.

The latest in Pennsy dining cars is depicted in October 1938. It was a part of the railroad's new "Fleet of Modernism" streamlined equipment that dominated much of the Pennsylvania Railroad's magazine advertising that year.

# FIRST TIME! NEW DE LUXE ALL-COACH TRAIN BETWEEN CHICAGO AND NEW YORK
## ...*Direct to World's Fair!*

### The Trail Blazer

### Travel Splendor at Low Coach Fares

Observation - Buffet - Lounge Car...Radio...Smart Diner ...Low-Priced Meals...Luxury Coaches...Reserved Seats... Completely Air-Conditioned ...Personal Service Galore!

FIRST RUN, JULY 28, 1939

**RELAX** in an Observation-Lounge Car which has glass-enclosed end, its own buffet and every modern appointment.

**NEVER BEFORE** on the speed lanes between Chicago and New York a train like this!

Complete "run-of-train" from end to end. Beverages of all kinds...tables at which to sip and play ...smart lounge chairs on which to relax and watch nature glide by—that's the spirit!

Grand dinners in the smartest of Diners—75 cents; luncheon—65c; breakfast—50c. Alert, gracious coach attendants at your beck and call—day or night. Soft, billowy pillows if desired at small charge. Lights dim at night—no glare. Modern washrooms.

Get off in the heart of New York or in the heart of The Fair—the choice is yours. Eastbound enjoy the special fare, Chicago to New York for the World's Fair—*$28.20 round trip; westbound enjoy the new low fare now in effect—$30.90 round trip. Save in either direction! And note the fast running time shown in schedule panel at the right.

While you now enjoy Luxury Coaches . . . with their deep-cushioned reclining seats . . . on principal Pennsylvania trains between West and East, the magnificent TRAIL BLAZER offers a *breadth* of luxury at low cost unprecedented in West-East travel. Be among the *first* to reserve a seat on it!

| DAILY SCHEDULE OF THE TRAIL BLAZER | |
|---|---|
| **TO THE FAIR!** | Standard Time |
| Lv. Chicago (Union Station) | 1:30 P.M. |
| Ar. North Philadelphia | 6:08 A.M. |
| Ar. New York (Pennsylvania Station) | 7:55 A.M. |
| Ar. World's Fair Station | 8:30 A.M. |
| **WESTBOUND!** | |
| *(And no Easterner should forego the experience)* | |
| Lv. New York (Pennsylvania Station) | 5:25 P.M. |
| Lv. North Philadelphia | 6:57 P.M. |
| Ar. Chicago (Union Station) | 9:25 A.M. |

THE TRAIL BLAZER makes stops to receive or discharge passengers at Pittsburgh and a number of principal intermediate stations.

Seats must be reserved before boarding train. For complete information and connections consult your local ticket agent.

*From Pennsylvania Station, New York, to World's Fair. 5c each additional each way.

**YOUR LUXURIOUS** Coach seat reclines at just the angle most conducive to your comfort—you can SLEEP RESTFULLY!

**WHAT ABOUT HAND BAGGAGE?** If you're going through to the Fair on the Trail Blazer an attendant takes care of your hand baggage aboard...check it, for a small charge, at Pennsylvania Station, New York...hand you duplicate check...you pick it up there when you please.

# Pennsylvania Railroad

*SHORTEST WEST-EAST ROUTE . . . THE DIRECT ROUTE TO THE NEW YORK WORLD'S FAIR*

While the *Broadway Limited* represented the top end in overnight sleeper comfort, it wasn't the only service Pennsy offered in the Chicago-New York corridor. Beginning in July 1939 (when this ad appeared), the railroad debuted the fast and comfortable all-coach *Trail Blazer*. The service was both more democratic and more affordable: Any passenger could walk back and enjoy the observation lounge and a dinner in the diner cost just 75 cents.

# NOW YOU CAN LIVE
## *Upstairs* OR *Downstairs*
# WHEN YOU TRAVEL

**Ever see** anything like this in your travels? Very novel! And *most* comfortable. "Duplex Rooms" they're called . . . private rooms on two different levels of a Pullman car. An exciting innovation which Pennsylvania Railroad presents on a great fleet of trains speeding on the shortest route between East and West.

**Every homelike comfort** right there! Whether you live "up or down". A long soft sofa which opens at night into a broad bed. Your own toilet facilities . . . washstand . . . mirror . . . folding table for writing or meals . . . individual air-conditioning. Its cost? Surprisingly little for such comfort and luxury.

◄ **This diagram** shows how upper and lower rooms dovetail. The daytime and nighttime arrangement is clearly depicted. Notice that the sofa has a well-tufted center arm rest, which may be folded back if you wish. How about head room? No stooping no matter how tall you are! Day or night, plenty of room to move about.

**But that's not all!** Enjoy other modern Pullman private rooms, too! Roomettes, Bedrooms, Compartments, Drawing Rooms, Master Rooms. In addition to spacious Section Sleepers and *Luxury Coaches* with soft, reclining seats on all but all-room trains. What's more, however you go, Pullman or Coach, you pay surprisingly little, as fares never were lower! So go on the Pennsylvania—more luxury at less cost!

**Ask about Low Fares**

## PENNSYLVANIA RAILROAD

**SHORTEST EAST-WEST ROUTE**

**Route of "The Luxury Fleet"** . . . Broadway Limited (*all-room train*) and The General, *New York, Philadelphia, Chicago*..."Spirit of St. Louis", *New York, Philadelphia, St. Louis*. . . Liberty Limited, *Washington, Baltimore, Chicago* . . . The Pittsburgher (*all-room train*), *New York-Pittsburgh* . . . The Golden Triangle, *Pittsburgh-Chicago*.

**For your New York World's Fair Visit...** *Take The* **DIRECT ROUTE**

**It goes "Straight to the Gate".** And don't forget Pennsylvania Railroad is the shortest route, with connecting lines, to the West and the San Francisco Fair.

A detailed peek into the Pennsylvania's Duplex Pullman car was printed in September 1940. Precious space aboard was conserved, and more compartments were possible in each car with this overlapping split-level arrangement. Note that both World's Fairs (New York and San Francisco) were still open at this time.

The Pennsylvania Railroad commissioned artists including Greenwich Village's Louis Bouche to deco-rate its streamlined club cars with picturesque murals of both historical and contemporary scenes. And other artists who painted winter scenes such as the one at top were successful in capturing the excite-ment of railroad travel. (February 1941)

Artistic license is evident in this eye-catching rendition of a Pennsy streamliner racing across America's rich heartland in June 1941. Note the exaggerated length on the stream-shrouded steam engine pulling the train. But, the four mainline tracks are not an exaggeration; Pennsy was proud of its quad-track "broadway," the true inspiration for the name of its crack *Broadway Limited*.

A memorable presentation by the Pennsylvania Railroad appeared in America's leading magazines during July and August of 1941. It was prophetic because war clouds, like the storm clouds seen here, were looming dangerously close. At any rate, a strong point was emphasized here: summer storms were no threat to trains, which managed to get through in weather that would ground all planes.

America

has the trains —

modern, fit, ready !

*This war* will be won not alone through greater and superior production, spirit and courage—it will be won also by the ability and capacity of the railroads to keep troops, materials and supplies rolling. Count on the Pennsylvania Railroad to play its part!

You may not realize it, but in keeping with its traditional policy of farsightedness, the Pennsylvania has over the past 12 years spent nearly $670,000,000 in improving its system and enlarging its equipment. Never in point of technical efficiency and state of equipment has it been so fit for the added responsibilities of war.

Yes, and its skilled army of 140,000 men will see that everything rolls swiftly, safely, smoothly!

To the extent wartime demands permit, the Pennsylvania will continue to make available in public travel those comforts, luxuries and innovations which have made travel over its lines so great a pleasure.

**LEADERS OF THE FLEET!**

BROADWAY LIMITED *(16 hour All Room Train)*

THE GENERAL    THE ADMIRAL    THE PENNSYLVANIAN

New York . . . Philadelphia . . . Chicago

**"SPIRIT OF ST. LOUIS"**

New York . . . Philadelphia . . . St. Louis
Washington . . . Baltimore . . . St. Louis

LIBERTY LIMITED          THE PENNSYLVANIAN

Chicago . . . Baltimore . . . Washington

THE PITTSBURGHER          THE GOLDEN TRIANGLE
*All Room Train*

New York . . . Pittsburgh      Pittsburgh . . . Chicago

And daily trains serving Cleveland, Cincinnati, Detroit, Columbus, Dayton, Akron, Louisville, Indianapolis and other cities. *40 trains daily between New York and Washington*

**FARES ARE LOW**

SHORTEST ROUTE BETWEEN EAST AND WEST

Serves America's largest cities. Through cars to New England and the South. Convenient connections to the West.

Pennsylvania Railroad

SERVING THE NATION

**Enjoy modern Pullman comforts!** In addition to attractive Pullman Lounges which have among their modern touches, radio, so you can keep up with the news—the Pennsylvania offers up-to-the-minute accommodations: Roomettes, Duplex Rooms, Bedrooms, Compartments, Drawing Rooms, Master Rooms, Section Sleepers also.

**Ride all-coach trains at low fares!** *The Trail Blazer*, New York—Chicago; *The Jeffersonian*, New York—St. Louis; *The South Wind*, Chicago—Miami. Observation-Buffet-Lounge; reserved reclining seats; low-priced meals; attendants; train passenger representatives. *The Trail Blazer* and *Jeffersonian* serve Washington, also.

There was a smooth transition to wartime advertising in April 1942, maintaining the unforgettable style of Pennsy's earlier ads. Here is another great composition in color.

## ROLLING
### TO
## VICTORY
**IN MILL.. ON RAIL!**

**UPON STEEL** the nation depends for its guns, tanks, ships, plane engines.

Upon railroads steel depends for its raw materials and the movement of finished products.

Steel production is at one of its highest points in history. Railroads are making records for tonnages carried. So the men who make the steel and the men who move it are coming through in true American fashion.

Pennsylvania Railroad is proud of its part in this program. Yet speeding war output is only part of our wartime job. Our passenger facilities must also move troops and business men engaged in wartime production. So demands on all of our equipment are extremely heavy.

To the best of our ability, we shall continue to provide fast, dependable travel for everyone. But should you occasionally encounter any inconvenience, please remember our main efforts are—and must be—dedicated to the cause of Victory.

*DEPENDABLE PASSENGER SERVICE. Pennsylvania Railroad operates a fleet of daily trains serving New York, Chicago, Philadelphia, Detroit, Cleveland, Baltimore, St. Louis, Pittsburgh, Washington, Buffalo, Cincinnati, Indianapolis, Louisville, Columbus, Toledo, Akron, Dayton and many other cities.*

# Pennsylvania Railroad
### SERVING THE NATION
★ *Buy United States Savings Bonds and Stamps*

The compelling, raw beauty of heavy industry and steam locomotive power combine as part of a July 1942 advertisement. Pennsy's steam locomotive power was both successful and unique, much of it having been built at the railroad's massive Altoona works. Model train buffs also loved locomotives like the Pacific pictured above. A.C. Gilbert's American Flyer Company produced an O Gauge tinplate version in the early 1940s and an S Gauge version from 1946 to the mid-1950s.

HOW *Women* HELP TO KEEP THEM ROLLING
ON THE PENNSYLVANIA RAILROAD

A WAR ROLE FOR WOMEN . . . as a trainman on the Pennsylvania Railroad. Women serve on short runs, as a rule.

RAILROADING has always been regarded as a man's calling.

But when war reached deeply into railroad ranks — taking from the Pennsylvania Railroad alone more than 41,000 skilled and experienced workers for the Armed Forces — women were employed to help keep trains rolling.

Today, on the Pennsylvania Railroad, approximately 22,000 women are serving in a wide variety of occupations—four of which you see illustrated here.

Positions such as trainmen, ticket sellers, train passenger representatives, ushers, information and reservation personnel call for intelligence, courtesy and a high degree of efficiency. Young women fresh from college and high school—after intensive training —have proved they can fill these roles most capably.

So, we're glad to have their help in the greatest job railroads have ever been called upon to do, *moving men and materials to Victory!*

AS A BRAKEMAN in freight yard operations, a woman fills a job that requires strength and coolness — in all weather.

AS AN USHER, a woman posts trains, announces departures and arrivals — answers the questions asked by travelers.

INFORMATION COUNTERS are besieged these days — so a woman's knowledge of travel must be extensive.

*BUY UNITED STATES WAR BONDS AND STAMPS*

**Pennsylvania Railroad**
*Serving the Nation*

★ *44,150 in the Armed Forces*     ★ *118 have given their lives for their country*

Several years before the railroads took a cue from the airlines and placed stewardesses aboard some trains, the wartime manpower shortage made it necessary to hire women for jobs once reserved for men. In this April 1944 ad we see the Pennsylvania Railroad placing women roles, including  strenuous brakemen's spots in freight yards.

# ON THEIR WAY

Shades are drawn down. Lights dim low. The landscape is blotted out . . . there's just the hum of the speeding train.

These boys know what it means — the troop train is approaching the troop ships.

Some draw a deep breath. A soldier fumbles for a letter. Another wonders if he can make a last telephone call. Another draws out a crumpled photograph.

No, travelers don't see this — but the trainmen of the Pennsylvania Railroad do, daily. And more so than ever now. As the swelling tide of American youth — fine and fit — streams overseas . . .

Of course, it takes a lot of equipment for these troop movements — but with what remains we are doing our best to serve all essential travelers . . . efficiently, courteously.

*BUY UNITED STATES WAR BONDS AND STAMPS*

## Pennsylvania Railroad
### Serving the Nation

★ *15,194 in the Armed Forces*   ★ *151 have given their lives for their country*

June 1944 was the month of the historic D-Day Allied invasion of France at Normandy Beach, a major turning point in the war. Thousands more soldiers were on their way to battle each month, as crowded troop trains carried the boys from one assignment to the next.

CROSSTIE

STONE BALLAST 18" DEEP

CINDERS 12" DEEP

SUBSOIL

## *Groundwork*

### Millions will be needed for "Deferred Maintenance"

TODAY's mighty war loads are riding on foundations like that pictured . . . "highways" into which the railroads have put more than 4 billion dollars for improvements since the last war. This groundwork is the necessary basis for carrying the greatest load in history.

Wear and tear on roadway, bridges, locomotives, cars and equipment have been terrific. And material and labor for needed maintenance are not obtainable now beyond the minimum necessary for safe, continued operation. As a result, much work that should be done has had to be deferred. So the railroads are wearing out 25 per cent faster than they can be restored.

If permitted, railroads would put aside money from current revenues for postwar replacement of things that are worn out in earning that revenue. But the tax law forbids. If money for needed repairs cannot be spent for those repairs as it is earned, it is considered "profit" and practically taxed away.

Money that should be spent for maintenance isn't profit. Actually it is "repair money" that ordinarily would be spent for that purpose. As such, it is the lifeblood of the railroads. To tax it away, simply because it cannot be spent now because of war conditions, threatens the backbone of American transportation.

Congressional amendment of the tax law to permit this money to be put aside for repairs and replacement would mean strong postwar railroads and thousands of jobs for returning fighting men in furnishing materials and restoring the railroads for the needs of tomorrow.

## PENNSYLVANIA RAILROAD
### *Serving the Nation*

★ *31,779 entered the Armed Forces* ☆ *647 have given their lives for their Country*
BUY UNITED STATES WAR BONDS AND STAMPS

The fascinating anatomy of track and roadbed, usually taken for granted, is detailed in an April 1945 ad that takes pains to hide its true purpose. Read the fine print and you'll discover that the ad is a subtle plea for a change in federal tax law that would help railroads rebuild after the pounding of wartime traffic. The railroads were essential to U.S. victory, but ironically many of the companies never fully recovered from the damage inflicted by wartime hauling compounded by a post-war drop in traffic and revenues.

## While the Storm rages . . .

### THE TRAIN GOES THROUGH !

The sky darkens . . . lightning crackles—soon comes the deluge, blotting out all visibility !

No matter—your Pennsylvania Railroad train takes weather as it comes . . . the good with the bad.

And if you've temporarily lost one horizon *outside*— you've gained another, new and more beautiful, *inside!*

For now those two famed all-coach streamliners—*The Trail Blazer*, New York-Chicago and *The Jeffersonian*, New York-Washington-St. Louis—and the *Liberty Limited*, Washington-Chicago, proudly welcome you to Pennsylvania Railroad's grand postwar coaches.

So roomy . . . only 44 seats to the car !

So magnificently lighted . . . fluorescent lights *four times* stronger, yet soft and . . . shadowless.

So much easier riding . . . credit that to the improved undercarriage and those new lightweight but sturdy steels.

Your window is a full 6 feet wide, the largest we've ever made . . . and the washrooms likewise are extra spacious, each with two toilet annexes and three washstands.

Even your coach doors admit you with an ease never before known—they're electro-pneumatic and open at a finger's touch.

From the ground up, from door to door, these postwar coaches invite you to enjoy not only new comfort, new riding ease, new beauty—but an utterly new experience in dependable low-cost travel. So step aboard ! . . . to a comfortable seat reserved for you at NO EXTRA COST!

## PENNSYLVANIA RAILROAD
### for *WEATHERPROOF* service

In the face of increasing competition from airlines, railroads had to grasp at whatever advantage they could find. "All-weather service" and "weatherproof service" (the latter seen in this August 1947 ad) were popular marketing slogans for the Pennsy, hoping to woo travelers still unsure about the concept of air travel.

# We've come a long way
## since the "Highball"

The first railway signals ever to be established on an American railroad were installed in the early 1830's on the old New Castle and Frenchtown Railroad, long a part of the Pennsylvania Railroad System.

Until then, a locomotive engineer had only a time card to guide him—there were no signals, no telegraph, no communication between stations, no way to transmit orders to a train.

But the spirit of railroad progress soon corrected that!

At stations along the line, poles were erected with crossbars projecting over the track—to which were attached pulleys and ropes.

As a train approached in the distance, the station agent ran up a big ball—much as you would hoist a flag.

White ball run clear to the crossbar meant "clear track." Black ball, run half-way up, meant "stop!"

Thus was born a phrase famous in railroading even in this day . . . "highball"—or clear track ahead.

In rapid succession over the years followed a host of improvements in the science of railway signaling—many of them pioneered by the Pennsylvania Railroad. The semaphore . . . the block signal system, inaugurated first on the Pennsylvania Railroad in 1863 . . . interlocking switches . . . automatic block signals . . . centralized train control . . . position lights . . . cab signals . . . and many others, the latest being the train telephone.

Now what have these forward steps meant to the American people? *The safest travel developed by man!*

Today, as the Pennsylvania Railroad begins a second century of transportation progress, its research and engineering staffs strive to adapt the latest discoveries in electronics and other fields to its signal and communications system, and thereby give passengers and shippers even better, safer service.

CAB SIGNALS automatically reproduce the wayside signals—a great aid to the engineer on stormy, foggy nights.

THE TRAIN TELEPHONE. Latest of Pennsylvania Railroad achievements, the train telephone enables an engineer to talk to other trains, wayside stations, freight cabooses—all while his train is pushing on.

AUTOMATIC POSITION LIGHT SIGNALS on crosstrack bridges tell Pennsylvania Railroad engineers the state of every track.

## PENNSYLVANIA RAILROAD

*1846* *1946*

ONE HUNDRED YEARS OF TRANSPORTATION PROGRESS

Ever wonder where the term "highball" originated? Pennsylvania Railroad celebrated its centennial in part with this July 1946 ad that educated readers on the evolution of signal systems. The ball-style sys-

tem deemed archaic in this ad was nonetheless effective. At least one ball signal remained in operation on the Boston & Maine (in Whitefield Junction, N.H.) into the 1980s.

## Room to Relax ... Room to Roam
### IN THESE NEW COACHES!

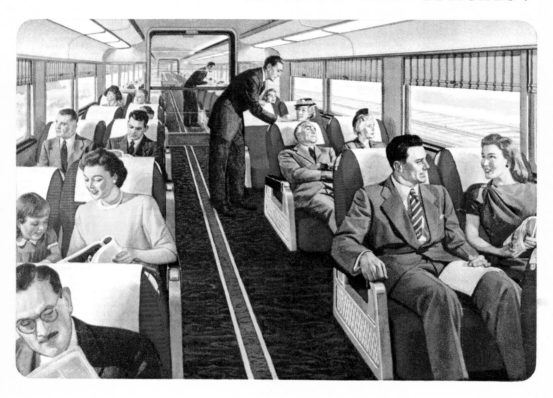

The thing you have always wanted in coach travel . . . *roominess!* Accomplished by Pennsylvania Railroad by installing *only 44 seats to the car*. More room to lean back . . . more room to stretch out. Fact is, more of *everything* for your enjoyment. Bigger panoramic windows . . . deeper luggage racks, with a compartment at the end for bulkier things . . . brilliant fluorescent lighting—yet easy on the eyes . . . electro-pneumatic doors that open at finger's touch . . . air-conditioning . . . and, above all, a ride . . . easy, quiet and smooth. Step aboard one of the fine Pennsylvania Railroad trains equipped with these new overnight coaches and enjoy thorough comfort every mile of the way!

## PENNSYLVANIA RAILROAD
*Serving the Nation*

**Enjoy these**
*Overnight Coaches on*

**THE TRAIL BLAZER**
*All-coach streamliner*
NEW YORK-CHICAGO

**THE JEFFERSONIAN**
*All-coach streamliner*
NEW YORK-WASHINGTON-
ST. LOUIS

**LIBERTY LIMITED**
*Premier train*
WASHINGTON-BALTIMORE-
CHICAGO

*at Low Coach Fares*

EXTRA LARGE WASHROOMS                    EASY-OPENING DOORS

Freedom is the underlying theme in this October 1947 ad, not surprising in a nation fresh off a mighty war to fend off tyrannical powers. "Room to roam" may have been a subtle attack on cramped airline travel, but this ad was probably speaking more to the growing democratization of travel.

In attempt to retain customers, railroads tried a variety of innovations. In May 1948, a recreation car was the hook for luring riders to Pennsylvania Railroad's New York-St. Louis *Jeffersonians*. The car featured a playroom for kids and even a small movie room.

# ALL DIESEL-POWERED!

**A GREAT FLEET** of overnight trains in Pennsylvania Railroad's East-West service now *Diesel-powered, west of Baltimore and Harrisburg!*

That's something new . . . *Electric power all the way!*

Between New York and Harrisburg, streamlined electric locomotives, drawing their energy from an overhead wire system.

Over the Pennsylvania Railroad's lines west of Harrisburg—giant, smooth operating Diesel locomotives generate their own electric power.

Besides the famous trains pictured above, others in the great Pennsylvania fleet now powered by modern Diesel-Electric locomotives include *The American, Pennsylvania Limited, Manhattan Limited, The Pennsylvanian* and *Gotham Limited.*

Here, indeed, is another great forward step in our constant effort to give you better passenger service.

Step aboard ! . . . *enjoy electric power all the way!*

## PENNSYLVANIA RAILROAD
*Serving the Nation*

By the time of this July 1948 ad, diesel power had become the rule for Pennsy's name trains. Interestingly, a year later, rival New York Central ran a very similar ad. The two competitors often followed each other closely in a variety of ways, so it is not surprising that they eventually merged, in 1968, to form the Penn Central Railroad. The union was a disaster and in 1976 the government cleaned up the mess of Northeastern railroading by forming Conrail, from the ruins of Penn Central, Erie-Lackawanna and other struggling carriers.

## HOLIDAY HOMECOMING...

*There's nothing quite so pleasant as coming home again . . .* Especially when it's "home for Christmas" . . . and when you take the train!

This is the happy season when Pennsylvania Railroad's great fleets of trains between East and West, North and South, assume a particularly festive air.

By Pullman, by coach, joyous families are going to visit the folks at home—carefree, comfortable, relaxed as they speed on their way.

For *your* holiday travels Pennsylvania Railroad offers a wide choice of daily trains . . . conveniently scheduled to fit your plans.

## PENNSYLVANIA RAILROAD

It's Christmas 1948: What more can be said about this heart-warming arrival?

*The New*
# BROADWAY LIMITED
## NEW YORK • CHICAGO
*Now in Service*

THE NEWLY-EQUIPPED Broadway Limited presents a completely new conception of travel . . . with new styling, appointments, riding ease and beauty . . . more comforts and conveniences than ever before, representing the finest that modern design and engineering can offer.

Beautiful new Lounge and Observation Cars . . . attractive new Dining Cars . . . distinctively new, all-room sleeping cars . . . plus the Broadway Limited's traditional hospitality — all for your personal travel pleasure! We invite you to make a reservation for your next trip.

**NEW MID-TRAIN LOUNGE AND OBSERVATION LOUNGE CARS** — Cheerful, spacious settings — richly appointed for leisure. Thick soft carpets . . . easy chairs and roomy settees. Magazine libraries. Buffet service for refreshments.

**NEW MASTER DINING CAR** — Attractive furnishings and decorations. Enjoy delicious food . . . meticulous service . . . a view of the passing scene through panoramic windows. Entire car is reserved for dining — with the kitchen in an adjoining car.

**DUPLEX ROOMS** — for one person. A restful full-length bed becomes a comfortable divan by day. Complete toilet facilities.

**BEDROOMS** — for one or two passengers — *now in three distinct styles*. Each has its own comfortable arrangement by day. Lower and upper beds . . . full-length wardrobe . . . enclosed toilet annex.

**COMPARTMENTS** accommodate two. By day — a wide sofa-seat and folding lounge chair. By night — lower and upper beds parallel the window. As in all rooms, lighting, heating and air conditioning are yours to control. Full-length wardrobe . . . enclosed toilet annex.

**DRAWING ROOMS** — ideal for three persons. Broad sofa and two folding easy chairs are replaced for slumber by three beds. Full-length wardrobe . . . enclosed toilet annex.

**MASTER ROOMS** — extra-spacious for two. Radio, four folding lounge chairs, two lower beds, bathroom annex *with shower*.

**ROOMETTES** for the individual. Easily lowered-from-the-wall bed . . . wide sofa-seat . . . enclosed wardrobe . . . complete toilet facilities.

## PENNSYLVANIA RAILROAD

In 1949, Pennsylvania Railroad completely re-equipped its flagship *Broadway Limited*; this ad from April of that year takes you on a tour of the new train an its amenities. Investing in new passenger equipment proved be a poor way to spend money. Despite its top-notch equipment, Pennsy's long-distance passenger trains failed to turn a profit for the railroad after 1946.

Ever since the early cinder-and-smoke days, kids and trains have mixed well. This picture appeared in June 1949, and even if you're too young to have taken a train ride that year, you can still look at this cheerful illustration and understand the little boy's delight as he boarded the big red Pullman.

THE
MORNING CONGRESSIONAL
*Washington • New York*

THE
SENATOR
*Washington • New York • Boston*

THE
AFTERNOON CONGRESSIONAL
*Washington • New York*

# ALL-NEW Through and Through!

NEW COACHES are roomy. Deeply upholstered *reclining seats*—plenty of baggage space. *Separate smoking compartment with 14 lounge chairs.* Complete washroom facilities.

These brilliant new Pennsylvania trains are the finest ever developed for daytime travel. Operating over the busiest tracks, the finest roadbed in the world—they serve the East's largest, most important cities.

Accommodations for Coach and Parlor Car passengers are of rich quality for the mood of the moment . . . to work, relax or dine as you travel. In addition to facilities pictured, newest creations in handsomely furnished lounge cars are available for all.

Latest-type air-conditioning, colorful decor, fluorescent lighting, panoramic windows, electro-pneumatic doors, enclosed telephone rooms—and more—sum up to the most satisfactory trip you've ever taken by rail.

Enjoy the fine daily service provided by these great streamliners. It will be a pleasant NEW experience!

NEW PARLOR CARS with soft-cushioned *reclining* swivel chairs, deep-piled carpeting, attractive draperies, ample luggage space, wide package racks. Private drawing room with enclosed toilet annex.

NEW DRAWING ROOM PARLOR CAR on *The Congressionals.* Private rooms with divans, lounge chairs, wardrobes. Removable partitions permit use en suite. Enclosed toilet annexes.

NEW DINING CARS with all-electric kitchens designed for more efficient cooking. Wonderful service in a setting of charm comparable to fine hotel facilities.

NEW COFFEE SHOP CAR for Coach passengers. Complete meals or snacks prepared on electric radarange and electric grill. Served at counter or tables. Separate section with lounge facilities.

PENNSYLVANIA RAILROAD
*Go by Train . . . Safety—with Speed and Comfort*

An ad touting new passenger equipment on the Northeast Corridor trains also provides an enduring image of the Pennsylvania Railroad—the venerable GG1 electric locomotive. The streamlined GG1s were yet another memorable product of industrial designer Raymond Loewy. The durable electrics, which were introduced in 1935, remained in service after the Penn Central merger and even survived into the Amtrak era.

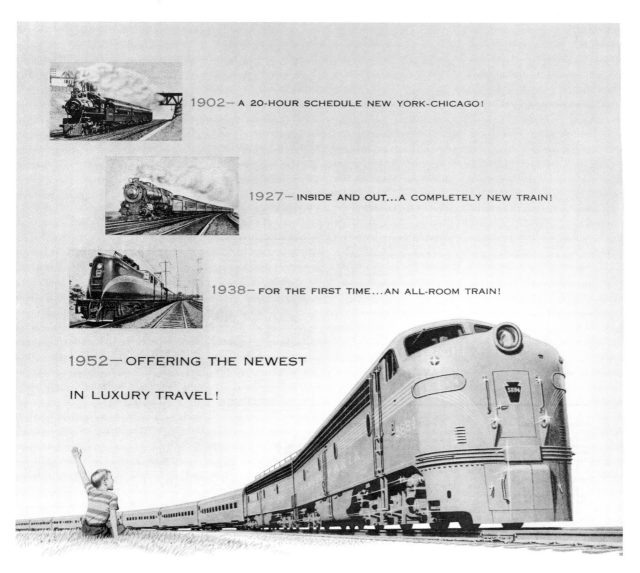

1902— A 20-HOUR SCHEDULE NEW YORK-CHICAGO!

1927— INSIDE AND OUT...A COMPLETELY NEW TRAIN!

1938— FOR THE FIRST TIME...AN ALL-ROOM TRAIN!

1952— OFFERING THE NEWEST

IN LUXURY TRAVEL!

# BROADWAY LIMITED
## NOW CELEBRATING ITS GOLDEN ANNIVERSARY

On June 15, 1902, Pennsylvania Railroad introduced a train between New York-Philadelphia and Chicago—the finest of its day! Now on its golden anniversary, the magnificent all-private-room *Broadway Limited* still sets the standard for dependable travel—a train unmatched in splendor, comfort and convenience. Within the streamlined *Broadway Limited* you'll find an exceptional range of accommodations with six types of rooms varying in size from cozy Roomettes to luxurious Master Rooms with *private bath and shower*. The color and charm of its handsome lounge cars fitted with buffets, easy chairs and divans . . . marvelous food served in a beautifully designed Master Dining Car and traditional *Broadway Limited* service and courtesy all add to the pleasure of your overnight trip. For the finest in travel between New York and Chicago—ride the *Broadway Limited*. You'll enjoy every restful mile!

PENNSYLVANIA
RAILROAD

*Go by Train . . . Safety—with Speed and Comfort*

A golden anniversary ad from July 1952 celebrates 1902 to 1952 milestones in the history of Pennsy's great *Broadway Limited*, which was originally known as the *Pennsylvania Special*. The train remained all-Pullman until 1967, and it survived both the Penn Central merger and the start of Amtrak. But, in 1995 the national rail passenger carrier finally discontinued once-venerable train.

a **PORTER FIRELESS LOCOMOTIVE**

can save up to **50%** of your switching costs

No Fire

No Smoke

No Noise

It's hard to believe, but here it is: A steam switching locomotive that carries no fire, makes no smoke, and does its work with no more noise than a gentle exhaust of steam! The Porter Fireless Locomotive operates on heat energy stored in its tank. The heat is supplied by excess steam from your stationary boilers. The Porter Fireless is so easy to handle, new unskilled employees—even women—can quickly learn to run it. Practically 99% availability. Few wearing parts make the maintenance expense almost negligible.

*ONLY PORTER BUILDS A COMPLETE LINE OF LOCOMOTIVES*

**H. K. PORTER COMPANY, INC.**
PITTSBURGH, PENNSYLVANIA

PITTSBURGH, PA.  **FACTORIES:**  NEWARK, N. J.
BLAIRSVILLE, PA.  NEW BRUNSWICK, N. J.

**LOCOMOTIVE DIVISION:**
Diesel, Diesel-Electric, Electric, Steam, and Fireless Steam Locomotives.

**PROCESS EQUIPMENT DIVISION:**
Agitators, Mixers, Blenders, Autoclaves, Kettles, Pressure Vessels, Driers, Ball and Pebble Mills.

**QUIMBY PUMP DIVISION:**
Screw, Rotex, Centrifugal, Chemical, and Steam Pumps.

**ORDNANCE DIVISION:**
Projectiles, Heavy Forgings, Breech Blocks.

PORTER
*Better Built*
Equipment
*Established 1866*

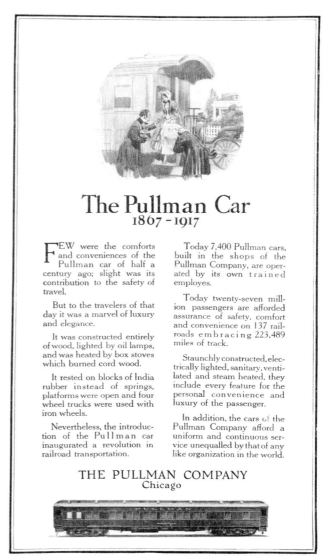

## The Pullman Car
### 1867 - 1917

FEW were the comforts and conveniences of the Pullman car of half a century ago; slight was its contribution to the safety of travel.

But to the travelers of that day it was a marvel of luxury and elegance.

It was constructed entirely of wood, lighted by oil lamps, and was heated by box stoves which burned cord wood.

It rested on blocks of India rubber instead of springs, platforms were open and four wheel trucks were used with iron wheels.

Nevertheless, the introduction of the Pullman car inaugurated a revolution in railroad transportation.

Today 7,400 Pullman cars, built in the shops of the Pullman Company, are operated by its own trained employes.

Today twenty-seven million passengers are afforded assurance of safety, comfort and convenience on 137 railroads embracing 223,489 miles of track.

Staunchly constructed, electrically lighted, sanitary, ventilated and steam heated, they include every feature for the personal convenience and luxury of the passenger.

In addition, the cars of the Pullman Company afford a uniform and continuous service unequalled by that of any like organization in the world.

**THE PULLMAN COMPANY**
Chicago

Two ads feature an interesting pair of curiosities. At left, a December 1943 advertisement from H.K. Porter Company Inc. of Pittsburgh shows its unique Porter Fireless switching locomotive, designed for use by industries that had railroad spur connections. At right, the ubiquitous "iron monster" Pullman car (pre-streamlined) was found on most railroads until the postwar transition to streamlined equipment. This Pullman ad appeared in September 1917, and many readers may be surprised to learn how little the basic design of Pullman cars changed until the 1930s.

## HERE ARE EXAMPLES OF THE LOW COST OF PULLMAN ACCOMMODATIONS

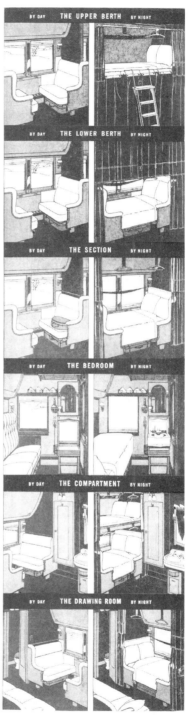

About one-half of those who use Pullman cars during the course of a year travel between places where the lower berth rate is $2.50 or less. A $2.50 lower berth rate covers a typical overnight journey—about 300 miles. These pages picture and indicate to you the cost of each of the various types of Pullman accommodations for such a typical overnight journey. For longer trips, of course, the rates are correspondingly higher, but the ones quoted will give you an idea of the relatively low cost of Pullman service. Pullman accommodations may be purchased by passengers holding transportation tickets required by the railroad company. The rates shown on these two pages are Pullman charges only and do not include the cost of railroad transportation tickets. Your ticket agent or the Pullman Company will gladly quote rates on available accommodations for your next journey.

*Where "tourist" cars are operated, berth and section accommodations are available at rates approximately half those charged between the same places in "standard" cars.*

THE PULLMAN COMPANY
CHICAGO

**Taking a 500-Mile Overnight Trip?**
*Your Pullman accommodation would cost about:*

| | |
|---|---|
| Lower Berth . . . . . . . . . . . . | $2.50 |
| Upper Berth . . . . . . . . . . . | 2.00 |
| Single Occupancy Section . . . . . . . . | 5.50 |
| Bedroom for one, $4.50; for two, each . . . | 2.50 |
| Compartment for one, $5.00; for two, each . . | 5.50 |
| Drawing Room for one, $6.25; for two, each . | 4.50 |

——— (Railroad fare is in addition to these rates) ———

*All testimonial statements in this advertisement were furnished without compensation*

**The UPPER BERTH**

"I've got to get plenty of sleep at night," says **Miss Helen Reese,** actress. "And I sure get it on a Pullman when I am on tour." Miss Reese always takes an upper berth (illustrated below) because that is the accommodation she prefers. Miss Reese's upper berth costs her only $2 for her usual overnight trip—20% less than she would pay for a lower berth for the same trip.

**The BEDROOM**

"Think of having a private room while traveling—it's just like home to us," declare **Madeleine Shannon** and her friend **Linda Yale.** Their favorite Pullman accommodation is the Bedroom (illustrated above), with desk, lavatory and toilet. A comfortable sofa, with concealed upper berth above, become commodious beds at night. When Miss Shannon goes on an overnight journey, the Bedroom costs $4.50. When Miss Yale is along, the price of the room is $5.00, or $2.50 each.

Though this ad appeared in June 1937, it showed the various types of standard Pullman accommodations found on heavyweight trains, which predominated through the end of World War II.

# GIRL GOES BACK TO COLLEGE

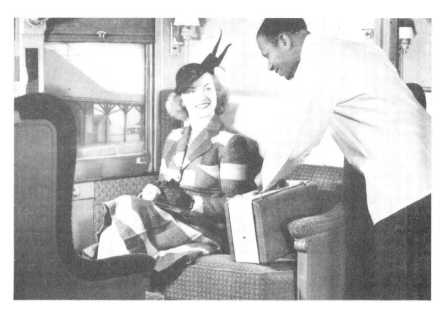

Last January 2, Clare Fisher, her Christmas holiday over, kissed Papa and Mama Fisher goodbye, set out to return to her classes at a well-known girls college in New England.

Her father had planned to drive Clare back. But weather was bad, so he put her on a Pullman, as being the safest, surest way for her to travel. Never having taken a Pullman before, she was a bit nervous. But all nervousness faded as the porter gave her a big, reassuring smile, told her to ring the bell if she wanted anything.

**CLARE NO SOONER** got settled than another girl came in. Clare found that her name was Ruth Murphy, that she was also going back East to college, and that she had the upper berth over Clare's lower. They hit it off together at once, went up to the dining car to have dinner together.

**DINNER OVER,** they wandered back to the lounge car. Here they got their first big kick of the trip; a famous movie actor was there! He left, but they hardly noticed, for they'd struck up an acquaintance and started a lively conversation with two army flyers (whose names you can't have—yet).

**AFTER BRIDGE** and much good talk with the flyers, Clare and Ruth retired to their car, washed faces and scrubbed teeth before bed. Clare discovered (by watching Ruth) that you *pull forward* the water faucets to turn them on, that the small bowl was the tooth-scrubbing bowl. She felt like an old hand!

**TO BED:** Ruth up above, Clare below. And those berths are shipshape as a Captain's Cabin! Hangers for clothes; a hammock and shelf for stockings, etc.; a dandy reading light; real air-conditioning; and, between those crisp, crackly sheets, *the divinest bed you ever tucked a toe into!*

**NEXT MORNING,** Clare was writing home: "Dear Dad and Mom . . . There never, never was anything like this Pullman trip for fun . . . I feel like a queen . . . I met the most wonderful people . . . I guess I'm spoiled for any other kind of travel." Try *Pullman.* You'll be spoiled, too.

FOR COMFORT, SAFETY, AND DEPENDABILITY
GO PULLMAN

A student makes her way back to college on board a Pullman car in December 1941. The pre-war era was about to end for Americans; note the military personnel on board.

**180**

**1. Private rooms at bargain prices!** That's what you'll get in new Duplex-Roomette cars like the one that is pictured above. There are going to be other new kinds of sleeping cars, too, but let's look now at all the luxury you'll get *at bargain prices* in . . .

# The car with the staggered windows

**2. A private sitting room!** That's what you'll ride in when these new sleeping cars go into service.

This air-conditioned *room of your own* will be equipped with every comfort and convenience that Pullman's mastery of travel hospitality can provide. And kept as spick-and-span as only Pullman's expert "housekeepers" can keep travel accommodations.

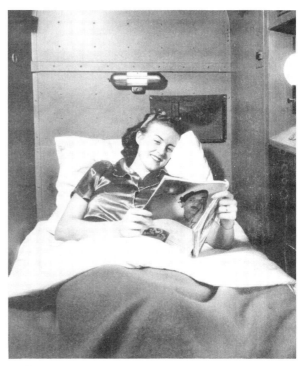

**3. A private bedroom!** That's what your air-conditioned sitting room becomes when it's time for some good, sound sleep!

Just touch a lever and presto! a big, soft bed comes out of hiding—with crisp, clean sheets all ready to slide into. What a wonderful rest you'll get as you speed *safely and dependably* toward your destination.

**4. A bargain price!** The *new design* of the Duplex-Roomette car (indicated by its staggered windows) brings the cost of private rooms *way down*. Between Chicago and Detroit, for example, you could enjoy all this luxury, at present rates, for *only 30¢ more than the price of a lower berth!*

# GO PULLMAN
THE <u>SAFEST</u>, MOST <u>COMFORTABLE</u> WAY OF GOING PLACES FAST—THE <u>SUREST</u> WAY OF GETTING THERE IN TIME!

Pullman's new Duplex-Roomette car was presented in this March 1946 advertisement. Easily identified by their staggered windows, the cars represented an attempt to capture the economy sleeper market, a vast departure from Pullman's traditional focus on providing luxury accommodations on rails.

# How to get a family vacation on the right track

**When you Go Pullman** with the family, you get a running start on a happy holiday. That's because your vacation begins the moment you step into this wonderful world on wheels.

With the children safe and sound in your accommodation, you can stroll down to the Club Car for some down-to-earth friendliness. You'll meet delightful people in comfortable surroundings, and soon learn that half the fun of going is *going* Pullman.

You're supposed to rest on a family outing. And with a big comfortable bed to stretch out in, here's a restful thought: You'll arrive where you're going *on time* —*relaxed* and *ready* for all the waiting fun.

The only time you lift a finger is to ring your Porter. He'll be glad to see to it that your every wish is granted . . . including breakfast in your own accommodation. Further proof that you're really on vacation when you Go Pullman.

## Have you discovered PULLMAN

With the decline of luxury and business travel by rail, Pullman reached out to vacationers and families with its later marketing campaigns, including this family-oriented ad from April 1953.

Though this November 1944 appeared during wartime, improvements were still made in railroad rolling stock, for comfort as well as for efficiency. In spite of emergency limitations, new day-nite coaches were fitted by Pullman-Standard. (In 1934, Pullman's domestic car-building factories had been consolidated under this name.) In these new luxury coaches, curtains could be drawn between the sets of reclining seats, for the privacy of those who wished to rest or sleep.

## ON THE SANTA FE---
## IN CARS BUILT BY PULLMAN-STANDARD

RIDE
BY
RAIL
SHIP

*The luxurious Observation Car pictured below is one of a large streamlined fleet Pullman-Standard is building for the Santa Fe. It comprises the last word in sleepers, chair, lounge, club, and observation cars—all expertly designed and engineered for your greater travel pleasure.*

● The minute you step aboard these new, spic-and-span streamlined cars, you'll be out of this world—into a world chock full of travel thrills. You'll ride Santa Fe to the romantic Southwest, the land of Indians, canyons and cowboys, pinto ponies and pueblos.

● Rail travel offers the best of all travel delights. You have fun. You have spaciousness; room to move around. You'll find it agreeably exciting to walk through the air-conditioned train, pause for refreshments and enjoy superb food and service. You'll meet interesting people and team up for games or stimulating talk, or just relax and enjoy the scenery *at eye level.* At night you'll sleep in deep-mattressed comfort and awake refreshed and relaxed, at peace with the world.

● Yes, you'll enjoy every moment as the miles go swiftly, smoothly by. On any trip in all America, when you ride in the new cars designed and built by Pullman-Standard, you are enjoying the best in modern transportation—*and the safest!*

## PULLMAN-STANDARD *Car Manufacturing Company*
**CHICAGO · ILLINOIS**     *Offices in six cities from coast to coast . . . also manufacturing plants at six strategic points*
*World's largest builders of modern streamlined railroad cars*

World War II put car construction on hold, but once it ended a flood of new streamlined equipment poured out of the major manufacturers' plants and onto railroad properties. Chicago's Pullman-Standard celebrated a year of world peace—and its prosperity—in August 1946 with an ad promoting cars it was building for Santa Fe. By February 1948, AT&SF had enough new equipment available that it was able to fully refit its *Super Chief* and *El Capitan* trains in Chicago-California service.

## Winter's TWO-WAY ROAD TO Summer

To those who have experienced a winter visit in Florida's delightful clime, this scene will recall the swift, smooth transition from winter to summer provided by the *Orange Blossom Special*, the *Silver Meteor* and other modern trains of the Seaboard's famed passenger fleet. It is also a reminder of the transportation comforts you can expect from the Seaboard in the future, when war's demands have been met.

Most folk, this winter, are remaining at home and for them we are happy to provide "packaged" Florida sunshine—golden citrus fruit and fresh grown vegetables in bountiful variety—brought speedily and regularly by Seaboard's crack freights—the *Marketer*, the *Greyhound*, the *Red Fox*, and others.

Whether you come to Florida or stay at home, the Seaboard Railway—*winter's two-way road to summer*—is always the dependable link between you and the delights of this magic clime.

## SEABOARD RAILWAY
### THROUGH THE HEART OF THE SOUTH

Starting in February 1939, Seaboard Air Line Railroad became the first carrier to offer a New York-Florida streamliner. The *Silver Meteor*, operated in conjunction with Pennsylvania Railroad north of Washington, D.C., was a rousing success and launched a pitched battle with dominant East Coast carrier Atlantic Coast Line. ACL countered with its own streamlined *Champion* in December 1939. The two railroads and their Florida streamliners remained immensely popular right up until they merged to form Seaboard Coast Line in 1967. Descendents of these original trains still ply the rails for Amtrak today. (February 1945 ad)

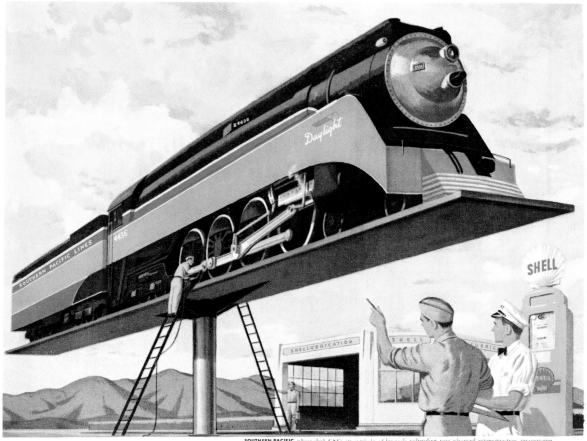

SOUTHERN PACIFIC, whose sleek GS4's are symbols of big-scale railroading, uses advanced automotive-type, pressure-gun lubrication to operate locomotives greater distances between service points. Shell supplies the special lubricant required.

# *Whose Loco ?*

FROM Portland, Ore., to Guadalajara, Mexico . . . San Francisco to Ogden . . . Los Angeles to New Orleans—Southern Pacific is a vital link carrying men, supplies, and war material for our two-ocean war.

No railroad is more strategically located than Southern Pacific . . . and none has more difficult problems involving operation across vast reaches of mountain and desert.

To meet its problems Southern Pacific has initiated far-reaching improvements of equipment and methods. More locomotives . . . more passing tracks and sidings . . . centralized traffic control . . . larger yards . . . all-around

greater capacity for the war effort, which will be helpful too when peace comes . . .

Less spectacular, but no less vital, is the novel lubrication system now built into 75% of Southern Pacific's 2200 locomotives. Many parts of these engines are now lubricated in the same fashion as a car—an advance from the old "grease-cup" method to modern pressure-gun lubrication.

**Southern Pacific called on Shell** to supply a pressure-gun locomotive lubricant which would withstand terrific strains and perform equally

well in temperatures from 40° below zero to 125° above.

**Shell Research developed** this Industrial Lubricant. Not only has it made possible longer runs between service points, but saved in both manpower and maintenance.

Constant improvement in lubricants is a major duty of the "University of Petroleum," Shell's research laboratories. Shell engineers apply these improvements in the field.

*Be sure your plant has the benefit of all that's new in lubrication. Call a Shell Engineer.*

*LEADERS IN WAR PRODUCTION RELY ON*
## SHELL INDUSTRIAL LUBRICANTS

First oil refinery to win the Army-Navy "E"— Shell's Wood River Refinery.

This is a bit of pure fantasy. No gas station ever had a lube rack for locomotives. But this May, 1944, advertisement by Shell Oil Company presents a fine view of a Southern Pacific streamlined steam *Daylight* locomotive, so technicalities are ruled aside for the sake of a good picture.

Established in 1894, Southern Pacific's (now Amtrak's) *Sunset Limited* is America's longest-running name train. The SP train connected New Orleans with California via the Sunset Route, the country's southernmost transcontinental rail line. As this 1926 ad attests, the train offered through service to Los Angeles, San Diego and San Francisco, though Amtrak's modern version terminates at L.A.

# SPEAKING OF NEW TRAINS···

**SOUTHERN PACIFIC** presents here seven swift new trains—seven gleaming standard bearers that symbolize the dynamic progress made by the West's Greatest Transportation System in 1937. 1—the fleet streamlined *Sunbeam*, just placed in service between Houston and Dallas. 2—celebrated Streamliner *City of San Francisco*, 39¾ hours between Chicago and San Francisco. 3—sleek streamlined *Daylight* on the beautiful seashore route between Los Angeles and San Francisco. 4—*San Francisco Challenger* (Chicago-San Francisco). 5—*Californian*, between Chicago and Los Angeles. (Both *Challenger* and *Californian* are new departures in money-saving chair car and tourist travel, are called Economy Trains.) 6—luxurious all-Pullman *Forty-Niner*, Chicago-San Francisco. 7—deluxe all-Pullman *Cascade*, Pacific Northwest-California.

**SPONGE** rubber seats (*above*), individual lights and ash trays, radio, extra-broad windows are chair car attractions of SP streamlined flyers, the *Sunbeam* in Texas, the brilliant *Daylight* in California.

**LUXURY** lounge cars, many of them brand new this year, are regular equipment on Southern Pacific's finest trains. One above on famed, all-Pullman *Cascade* is typical, has indirect lights, deep chairs, radio, bar.

**UPSTAIRS** bedrooms are a feature of the swift, all-Pullman *Forty-Niner*. This train and the Streamliner *City of San Francisco* offer super-speed service from Chicago to San Francisco every third day.

**CAPABLE** stewardess-nurses practice real Western hospitality, are on several SP trains including the *San Francisco Challenger* and the *Californian* . . . both reserved for chair car and tourist car passengers.

## ···AND WHERE THEY GO

Southern Pacific
FOUR SCENIC ROUTES
1 SHASTA ROUTE
2 OVERLAND ROUTE
3 GOLDEN STATE ROUTE
4 SUNSET ROUTE
WEST COAST OF MEXICO ROUTE

**GLORIOUS BACKDROP** for Southern Pacific's fleet of 15 transcontinental trains (all air-conditioned) are these Four Scenic Routes. Longest is the colorful SUNSET ROUTE: from New York to New Orleans on SP's gallant *S. S. Dixie*, thence through the deep South and the cowboy Southwest to California. GOLDEN STATE ROUTE lays shimmering tracks from Chicago direct to Los Angeles via the red mesas and purple peaks of the Rio Grande region. OVERLAND ROUTE follows the trail of the early Pony Express, is shortest, most direct rail line from Chicago to San Francisco. SHASTA ROUTE circles lofty ranges, azure lakes from the Evergreen Northwest to California. (West Coast of Mexico Route, only US-owned line in Mexico, cuts through a country rich in scenic grandeur on its way to Mexico City.) SP Routes embrace the West's finest collection of things to see: mysterious Carlsbad Caverns, mighty Yosemite, Great Salt Lake, Crater Lake, Mt. Shasta, Big Trees, many another picture-place in the Southwest, Pacific Coast and Mexico.

**WHEN WINTER COMES** to the Southwest, brings sunny days and crisp star-filled nights, dude ranches and desert resorts buzz with a new season's activity—range riding, barbecues, swimming, polite loafing. Only Southern Pacific has direct, mainline service to the dude ranches and resort hotels of Southern Arizona and to the desert resorts at Palm Springs. Winter vacationists take the GOLDEN STATE or SUNSET ROUTE to these places and Los Angeles.

**SEE TWICE AS MUCH** on your Western trip by going on one SP Route, returning on another SP Route. You ride fine trains like the *Daylight* (*above*) and its near-twin the Texas *Sunbeam*. And, generally, this *real* round trip costs no more rail fare.

**FREE TRAVEL GUIDE.** SP's new booklet, *How to See the Whole Pacific Coast* tells how you can see more when you make a trip West. 82 large pictures. For a free copy, write O. P. Bartlett, Dept. LE-102, 310 South Michigan Avenue, Chicago, Illinois.

## SOUTHERN PACIFIC
### THE WEST'S GREATEST TRANSPORTATION SYSTEM

Early color advertising was a boon to Southern Pacific, which boasted that it operated "the world's most beautiful train." This October 1937 ad gives a wonderful overview of pre-war SP routes, equipment and amenities, but the star is the newly streamlined *Daylight* in its splendid orange-red-and-black livery. The revamped *Daylight* and its overnight cousin the *Lark*, quickly became the trains of choice for traveling between Los Angeles and San Francisco.

# RIDE THIS NEW STREAMLINER TO SAN FRANCISCO

## Twice as big, twice as powerful, twice as luxurious!

**72 PEOPLE** sit comfortably in this sensational, full-length Dining Car. (The kitchen is in an adjoining car.) There is also a Coffee Shop.

**60 ROOMS** on the new Streamliner! There are six drawing rooms, eight compartments, 18 "roomettes," 28 bedrooms and 36 Pullman sections.

**THE CLUB** and Observation cars on this Streamliner are probably the most beautiful ever built. The chairs and lounges are cushioned with sponge rubber.

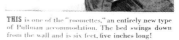

**5,400 HORSEPOWER** whip this giant over the 2,260 miles between Chicago and San Francisco in just 39¾ hours. Operated jointly by Southern Pacific, Union Pacific, North Western. Five departures a month. Extra fare.

**THIS** is one of the "roomettes," an entirely new type of Pullman accommodation. The bed swings down from the wall and is six feet, five inches long!

Ladies and gentlemen, we are proud to present No. 7 in Southern Pacific's sensational parade of new trains — the giant new Streamliner *City of San Francisco*, just placed in service between Chicago and San Francisco. Seventeen cars from tip to tip, *wider* than a standard train, it's twice as big, twice as powerful, twice as luxurious as the smaller *City of San Francisco* it replaces.

Words and pictures cannot do justice to this train. You must see it to realize what "luxury" means. No detail for your comfort has been overlooked. (For example, there are outlets for electric razors). The tremendous size of the cars gives you a feeling of roominess like in a great hotel.

This is the *seventh* brand new train recently inaugurated by Southern Pacific. In the year just past, the brilliant streamlined *Daylight*, the royal *Forty-Niner*, the thrifty *Californian* and *San Francisco Challenger*, the new *Cascade* and the *Sunbeam* in Texas joined the *Golden State Limited*, *Sunset Limited*, *Overland Limited* and the other famous trains that serve the Southern Pacific West.

### HOW TO SEE TWICE AS MUCH

Southern Pacific's Four Scenic Routes to California (see map) serve six national parks (Yosemite, Carlsbad Caverns, Crater Lake, Mt. Lassen, the Big Trees of General Grant and Sequoia National Parks) and most of the other top-ranking wonders of the West and South. By going to California on one of these routes and returning on another one, you'll see a different part of the United States each way. You'll see *twice as much* of California and the West. And from most eastern and mid-western places, such a "go one way, return another" SP ticket costs you not one cent more rail fare than the usual back-and-forth round trip!

**FREE TRAVEL SERVICE!** For Southern Pacific's liberally illustrated travel guide, *How to See the Whole Pacific Coast*, write O. P. Bartlett, Dept. SE-2, 310 So. Michigan Avenue, Chicago. He will also send you a post card for you to mail if you wish a detailed routing, with costs. No charge for this service. No obligation.

### FOUR SCENIC ROUTES TO CALIFORNIA

1 SHASTA ROUTE
2 OVERLAND ROUTE
3 GOLDEN STATE ROUTE
4 SUNSET ROUTE

Southern Pacific's representatives in principal eastern cities are authorities on the West. They will be glad to personally assist you plan your trip. See your telephone directory.

# SOUTHERN PACIFIC

## THE WEST'S GREATEST TRANSPORTATION SYSTEM

The streamlined *City of San Francisco* made its debut in 1936 as a joint operation of Chicago & North Western (Chicago-Omaha), Union Pacific (Omaha-Ogden) and Southern Pacific (Ogden-Bay Area). The train and its jointly owned equipment was a trendsetter. Its EMD E2 locomotives (two sets of three units) weren't custom-built, but "catalog" diesels that any road could buy. Its two Pullman-Standard trainsets had new styling and features that became standard for passenger car construction right up to the Amtrak era. (February 1938 ad)

# How to see twice as much of America
## on your train trip to **California!**

**Southern Pacific FOUR SCENIC ROUTES**

**1 Wouldn't you** like to know the picturesque Old South and New Orleans? Wouldn't you like to visit Texas... the border country along the Rio Grande... Arizona's garden desert... Los Angeles and San Francisco? Wouldn't you like to see America's highest mountains?

Southern Pacific, the West's greatest railroad, offers you an easy way to see more of America on your trip to California this year: go West on *one* of our Four Scenic Routes and return on a *different* S. P. route. Thus you see *twice* as much of America as you would by going and returning on the same route—for not 1¢ extra rail fare (from most eastern and midwestern places). Here's one example of such a trip:

**2 See New Orleans** and the Old South, then speed West across mighty Texas on Southern Pacific's romantic Sunset Route. Stopover at El Paso for the thrilling one-day tour to Carlsbad Caverns National Park.

**Southern Arizona** is next, with its purple mountains, its forests of giant cactus and its gorgeous desert sunsets. You pause briefly at Tucson and Phoenix, and at Yuma, where Indians come down to the station to meet your train.

**Then Los Angeles,** Hollywood and all of Southern California, with its miles of beaches beside the Pacific Ocean. (Your Sunset Route train will be the *Sunset Limited* or *Argonaut*, famous for southern hospitality.)

**3 Next,** you speed from Los Angeles up the California coast to San Francisco on Southern Pacific's streamlined *Daylight*, the most beautiful train in the world. See 113 miles of Pacific Ocean. Or go via the San Joaquin Valley and see Yosemite and the Big Trees.

**4 See San Francisco,** then return home through a different part of America on our Overland Route. Ride the swift Streamliner *City of San Francisco,* the *Overland Limited,* the scenic *Pacific Limited* or the money-saving *San Francisco Challenger* (good meals for 90¢ a day).

**High Sierra,** the Gold Country, Reno and the Rockies are just a few of the thrills on Southern Pacific's pioneer Overland Route, first railroad to span the continent. Another thrill is your "sail by rail" across Great Salt Lake on the spectacular Lucin Causeway—32 miles from shore to shore!

**5 New Color Guidebook!** We have just prepared an attractive new 32-page booklet, illustrated with 64 natural color photographs. It describes the territory along our lines and the service on our trains. We have tried to make this booklet honest and factual so it will be helpful in planning your western trip. Mail the coupon and we'll send this booklet to you free. This offer is restricted to grown-ups.

---

O. P. Bartlett, Dept. LE-31, Southern Pacific, 310 So. Michigan Ave., Chicago, Illinois. Please send me your new free western guidebook.

*Your Name*_____

*Address*_____

*City*_____ *State*_____

*If child, please give age*_____

Note: If you live on the Pacific Coast, you can enjoy a "go one way, return another" trip to the East. See your nearest Southern Pacific agent.

**S·P** **The Friendly Southern Pacific**

This beautiful color page from March 1941 gives a stylized view of the graceful, steam-powered *Daylight*, the recognized star of the Southern Pacific's huge fleet of passenger trains. The various points of interest extolled by the ad reveal just how vast and varied a territory the "Espee" covered.

# How to see twice as much of America
## on your train trip to California!

Southern Pacific
**FOUR SCENIC ROUTES**

**1** **How much** have you seen of your own America? Have you thrilled to mountains that are more than two miles high . . . a flaming sunset on the Arizona desert . . . San Francisco's mighty bridges . . . the virgin forests of Oregon and Washington? Do you know how blue the Pacific Ocean really is? Have you ever seen an Indian?

Southern Pacific, the West's greatest railroad, offers you an easy way to know your country better. When you go to California this year, go on *one* of our Four Scenic Routes (see map) and return on *another* S. P. route. Thus you see an entirely different part of the United States each way. You see *twice* as much of America as you would by going and returning on the same route . . . for not 1¢ extra rail fare (from most eastern and mid-western places). For example:

**2** **You can go** on Southern Pacific's Golden State Route, through the Mexican Border country along the Rio Grande. Stopover at El Paso for the thrilling one-day tour to Carlsbad Caverns National Park ($9.75 all-expense).

**Cowboys** meet the train in New Mexico and Arizona! Your Golden State Route train will be the famous *Golden State Limited* (extra fine service for no extra fare) or the money-saving *Californian* (good meals for $1.25 a day).

**Next stop, Los Angeles!** Miles of palm-fringed beaches, Hollywood, movie stars. Then you speed up the California coast to San Francisco on Southern Pacific's thrilling streamlined *Daylight*, most beautiful train in the world.

**3** **This** is the Tavern Car on Southern Pacific's streamlined *Daylight*. Through these enormous windows you see 113 miles of blue Pacific Ocean, oil wells in the surf, Mission San Miguel, valleys, mountains. Free side trip, if you wish, to Del Monte on the lovely Monterey Peninsula.

**4** **See San Francisco,** then speed north on Southern Pacific's Shasta Route to the evergreen Pacific Northwest. Low cost side trips show you the giant trees of the Redwood Empire or magnificent Crater Lake National Park.

**Your** Shasta Route train will be the luxurious, all-Pullman *Cascade* or the money-saving *Beaver* (breakfast 35¢, luncheon 40¢, dinner 50¢). From the Pacific Northwest, you can return to your hometown on any northern railroad line you choose.

*Note: If you live on the Pacific Coast, you can enjoy a "go one way, return another" trip East. See your nearest S. P. agent.*

**5** **New Color Guidebook!** We have just prepared an attractive new 32-page booklet, illustrated with 63 natural color photographs. It describes the territory along our lines and the service on our trains. We have tried to make this booklet honest and factual so it will be helpful in planning your western trip. Mail the coupon and we'll send this booklet to you free. This offer is restricted to grown-ups.

O. P. Bartlett, Dept. LE-41, Southern Pacific, 310 So. Michigan Ave., Chicago, Illinois. Please send me your new free western guidebook.

Your Name_____
Address_____
City_____ State_____
*If child, please give age_____*

**S·P** The Friendly
Southern Pacific

If a trip like this wouldn't excite you, what would? The center of interest on this page is the spectacular coastal view from Southern Pacific's *Daylight*, as the long (sometimes 19-car) luxury train threads northward toward San Francisco. (April 1941)

.

## WAR RECORD of Southern Pacific's Daylights
### -"the most beautiful trains in the world"

'Way back in 1937, Southern Pacific introduced the streamlined *Daylights*, streaking along the blue Pacific shore between San Francisco and Los Angeles.

The trains "caught on" at once, and were soon among the most popular in America. Pleasure-travelers clamored to ride these "most beautiful trains in the world," as they were soon called, and thrilled at the 470-mile daylight journey through orchards and valleys, and along the blue Pacific shore for more than a hundred glorious miles.

Tourist travel on the streamlined *Daylights* ended soon after Pearl Harbor. Now these famous coastal trains, and their companion *Daylights* through the San Joaquin Valley, are carrying nearly 3,500 passengers a day, including many in uniform. Their war record: 833,510 passengers in 1942; 1,153,585 in 1943; 1,268,008 in 1944!

Temporarily the *Daylights* will be busy moving the thousands of war-weary veterans from Europe and the Pacific. We intend to take care of these men.

Soon vacation travelers who "go one way, return another" on S.P.'s famed Four Scenic Routes to California will trace the Mission Trail between San Francisco and Los Angeles on the *Daylight*, through Santa Barbara and near the Monterey Peninsula. Or they may go by night on the luxurious *Lark*, or through California's great central valley on the *San Joaquin Daylight*, near Sequoia and Yosemite National Parks.

But now our most important traveler is the homeward bound veteran.

Now night and day the troop trains roll on Southern Pacific's 15,000 miles of line—on our SHASTA ROUTE from the evergreen Pacific Northwest, over the high Cascades and down past Shasta Dam to San Francisco; on our SUNSET ROUTE from New Orleans through the Old South, Texas, New Mexico and Arizona to California; on our OVERLAND ROUTE from Chicago straight across mid-continent; on our GOLDEN STATE ROUTE through El Paso and Southern Arizona.

## S·P
### The friendly Southern Pacific
*Headquarters: 65 Market Street, San Francisco 5, California*

September 1945 brought victory as expressed in a beautiful rendering of *Daylight*, flashing northward on the scenic Coast Route. These long trains carried 500 passengers each and, in 1946, were rated the most popular and profitable streamliners in the U.S. In that era, four Daylights were running in each direction: The *Morning Daylight*, the *Noon Daylight*, the *San Joaquin Daylight*, and the *Sacramento Daylight*.

# NOW! San Francisco-Chicago only 48½ hours on the OVERLAND LIMITED

*Over the High Sierra by daylight!*

## NO EXTRA FARE!

Just before noon every day, the sleek, modern *Overland Limited* glides away from the Golden Gate. By dusk it has completed one of the most spectacular rail trips in America—over the High Sierra by daylight. Only 48½ hours after leaving San Francisco, this luxurious train pulls into Chicago—the fastest no extra fare schedule in history for this route. Westbound, the trip is made in 49⅓ hours, again with a daylight crossing of California's rugged mountains.

The new, faster *Overland Limited* carries streamlined Pullmans to Chicago and St. Louis, and streamlined chair cars to Chicago. Later, as additional light weight cars become available, the *Overland Limited* will be completely streamlined with the most modern equipment. Lounge cars, dining cars and coffee shop cars have already been modernized and redecorated.

Through Pullmans to New York are carried on the *Overland Limited.*

## The friendly Southern Pacific

### OTHER S. P. TRAINS FASTER, TOO!

**GOLDEN STATE LIMITED,** 48½ hours, Los Angeles to Chicago. No extra fare. All Pullmans and chair cars streamlined. Through Pullman to New York.

**SUNSET LIMITED,** 49¾ hours, Los Angeles to New Orleans, Southern Pacific all the way. No extra fare.

**PACIFIC LIMITED** now on much the same schedule as former *Overland Limited.* Carries through Pullman to Washington, D. C.

**CITY OF SAN FRANCISCO,** crack extra fare streamliner between San Francisco and Chicago, now back on pre-war 39¾ hour schedule, leaving every three days.

**SAN FRANCISCO CHALLENGER,** popular economy train for chair car and tourist Pullman passengers, has been speeded up.

**CALIFORNIAN,** friendly Golden State Route train, now runs in two sections and has been speeded up.

The *Overland Limited* was another SP/UP/C&NW train offering Chicago-San Francisco service. The striking artwork from this July 1946 ad reveals two of SP's better-known trademarks: Sierra scenery and cab-forward steam locomotives, which are closely related. SP's mountainous Sierra crossing—built for the first transcontinental railroad—is the stuff of legends, but it was a tunnel-heavy, arduous route. SP's articulated, cab-forward oil-burners (it rostered nearly 200) were a perfect match for the mountain grades and they kept the crew comfortable—in front of the smoke—and afforded a better view of the tracks ahead.

In April 1949, Southern Pacific unveiled an extension of the *Daylight* fleet that some would argue was the ultimate expression of the concept. The *Shasta Daylight* linked Oakland and Portland, 714 of the most scenic rail miles in the West, with daily service. Equipment for the "Million Dollar Train" came in the form of 29 new Pullman-Standard cars, including the memorable (and articulated) diner/kitchen/coffee shop cars. Providing power were Alco PA diesels, resplendent in their *Daylight* orange-and-red stripes.

★ Golden State, *Southern Pacific-Rock Island streamliner, Chicago to Los Angeles via El Paso, Tucson, Phoenix, Palm Springs.*

# Come to Arizona and California

## ...on the swift Golden State

★**GOLDEN STATE** is the *only* streamliner direct to Tucson, Phoenix and Palm Springs. It starts you on this wonderful Great Circle Tour of the West, which you can combine with your next Arizona-California trip:

**From Chicago** take our swift *Golden State*—"smoothest streamliner to the Pacific Coast"—via El Paso (where you stopover for Carlsbad Caverns National Park if you wish), Douglas, Bisbee, Tucson and Phoenix. Bask in Arizona's famed desert resort country. Then Palm Springs and Los Angeles, San Diego, Old Mexico.

**From Los Angeles,** go North on our scenic *California Daylight* streamliner via Santa Barbara—470 miles of lovely Pacific surf, valley and mountain—to San Francisco. See the Golden Gate.

**Then home** via Reno, Ogden, Omaha and Chicago on our luxurious *City of San Francisco*—"fastest thing on wheels between the Golden Gate and Chicago".

**Or go North** from San Francisco on our new *Shasta Daylight* streamliner, past 14,161-foot Mt. Shasta, through beautiful Oregon to Portland, thence home by the U.S. or Canadian line of your choice.

**If you prefer,** go home via New Orleans. From Arizona or Los Angeles take our fast *Sunset Limited* to El Paso, Texas resort country, San Antonio, Houston, New Orleans. (All-Diesel now, the *Sunset* will be a completely new, 42-hour streamliner later this year.)

**Only Southern Pacific** brings you to California one way, returns you another. You *see twice as much* on an S.P. Western trip. The two photo folders explain fully. Send for them today.

**SOUTHERN PACIFIC'S FOUR SCENIC ROUTES
SHOWING THE GOLDEN STATE ROUTE IN RED**

SOUTHERN PACIFIC, Dept. HY-2
310 So. Michigan Avenue, Chicago 4, Illinois.

Please send me, free, the photo folders, "Your Vacation in Arizona" and "How to See Twice as Much on Your Trip to California".

NAME

ADDRESS

CITY _____ STATE

(If school student, state grade _____ )

## S·P  The friendly Southern Pacific

➡ ➡ ➡

Another jointly operated transcontinental service for Southern Pacific was the Chicago-L.A. *Golden State*, run east of Tucumcari, N.M., by Rock Island. The train was originally established in 1902, was dropped for a time, went daily in 1910, then reached its heyday in the 1920s. This February 1950 ad features a newly equipped (in 1947) train, but by this time top-rate UP and Santa Fe trains had garnered much of the remaining passenger traffic. The *Golden State* rolled off into the sunset—and history—in February 1968.

*Southern Pacific's Sunset Limited, New Orleans to Los Angeles via Houston, San Antonio, El Paso, Tucson, Phoenix and Palm Springs.*

*Sensational! New!*

# SUNSET LIMITED NEW ORLEANS - LOS ANGELES

*The Streamlined Train with the Southern Accent*

Here is America's newest travel sensation, the red-and-silver diesel-powered *Sunset Limited!* Daily this great streamliner flashes east and west over Southern Pacific rails between New Orleans and Los Angeles.

In just 42 hours, at very little extra fare, she takes you "West by South" to California, or returns you "home the Southern Way." It's new. You see Arizona, booming Texas, Louisiana bayous. At New Orleans you should stop over to enjoy the famed cuisine and French Quarter shopping. You connect there with fine streamliners to and from Chicago and New York.

You'll thrill to the interiors of this Budd-built "Streamlined Train with the Southern Accent." She's styled to scenes and colors of the Old South...World's finest sleeping accommodations, newly designed bedrooms and roomettes...Luxury Chair Cars too... $15,000,000 worth of *Sunset Limiteds*, five of them, to assure you this glorious trip, any day, either way!

Want a preview of your *Sunset Limited* journey to California? Just mail us the coupon.

**S·P** The friendly Southern Pacific

**FRENCH QUARTER LOUNGE** *car has watermelon walls, white grill work.*

**THE AUDUBON DINING ROOM** *has gulf-green ceiling, features Audubon prints.*

**PRIDE OF TEXAS COFFEE SHOP** *car has gay longhorn and cattle brand designs.*

Mr. L. C. Ioas, Southern Pacific, Dept. HY-9, 310 South Michigan Ave., Chicago 4, Illinois.

Please send me, free, your 24-page, full-color booklet "The New Sunset Limited," including map and route description.

NAME _____

ADDRESS _____

CITY & ZONE _____

STATE _____

(If school student, please state grade _____)

SP's popular *Sunset Limited* entered a dramatic new era in August 1950 with the arrival of five full sets of new Budd-built, streamlined equipment. The new cars were fluted stainless steel accented by a broad red stripe on the outside, and they offered modern amenities and outstanding comfort on the inside. The glory years lasted for another decade, but the luxury disappeared in the 1960s and the train limped into the 1970s. Under Amtrak management, the train has enjoyed renewed success; after being extended east to Florida, the train became the carrier's only true transcontinental train.

## Next time, try the *City of San Francisco*

### Chicago-San Francisco

**O**n your next trip to or from California, try the extra fine, extra fast, extra fare streamliner, *City of San Francisco* (SP-UP-C&NW), Golden Gate to Chicago in 39¾ hours.

Take your choice of the finest in luxury-Pullman room accommodations. Delicious meals and new Pullman, dining, coffee shop and lounge cars add to your enjoyment. Or, for the last word in comfort with economy, try the foam-rubber, reclining Chair Car seats, with leg rests.

The "City" and no-extra-fare sister streamliner *San Francisco Overland* are hours faster than any other trains to San Francisco. They follow the direct Overland Route, via Ogden, Reno and California's rugged High Sierra.

S. P. has just completed a $316,000,000 new equipment program, placing great streamliners on each of its Wonderful Ways West. (See map and list of "name trains" below.) For free folders and information, write Mr. L. C. Ioas, Dept. 101, 310 S. Michigan Ave., Chicago 4, Illinois.

**S·P** AMERICA'S MOST MODERN TRAINS

City of San Francisco—"fastest thing on wheels," Chicago-San Francisco.

Pullman room on the "City"—like traveling in your own living room.

### GREAT SOUTHERN PACIFIC TRAINS

| | | |
|---|---|---|
| SUNSET LIMITED . . . . . New Orleans-Los Angeles | GOLDEN STATE . . . . . . . . Chicago-Los Angeles | |
| LARK, DAYLIGHTS, STARLIGHT . Los Angeles-San Francisco | SUNBEAM . . . . . . . . . . Houston-Dallas | |
| OVERLAND, CITY OF SAN FRANCISCO . Chicago-San Francisco | CASCADE, SHASTA DAYLIGHT . . San Francisco-Portland | |

In a June 1951 ad, the *City of San Francisco*, powered by Southern Pacific Alco PA diesels, ticks of the first few miles of an exciting trip eastward. The joint SP-UP-C&NW operation managed to remain one of the leading passenger trains throughout the pre-Amtrak era, in part because of the popularity of vacation travel to the West, but also because of timely equipment purchases. First streamlined in 1936, more new cars were added after World War II and again in the mid-1950s, including the train's first domes. Service cutbacks finally started to take their toll in the 1960s, but the train survived up to—and beyond—the start of Amtrak in 1971.

These hand-sketched ads from July (left) and November 1952 capture the spirit of the Southern Pacific in California during the 1950s. Look carefully at the San Francisco cable car: You'll note a strategic placement of SP's famous "Next time, take the train" slogan.

## TREMENDOUS SCENERY

High and mighty Mt. Shasta (14,161 ft.) towers above you during afternoon hours on the *Shasta Daylight* (San Francisco-Portland). And there's no better vantage point for eyeing the West's scenic splendors than a big picture window of an S. P. streamliner. Always lots to see, always a relaxing ride, always travel that is truly pleasure.

## TREMENDOUS FREIGHT

Early this year the longest one-piece freight load that ever rode a U. S. train was moved by S. P. from Texas to Louisiana. It was a rigid steel oil-refinery tank 208½ feet long. It required six flatcars and *very* careful handling. The ride was a huge success—thanks to S.P. planning, preparedness and skill in meeting shippers' needs.

# Southern Pacific

serving the West and Southwest with
TRAINS • TRUCKS • PIGGYBACK • PIPELINES

The 8-state Golden Empire served by Southern Pacific is one of the fastest growing, most productive areas in the United States. S. P.'s job is to match this vitality with dynamic railroading. We hope our customers and neighbors feel that we are doing so.

By September 1958, freight hauling had become more important to the SP than passenger service. Gone were SP's colorful passenger train advertisements of a few years earlier. As important as the split-level dome lounge is a picture of a record-setting freight shipment (America's longest one-piece load at that time): a 208-1/2 foot, rigid refinery tank, longer than anything previously moved by train.

Great Trains of America—"*Streamliner No. 1*" westbound by Weather Bureau Rock, near Stevenson, Washington

## The secret that helps No. 1 cover its tracks

Cruising the water grade route along the mighty Columbia River . . . past Bonneville Dam, through the heart of the Cascade Range to the lands of Lewis and Clark . . . Spokane, Portland and Seattle Streamliner No. 1 links the Pacific Northwest with an entire continent. And the strength of this link is Diesel power. Guarded by a special chemical in RPM Diesel Engine Lubricating Oil that helps them stay on the job more than 90% of the time, No. 1's Diesel locomotives turn miles into minutes to roll into Spokane on time. In RPM DELO Oil this carbon-fighting compound keeps Diesels clean and powerful, piston rings un-jammed. With RPM DELO Oil, Diesels now run 3 to 5 times longer without repairs . . . to bring East and West closer together than ever before.

DIESEL ENGINE LUBRICATING OIL

RPM DELO ran a series of attractive railroad-oriented advertisements in the late 1940s and early 1950s. The ad from March 1949 features Pacific Northwest regional carrier Spokane, Portland & Seattle. SP&S was jointly owned by Great Northern and Northern Pacific, and in 1970 was blended together with those railroads to form Burlington Northern. SP&S *Streamliner* No. 1 carried passengers from Portland to Spokane, giving them an eye-popping view of the Columbia River Gorge, before some cars were blended into the consist of GN's eastbound *Empire Builder*, bound for the Twin Cities and points beyond.

*Great Trains of America—The luxurious "Lark" slips through Santa Susana Pass enroute to Los Angeles*

## The tonic that makes such Westerners rugged

It's fitted with million-dollar accommodations, but the *Lark*'s no pampered dude when it comes to work. It runs a tight nightly schedule between northern and southern California... and its big Diesel engines are seldom turned off. Diesels like these can go a quartermillion miles without overhaul!... RPM DELO Oil, perfected to cure Diesel ring-sticking troubles, bearing corrosion and excessive wear, keeps carbon and other impurities harmlessly dispersed, resists acid- and gum-forming oxidation. RPM DELO Oil makes Diesel locomotives long on work, short on maintenance—enables high-speed Diesels everywhere to deliver more and cheaper power.

**DIESEL ENGINE LUBRICATING OIL**

From the laboratories of

## STANDARD OIL COMPANY OF CALIFORNIA

Subsidiaries: THE CALIFORNIA OIL COMPANY · STANDARD OIL COMPANY OF TEXAS
THE CALIFORNIA COMPANY · STANDARD OIL COMPANY OF BRITISH COLUMBIA LIMITED

The ad (from September 1949) is for Standard Oil but the train is Southern Pacific's venerable *Lark*, which is often remembered as the *Daylight's* overnight cousin. In fact, the Lark came first, debuting in 1910, 12 years before the better-known *Daylight*, and in the 1920s became one of SP's premier trains. In 1941, the streamlined *Lark* became the West's first private room train, notable for its two-tone gray paint. The train eventually fell victim to airline competition and lost its all-Pullman status in 1957. The train was dropped for good in April 1968.

A few months after the unveiling of the M-10000, Union Pacific took delivery of its first dedicated long-distance streamliner, the M-10001 *City of Portland*, in May 1935. In 1947, with the introduction of new, conventional streamlined equipment (as shown in this January 1950 RPM DELO ad), the *City of Portland* became the first UP transcontinental train to expand to daily service.

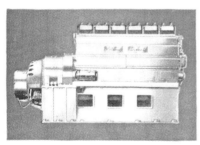

Self-propelled railcars (known as "doodlebugs" in railroad parlance) became popular in the 1920s and 1930s for providing economical branchline passenger service. Most of the early doodlebugs were powered by gas-distillate engines, but many were refitted with more-reliable and cheaper-to-operate diesel engines. Rock Island 9049 was one such example, having received a 275-h.p power plant manufactured by Sterling Diesel, sponsor of this May 1946 ad.

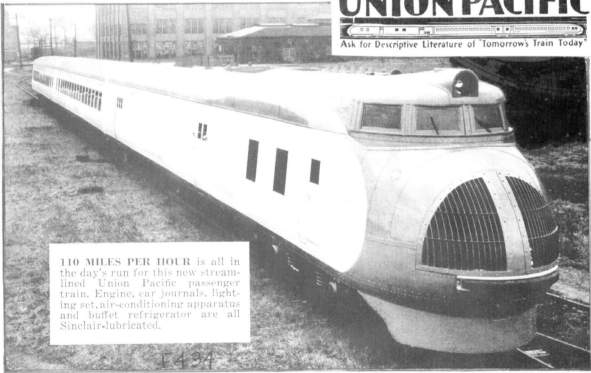

110 MILES PER HOUR is all in the day's run for this new streamlined Union Pacific passenger train. Engine, car journals, lighting set, air-conditioning apparatus and buffet refrigerator are all Sinclair-lubricated.

Here is one of two trains that heralded the era of streamliners on America's railroads—the famous Union Pacific M-10000 as it looked in April 1934. Finished in yellow and brown, the carbody was built by Pullman-Standard of lightweight aluminum alloys—with power unit by Electro-Motive Corporation subsidiary Winton Engine Company. A 600-hp gas distillate engine could haul the three-car, 124-ton consist at speeds up to 110 mph. After a successful cross-country tour, UP initially planned to use the train in an ambitious 24-hour Chicago-California schedule, but opted for more modest—albeit successful—Kansas City-Salina/Topeka service starting in January 1935.

# We didn't know THIS FAMILY!

*When this family boarded a Union Pacific train—*

*we didn't know them nor, for that matter, did they know us. But it is a Union Pacific policy to treat each passenger with the friendly courtesy you would extend to a guest in your home.*

● It's possible that it isn't necessary to adopt such a policy. Perhaps it *is* enough to provide dependable service, modern equipment and good food at reasonable prices; to be simply civil to our patrons.

Nevertheless, Union Pacific will continue to go a step further; to do everything possible to make our guests feel at home when they place themselves in our hands; to imbue them with the feeling that

Union Pacific is more than "just another railroad."

How this is accomplished isn't so easy to explain. A friendly greeting . . . a smile . . . a sincere desire to be helpful . . . those *little things* that cause patrons to say "I certainly enjoyed my trip."

May we suggest that you "find out for yourself."

Try Union Pacific next time!

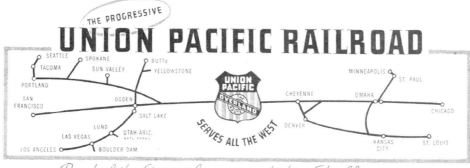

THE PROGRESSIVE

# UNION PACIFIC RAILROAD

*Road of the Streamliners and the Challengers*

The Union Pacific built the eastern end of the first transcontinental railroad, then fell into years of debt and scandal punctuated by Congressional inquiry into the shady financing that supported construction of the road. Then, in 1897, Edward H. Harriman gained control of the company and turned it into one of the world's greatest railroads, a position it firmly held at the time of this January 1938 ad.

Today, most folks think of the *Challenger* as UP's gigantic 4-6-6-4 steam locomotives, but in May 1941 it was also the name of a mostly coach-equipped Chicago-Los Angeles/Oakland train. The train had been streamlined in 1937, but in 1947 it was discontinued. UP used the train's equipment to expand its premier fleet of *City* trains to daily service.

**AMERICA SAYS** "keep 'em flying." But to keep 'em flying we must keep 'em rolling—on the rails. Materials, thousands of carloads, for planes, tanks and guns must be rushed to production and assembly plants. Completed armament also must be transported.

Union Pacific is powered to do the job. Twenty "Big Boys," largest steam locomotives ever built, have recently been added to the large fleet of other super-powered rail giants placed in service during the past five years.

Millions of dollars also have been invested in freight cars, new rails and property improvements. For defense as well as industry's normal needs, Union Pacific—the Strategic Middle Route connecting East with West—supplies the demand for dependable transportation.

*The Progressive*
# UNION PACIFIC RAILROAD
*The Strategic Middle Route*

The king of the steam locomotives is on display in an April 1942, ad. Heavier wartime loads were capably handled by Union Pacific's "Big Boy" fleet, largest and mightiest steam locomotives in the world. Alco built 20 of these for UP in 1941 and a few more in 1944. They weighed 386 tons each and developed 7,000 horsepower. Wheel arrangement of these articulated giants was 4-8-8-4.

SYMBOL OF PROGRESS

Like radio, electric refrigerators and many other modern conveniences, the streamlined train has become an accepted part of our lives. It symbolizes the progressive spirit of American industry—of individual enterprise.

Union Pacific developed the first streamlined train *during the depression era;* an outstanding example of farsighted engineering and executive genius. It is largely due to this same spirit of progress that miracles in war production have been achieved by our country's industrial plants; it is the spirit that has spurred our railroads to accomplish seemingly superhuman tasks in the transportation of war materials and troops.

It is this spirit of progress, this truly American characteristic, that will eliminate the Axis. Union Pacific, for its part, will continue to "keep 'em rolling."

*The Progressive*
UNION PACIFIC RAILROAD
ROAD OF THE STREAMLINERS AND THE CHALLENGERS

Union Pacific's M-10000 ushered in the era of streamlined trains and the railroad was so pleased with the design that in 1935-36 it took delivery of seven more trainsets for its *City* trains, albeit with diesel power plants. The tone of this July 1943 ad is almost nostalgic towards the distinctive trains, despite their relative youth. But, the short heyday of these trains was truly past—their articulated (permanently connected cars) design was inflexible and had been superceded by mix-and-match, off-the-shelf locomotives and cars. This diesel locomotice was replicated in O gauge "tinplate" train sets by the three leading toy train manufacturers—*Lionel, American Flyer,* and *Marx*—in shortened proportaions.

### The Man with the "Thousand Track" mind

Along the Union Pacific are many types of locomotives —tons of pulsating power — designed for particular tasks.

It's the job of the train dispatcher to know, at all times, what locomotives are available and to assign their "runs."

Heavy wartime traffic—the movement of troops and war materials—has greatly added to the dispatcher's responsibilities. More than ever before, he must be exacting, alert and resourceful—a man with a "thousand track" mind.

Dispatchers, like hundreds of other Union Pacific employes in key positions, are especially trained to handle the heavy traffic which flows over "the strategic middle route." They have the experience and ability. They know that hard work and initiative are recognized and rewarded.

Today, 60,000 Union Pacific workers are carrying on the tremendously important wartime transportation job. An additional 12,000 employes are in the armed forces. Their common objective is victory — to maintain the spirit of freedom, individual enterprise and equal opportunity for all.

★ *Help the war effort by not dealing with black markets nor paying over-ceiling prices.*

*THE PROGRESSIVE*

## UNION PACIFIC
### RAILROAD

Brute power during wartime in the Union Pacific yards is a study in steam (March 1944). There wasn't much concern about smoke pollution, especially when the war effort was at stake!

You say where...

We'll take you there

*in* Cool Comfort

**H**ere's an easy way to decide where to go this summer...and a suggestion as to the most enjoyable way to go. • First, select the region, or regions, in which you are interested and mail coupon for Union Pacific booklets containing beautiful color photos and interesting descriptive matter. • Then, ask your nearest Union Pacific representative—or travel agent—to help you plan your trip, make train reservations, etc. • On Union Pacific's Streamliners or other fine trains, you'll ride smoothly, safely, in air conditioned comfort.

UNION PACIFIC RAILROAD

Union Pacific Railroad
Room 317, Omaha 2, Nebraska
I am interested in a rail trip to the vacation region named below. Please send free booklet.

(Fill in name of region)

NAME
STREET
CITY_____STATE_____
Also send information on Escorted Tours ☐

Despite the post-war slump in passenger traffic thanks to competition from other transportation modes, UP was successful into holding onto a significant percentage of vacationers bound for a variety of Western destinations served by the railroad. Plus, its great service was a plus. Dinner on a UP train, even after dark, was a special delight with both great food and the chance to meet interesting new friends. (March 1950 ad)

At left, an appetizing fruit plate was just one of many great entrees offered by Union Pacific dining cars (August 1953). At right: A view of a UP Club Lounge Car shows that letter-writing was a convenience available to train passengers who wanted to keep in touch with the folks at home. UP passenger trains rode on some of the nation's best track; smooth rides made writing easy. (October 1953)

A distinctive new club car "The PUB" is an invitation to relaxation on the Streamliner "City of Denver" providing overnight every night service between Chicago and Denver for Pullman and Coach passengers.

## UNION PACIFIC RAILROAD
ROAD OF THE *Daily* STREAMLINERS

In a homey, wood-paneled room such as this, in Union Pacific's new "Pub" car, you could almost forget that you were aboard a train. (June 1954)

Dinner in UP's Astra Dome created more work for the waiters, who had to bring the meals to the upper level, but the grand table-side views made it seem worthwhile. There were also downstairs dining rooms, including one for private groups with seating for up to 10 people. (August 1955)

*An Invitation to Dine in Luxury*

*The stairway in background leads to the upper dome level where you can dine under the open sky.*

This Astra Dome dining room has a rare charm revealed in soft, pleasing colors and textures...in exquisite table ware. Guests enjoy truly marvelous meals prepared from the finest of fresh foods, graciously served.

The Astra Dome dining cars are in service between Chicago and the Pacific Coast on the "CITY OF LOS ANGELES" and "CITY OF PORTLAND" Domeliners. These luxurious dome dining cars are an exclusive Union Pacific feature.

When arranging your next trip through the West, we suggest you **ask** to be routed on a Union Pacific Domeliner.

There is no extra charge — just extra pleasure.

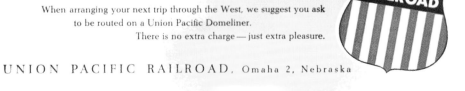

UNION PACIFIC RAILROAD, Omaha 2, Nebraska

Union Pacific's Astra Domes offered the only regularly scheduled dome car dining experience available in the pre-Amtrak era. Eating under glass was the highlight, but as this September 1955 ad attests, the dining experience in the main level seating era was no less elegant.

**214**

*The "City of Portland" Domeliner skirting the Columbia River Gorge*

## Miles and Miles of this...

Green forests coming down to meet the majestic Columbia River, waterfalls lacing high rugged rock. Your eyes drink in the ever-changing panorama through wide windows of Union Pacific Domeliners on your way to or from the Pacific Coast.

You can dine in the Astra Dome Dining Car, enjoy the luxurious Astra Dome Lounge, or relax in the restful Astra Dome Coach. All the extra pleasure at no extra cost.

Whenever you travel through the West, ask for reservations on *Union Pacific Domeliners* and *Streamliners* ... between Chicago and Los Angeles, San Francisco, Portland and Seattle, as well as many other western cities and National Parks.

UNION PACIFIC HONORS RAIL TRAVEL CREDIT CARDS

UNION PACIFIC
*Domeliners*

"CITY OF PORTLAND"
"CITY OF LOS ANGELES"
"The CHALLENGER"

*Between Chicago and the Pacific Coast*

*Let us help you*

PLAN YOUR
TRIP THROUGH
THE WEST

USE THE COUPON

**UNION PACIFIC**
RAILROAD

Room 753, Omaha 2, Nebraska

I am interested in a Domeliner trip to California ☐
To Pacific Northwest ☐  Send descriptive booklet.

Name_____

Address_____

City_____Zone_____State_____

Phone No._____

Union Pacific was a relative latecomer to the dome car business, but once it embraced the popular cars, starting in 1954, it marketed them aggressively and soon all UP trains with at least one dome came to be known as a "Domeliner." The *City of Portland* (featured in this October 1956 ad), the *City of Los Angeles* and the *Challenger* were the first to receive domes. The *City of St. Louis* was added to the list in 1958, and finally in 1960, the UP added domes to its segment of the *City of San Francisco*.

## A *recreation* ROOM
### THAT WOULD GRACE ANY HOME

*Beautiful* is the most appropriate word to describe this unusual Redwood Lounge on the "CITY OF LOS ANGELES" and "CITY OF PORT-LAND" Domeliners. Side walls are paneled in natural redwood and cedar. End walls are of brick, and there's a beam-type ceiling. This distinctive decor gives you a restful "at home" feeling.

You'll enjoy riding the Domeliners between Chicago and the Pacific Coast. In addition to the Redwood Lounge they feature an Astra Dome observation lounge and an Astra Dome dining car serving the finest of freshly prepared foods. The service is friendly and gracious.

Both of these luxurious Domeliners offer the very latest type of Pullman and Coach accommodations.

### Union Pacific Railroad
*Omaha 2, Nebraska*

In addition to their obvious scenery-viewing opportunities, UP's lounges were noted for their unique interior styling. This April 1956 ad extols the virtues of wood paneling, beam ceilings and brick accents—décor that any homeowner of the era would have wanted for a stylish rec room.

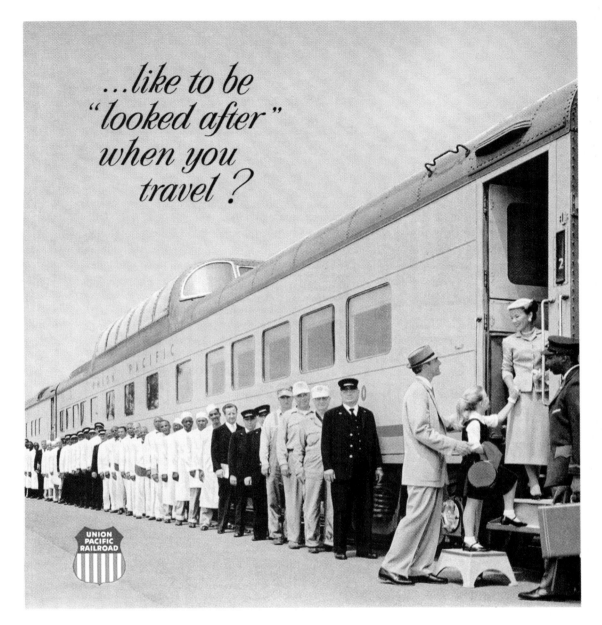

### SERVING YOU AND YOURS . . .

is the pleasant duty of the 35 highly trained employees comprising the personnel on Union Pacific Domeliners.

They look after your comfort and safety . . . prepare taste-appealing meals for your enjoyment. Your wish is their command and we're proud of the way they reflect true western hospitality.

*On your next trip to or from the West enjoy the finest in accommodations and service on a Union Pacific Domeliner—or Streamliner. There is no extra fare.*

## UNION PACIFIC
### *Railroad*

Dependable Freight and Passenger Service

This November 1959 ad reveals something that may shock contemporary travelers—it required 35 people to crew a UP domeliner. Passenger trains were labor-intensive operations, which is one reason that they struggled mightily in the face of competition, and why railroads quickly shifted their focus to lucrative freight operations in the 1950s.

Have you noticed the new small color-striped panels now being installed on our freight cars? Each stripe is a code. In a fraction of a second, as a highballing freight train passes a track-side scanner, a "magic eye" will record the car's identification, place, time and direction of movement. The information will be automatically transmitted to our computerized COIN* "bank." It will not only provide accurate car location information, almost to the minute and mile, but facilitate faster, more efficient equipment availability forecasts to meet short-notice needs and seasonal peaks. It's another reason you can depend on Union Pacific to speed tomorrow's commerce today!

*COIN is an acronym for **C**omplete **O**perating **IN**formation system now in operation.

# HIGH
# SPEED
# COLOR
# SET

Even as the passenger train era waned, Union Pacific was one of the few railroad's that stayed in the public eye through mass market advertising. In April 1970, the UP proudly explains its COIN computerized freight tracking system.

Travel to California
aboard the train
chosen to star in
"Cinerama Holiday"!

THE MOST
TALKED ABOUT
TRAIN IN
THE COUNTRY

Chances are you'll never find yourself hurtling down a Swiss mountainside on a bobsled, or zooming through space in the cockpit of a jet fighter plane, but there's one travel adventure in "Cinerama Holiday" you can enjoy in person. And that's to cross the country aboard the famous Vista-Dome streamliner, the California Zephyr.

Upstairs in one of the five Vista-Domes, you look up, look down, look all around as the magnificent scenery unfolds before you. You travel for hundreds of miles through the mighty Colorado Rockies...cross the High Sierra...wind down the entire length of California's Feather River Canyon. What's more, you see *all* this unspoiled wilderness during daylight hours!

Pullmans...Chair Coaches...Two Lounge Cars...through Pullman New York-San Francisco

**VISTA-DOME** *California Zephyr*

CHICAGO · DENVER · SALT LAKE CITY · OAKLAND-SAN FRANCISCO

## WESTERN PACIFIC

For illustrated California Zephyr booklet, write Jos. G. Wheeler,
Dept. H, Western Pacific, 526 Mission St., San Francisco 5.

The star of "Cinerama Holiday" was the *California Zephyr*. The Cinerama series of panoramic-screen movie spectaculars was launched to an eager audience in 1953, with "This is Cinerama." The realism was unequaled, as the spectator felt the illusion of being directly involved in the action, surrounded by a broad, semi-circular screen and bombarded everywhere by thunderous stereophonic sound! (From a December 1955 ad, seen again in February 1956)

# The "PRIVATE CAR"

## OF MR. AND MRS. HENDERSON
## OF CHICAGO

*Mr. Henderson, a young businessman and very smart traveler, knows you no longer have to be a tycoon to cross the country in complete privacy and luxurious surroundings.*

**This spacious living room** — a deluxe bedroom suite — gives the Henderson family loads of room. What's more, they enjoy such travel "extras" as room service, recorded music and radio reception, individual heat control, and the same standard of privacy they enjoy in their own home. And by taking advantage of Family Fares, they save $76.95 on their round-trip to San Francisco!

**"Reserved for the Hendersons".** Thanks to the unique system of advance dinner reservations, there's no waiting in line for a table in the California Zephyr's famous Dining Car.

**Scheduled for sightseeing,** the California Zephyr travels through the Colorado Rockies and winds down Feather River Canyon in daylight hours.

**When night falls,** a folding partition can convert the Henderson's living room into two separate bedrooms. Each bedroom has two comfortable beds and private lavatory.

**With the children in bed downstairs,** Mr. and Mrs. Henderson relax in one of the five Vista-Domes as the California Zephyr glides swiftly through the moonlight.

VISTA-DOME *California Zephyr*

**CHICAGO TO OAKLAND-SAN FRANCISCO**
over the Burlington, Rio Grande and Western Pacific
**via Denver and Salt Lake City**

# WESTERN PACIFIC

For illustrated California Zephyr booklet, write James J. Hickey, Dept. H-2, Western Pacific, 526 Mission St., San Francisco 5.

The *California Zephyr* was a hit with families, as expressed in a Western Pacific-sponsored ad from October 1956. The popular Chicago-Oakland (San Francisco) train was operated by WP—known fondly as "The Wobbly" by its many West Coast fans—west of Salt Lake City. Despite its limited reach and stiff competition from Southern Pacific, the Western Pacific soldiered along into the 1980s before being swallowed by Union Pacific.

# Take the time to take the train

## and enjoy such luxuries as breakfast in bed

Cross-country travel can be restful and fun . . . a fine way to relax, a chance to work in privacy, to live in the lap of luxury.

A good many executives have decided that speed alone is highly overrated. They prefer to take the time to take the train, particularly such a train as our Vista-Dome California Zephyr. They are waited on hand and foot; they eat what they like, when they like; and upstairs in a Vista-Dome they look all around at the most magnificent scenery in the entire West.

Next time you make a business trip across the country, let us show you how travel can be a wonderful experience, *not* just a means to an end. General Offices: 526 Mission Street, San Francisco 5.

# WESTERN PACIFIC
## ROUTE OF THE VISTA-DOME *California Zephyr*

### SAN FRANCISCO-OAKLAND TO CHICAGO via Salt Lake City and Denver (WP, D&RGW and CB&Q)

In March 1958, Western Pacific attempts to hold on to the *California Zephyr's* share of the lucrative business travel market that was being lost to airliners. Where else but on a train could you be served breakfast in bed while racing through some of the world's greatest scenery?

**CONTROLS AND INSTRUMENTS:**

1. Application pipe (train brake) 2. Transition lever ("shift") 3. Horn cords 4. Reverse lever 5. Bell valve 6. Speed recorder 7. Independent brake valve (engine only) 8. Control switches (electricity to motors, fuel pumps) 9. Transition indicator (measures power to traction motors).

Thank you for coming along. We hope you've thoroughly enjoyed this pleasant nostalgic trip through the United States and Canada aboard many of the great streamlined name trains of the 20th Century. And in case you were wondering how a 1950s-era diesel locomotive is operated, here's a close look inside the cab of a Northern Pacific unit from an April 1953 advertisement, with veteran engineman Frank Pugleasa showing you the controls.

# *BIBLIOGRAPHY*

Dubin, Arthur D. *More Classic Trains.* Milwaukee: Kalmbach Publishing, 1974.

King, Ed. *The A.* Glendale, Calif.: Trans-Anglo Books, 1989.

Kirkland, John F. *Dawn of the Diesel Age.* Glendale, Calif.: Interurban Press, 1983.

Kirkland, John F. *The Diesel Builders, Volume Two.* Glendale, Calif.: Interurban Press, 1989.

Nowak, Ed. *Ed Nowak's New York Central.* Glendale, Calif.: Interurban Press, 1989.

Pope, Dan and Mark Lynn. *Warbonnets.* Pasadena, Calif.: Pentrex, Inc., 1994.

Rattenne, Ken. *The Feather River Route One.* Glendale, Calif.: Interurban Press, 1989.

Repp, T.O. *Main Streets of the Northwest.* Glendale, Calif.: Trans-Anglo Books, 1989.

Schafer, Mike. *Classic American Railroads.* Osceola, Wis.: Motorbooks International, 1996.

Schafer, Mike and Joseph M. Welsh. *Classic American Streamliners.* Osceola, Wis.: Motorbooks International, 1997.

Scribbins, Jim. *The 400 Story.* Glendale, Calif.: PTJ Books, 1982.

Solomon, Brian. *The American Diesel Locomotive.* Osceola, Wis.: MBI Publishing Co., 2000.

# INDEX